The Self-Directed School:
Empowering the Stakeholders

Ronald G. McIntire

AND

John T. Fessenden

SCHOLASTIC

LEADERSHIP POLICY RESEARCH™

New York • Toronto • London • Auckland • Sydney

ISBN 0-590-49267-5

12   11   10   9   8   7   6   5   4   3   2   1   1   2   3   4   5/9

Printed in the U.S.A.

Library of Congress Cataloging-in-Publication Data
McIntire, Ronald G.
    The self-directed school: empowering the stakeholders /
Ronald G. McIntire and John T. Fessenden.
        p.   cm.
    ISBN 0-590-49267-5 : $29.95
    1. School management teams—United States.   2. Decision making,
Group—United States.   I. Fessenden, John T.   II. Title.
LB2806.3.M35   1994
371.2'00973—dc20   93-34345
                                                            CIP

To Kathy, Kym, and Megan for lost time.

R.G.M.

To my kids at McQueeney, who have shared with me their lives, their enthusiasm, and their love—and who have taught me far more than I could ever teach them.

J.T.F.

Contents

Preface

Why Write?

In sitting down to write a book, authors must first deal with the issue, Why write? What is it that compels authors to devote the time and effort necessary to produce a book? After all, writing a book is not easy. It takes commitment, discipline, courage, and creativity. To produce a finished book, the authors must be sufficiently motivated by some concept or message to sustain the energy necessary to survive the process of creating, writing, rewriting, and dealing with editors and publishers.

In our case, our motivation is our vision. Not unlike Martin Luther King, Jr., we have a dream. Unfortunately, our dream begins as a nightmare. As participants in the educational system, we have seen how the current educational system in the United States works— or, perhaps better stated, how it doesn't work. Our current system of public elementary and secondary education is leaving approximately half of our children woefully unprepared for life. If our country is to survive, it is critical that our system of education be reformed.

This is where our nightmare ends. We believe that reform is possible. Not only is it possible, it has already started. Educators throughout the country have begun to reshape schools to incorporate many of the concepts of collaborative decision making that have been so important in rescuing and salvaging the many United States corporations that began to feel the pressures of competition beginning in the early 1970s.

Our vision, and the vision of those leaders who have begun to incorporate into their schools and school systems the principles of collaborative decision making, is one of innovation and cooperation. In this new vision, school leadership is transformed from a hierarchical, top-down management structure to an integrated system that depends on, and takes advantage of, the collaboration of all of the parties involved in the operation of a school: principals, teachers, parents, community members, business leaders, and students (the people we refer to in this book as the Stakeholders).

Our vision is a vision in which the Stakeholders of a school are given the responsibility and authority to make key decisions. Teachers become leaders and important participants outside the four walls of their classrooms. Parents are given more responsibility for their children's education. And business leaders and community members are encouraged to become involved as valuable contributors to the educational process.

Perhaps most importantly, our vision is of a school that has self-directed, empowered, and involved students. Since our vision depends on a sharing of power and authority among all of the parties involved in the educational process, it is essential that students be included as valued participants. Students must be afforded both the right and the responsibility to participate in forums where the constitution and content of the school and the classroom are forged. Only then will our vision truly come into existence. Only then will our schools be able to produce students who are prepared for the challenges of the twenty-first century.

A major obstacle to our vision, and to what we believe is effective school reform, is the traditional hierarchical structure of our public education system—the sheer inertia of the established educational bureaucracy that currently controls our schools. This bureaucracy deprives the school staff and community of the necessary strength, flexibility, and creativity to provide quality education. The traditional structure has not only outlived its usefulness, it presents a danger to the welfare of all of us.

Reform is coming, as it must if the United States is to survive. Many states have already taken steps legislatively to mandate the implementation of site-based decision making at the local school level. In these states, some school systems have already begun to institute site councils, teacher-empowered clusters, and many of the other manifestations of successful collaborative and shared decision making.

So if reform is on its way, why is this book necessary? The answer lies in the fact that reform cannot occur unless the participants in the reform process are provided with the information necessary to effect the reform. Whereas a great deal has been written about the theoretical underpinnings of site-based, or collaborative, decision making, the existing literature is woefully lacking in systematic descriptions of how to implement a collaborative decision-making system. The reader, then, is typically left with a compelling case for collaborative or shared decision making, but with no practical suggestions or guidelines for making such a system work.

Our goal in writing this book is to provide a useful guide for implementing collaborative decision making in the public educational system. As such, we discuss the types of skills that participants will need in the system. We also present examples to illustrate ways that a collaborative decision-making model might deal with particular issues.

This book is intended to be used by anyone involved in a collaborative decision-making system—teachers, principals, district administrators, school board members, parents, community members, business leaders, and students. From site councils to empowered clusters, this book is intended to quench the thirst for information of the literally millions of individuals who may be currently involved, or who may in the future become involved, in the collaborative decision-making process in our nation's schools.

What This Book Is Not

There are without question a number of excellent schools in the United States that have learned to be clever and shrewd enough to circumvent the rigid bureaucratic structure that typically strangles creativity, ingenuity, and progress. These schools are entrepreneurs, innovators, system beaters, and rule benders. To use David Kearns' and Dennis Doyle's apt phrase, they are "canny outlaws"—playing the rules, not playing by the rules. These schools are, by necessity, persistent. Were it not for their persistence, they would simply roll over and be crushed by the overwhelming power and weight of school system bureaucracy. Although these schools are typically not prized by their district offices, their performance is usually outstanding. Not surprisingly, however, given the liking for "normalcy" that pervades public education in the United States, in some of these schools the principals have been fired. Where this has happened, the school in question has generally made the circle back to conformity—to the detriment of the students, the teachers, the district, and, ultimately, society.

Although we believe quite passionately that reform of the current system of education is vital to the survival of this country, this book is *not* about bending rules or beating the hierarchy. Rather, it is about how site councils and self-directed cluster teams can be entrepreneurial and innovative without breaking the rules.

This book presents a model for developing and implementing a Self-Directed School by working within the present organizational system. However, the present hierarchical system will need to make some major changes in its philosophy to allow and create an environment in which the Self-Directed School can be successful.

A Word About Models

At the beginning, we believe that it is critical to define what we mean by the term "model." Some people define a model as a structure that purports to represent a reproducible solution to a particular problem. So defined, a model is simply a solution that can be duplicated, with few or no changes. If the problem to which the model applies arises, the model is duplicated and the problem is solved.

In our view, a model is simply a collection of ideas—a skeletal presentation of the basic parameters of a particular proposal. By its very nature, a model cannot be reproduced. Instead, in following the model one must evaluate each step based on the particular nuances of the situation one is confronting. Accordingly, a solution devised by one person following a model may be quite different from that developed by another. Both solutions will, in their structures, have some commonalities—but the details of the solutions can differ significantly.

The model presented in this book should be used only to gain ideas that might be useful in building site councils and self-directed cluster teams. No single model should be used to develop self-directed and self-managed schools.

We acknowledge that the American tendency is to package and "franchise" an idea or system. However, in this case, the notion of a "uniform model" contradicts the very assumptions that underlie the rationale for restructuring schools in the first place. *Schools should be different.* When individual schools (through site councils made up of staff members, parents, business leaders, and the principal) develop their own programs without negative interference from administrators and bureaucrats, who are not in a position to evaluate effectively the needs of the individual school, each school *will* be distinctly different. Each school will have its own personality and character, which will reflect the strengths of the staff, the school, and the community. Many of our educational goals at the national, state, and local levels should be the same, but it should be the responsibility of individual schools to establish the environment and instructional techniques for meeting these goals. It is our belief that this individual school personality and character will translate directly into better education and better preparation of our children for the next century.

A Map of This Book

The Self-Directed School is designed for a varied audience. It contains useful information for all those who have assumed or been given the responsibility for implementing site councils and self-directed teams in their schools. Accordingly, this book should serve as a reference for school principals who are responsible for bringing the vision of teamwork and staff empowerment to their schools. But *The Self-Directed School* is more than just a how-to manual for principals. It should also prove useful to teachers, parents, community members, and business leaders who wish to become involved in their schools. These individuals will find many practical examples of how teams in a Self-Directed School can work together to solve problems and develop new programs.

Teachers will also find in this book many creative ideas for developing self-directed students in their classrooms. If reform is to be successful, the same ideas expressed in this book about staff empowerment and employee and community involvement must also be applied to students. Our goal, ultimately, is to a have a self-directed, creative-thinking, cooperative society. If we are to achieve that goal, we must have self-directed students. Much of this book, then, can be applied in the classroom to reach that end.

The Self-Directed School will also serve as a guide for local school superintendents and school boards as they develop an organizational structure that can facilitate Self-Directed Schools. Again, it is our belief that reform has to occur throughout the system. "Fixing" a handful of schools will not work. The entire organizational structure needs to be reformed, and the ideas discussed in this book can help to achieve this objective.

Finally, this book will be useful to those business leaders who believe that the present educational system puts the United States at a competitive disadvantage and who desire to find an avenue for constructive involvement in our nation's schools. The input of business and community leaders is critical to successful school reform. For too long our educational system has been operating in a vacuum, tied to staid techniques and obsolete practices. The students currently being produced by our educational system do not have the skills needed by business and industry. It is time to listen to business leaders. This book should assist business and community leaders in their attempts to become involved as active and meaningful participants in the educational process.

This book opens with a Prologue, "The Coming of the Self-Directed School. . . ." Here we discuss the historical background of educational reform in America and set the stage for our discussion of why radical school reform is necessary and why we believe it must begin reform at the individual school level. Our educational system can change only one school at a time. We believe that Self-Directed Schools will become the standard—not the exception—within this decade.

The nine chapters following the Prologue are divided into three parts. Part I, containing Chapters 1 through 3, introduces the concept of empowerment in schools and describes how collaborative teams allow individuals to take initiative in a collaborative and cooperative environment.

Chapter 1, "Rethinking Leadership Responsibilities in Schools," examines the types of structural relationships that are most effective in facilitating Self-Directed Schools. In Chapter 2, "Clusters: The Heart of the Self-Directed School," we look at ways to create a school culture that is conducive to developing empowered, collaborative clusters, and we examine how site councils involve teachers, parents, community members, and business leaders in establishing the mission and goals of a school. Chapter 3, "Teamwork and Team Players," discusses what an effective team player is and how team players contribute to the success of the Self-Directed School.

Part II, which includes Chapters 4 through 6, covers an essential element for the success of the Self-Directed School—skills for collaboration. These chapters discuss the type of training that will be required in order to develop the collaborative skills necessary for team members and team leaders to function productively.

Chapter 4, "Training for Self-Directed Schools," examines a number of fundamental principles that should be considered when developing training programs for a Self-Directed School. Chapter 5, "Group Interaction Skills: Communication, Coordination, and Conflict Resolution," looks at the skills that form the backbone of the collaborative decision-making process. As individuals begin to work together, conflict will inevitably occur. Learning how to communicate and how to deal with the conflicts is critical if the Stakeholders of a school are going to be successful in implementing the Self-Directed School model. Chapter 5 also deals with planning, holding, and coordinating effective meetings. As we shall see, meetings are the lifeblood of the collaborative process. Unless the participants learn how to hold effective meetings, the collaborative process will collapse. Chapter 6, "Making Decisions and Reaching Agreement in Clusters," discusses the process of making decisions and reaching agreement in teams. Reaching consensus in group activity is a skill that needs to be developed. In Chapter 6, we outline an integrated model for group problem solving and decision making that will assist in the process of getting groups to reach agreement.

Part III, which contains Chapters 7 through 9, examines the issues that must be dealt with by the Self-Directed School as well as the overall educational system in order to facilitate the empowerment of the Stakeholders at the individual school level. Chapter 7, "Deciding Who Decides: Determining Which Decisions Are Made at Which Levels," outlines a plan for assisting both the school district and the Self-Directed School in determining who will make what decisions. Chapter 8, "What's Left for the Principal to Do?" examines the changing role of the school principal as schools move toward self-directedness. Surprisingly, perhaps, the principal's role is actually expanded as a school moves from being a traditional school to being a Self-Directed School. Chapter 9, "Facilitating the Self-Directed School," looks at the ways district offices can be organized to assist the development and implementation of Self-Directed Schools.

This book closes with an Epilogue, "Moving Forward: The Self-Directed Learner." The Epilogue considers how the Self-Directed School can best facilitate the development of self-directed learners and describes ways to transfer some of the newly found school and teacher power to students. We must all realize that the empowerment of the adult Stakeholders at the individual school level is only the first step in accomplishing the ultimate mission of our society— creating self-directed learners.

We believe that Self-Directed Schools will not be another educational fad but will become the standard way schools operate in the future. We hope that you will benefit from *The Self-Directed School* as you successfully empower the Stakeholders in your organization. As you will see, the journey is a long one with few shortcuts. But getting there can be fun. And once you have arrived, the payoffs for you, as well as for our children and society, can be tremendous.

Waco, Texas   R.G.M.
March 1994   J.T.F.

Prologue

The Coming of the
Self-Directed School . . .

Public education in America today is in a state of crisis. Study after study has identified weaknesses in our current educational system. Numerous books have detailed the abysmal and embarrassing performances of U.S. students, both in an absolute sense and in comparison with students from other countries. Are these studies and books mere harbingers of doom? Must we resign ourselves to the inevitability of decline, to repeating the cycle of rising and falling experienced by other great civilizations in history? We think not. Educational reform *can* be accomplished—if we maintain our perspective and remain sensitive to changes in society that demand or dictate changes in our schools.

As a beginning point we believe it is essential to note that controversy and debate over the state of public education are by no means a modern phenomenon. In fact, people have been arguing about the goals, purposes, and objectives of public education for thousands of years. The controversy centers around a dilemma as old as formal education itself. More than two thousand years ago, Aristotle summarized the dilemma as follows:

> From the present mode of education we cannot determine with the certainty to which men incline, whether to instruct a child in that

1

which will be useful to him in life, or what tends to virtue, or what is excellent; for all these things have their separate defenders.[1]

Throughout the ages men and women have struggled with the proper role of education in society. The Greeks, through the teachings of Aristotle and Socrates, placed a strong emphasis on intellectual development and the power of the human mind. Plato, Pythagoras, and Euclid are but a few of the great thinkers who emerged from this society of educational enlightenment. During the Middle Ages, education was severely restricted and served primarily as a means of imposing morality rather than challenging the intellect. With the Renaissance and the Age of Enlightenment came a renewed emphasis on education as a means of promoting human growth and progress. Education was highly valued, and it soon became synonymous with power. Those who were educated survived and flourished, whereas the uneducated remained subservient and fell behind.

In the United States, education, particularly public education, has existed as a priority from the time of the first European settlers. The pilgrims in New England and the colonists in Virginia established public schooling almost immediately after their arrival. Harvard University (established as Harvard College in 1636) and The College of William and Mary (established in 1693) stand as examples of the emphasis the settlers placed on education.

Even though public education is an integral aspect of American culture, it cannot be said that the purposes of, or the emphasis on, education has remained constant throughout our history. To the contrary, our system of public education has reflected the ebb and flow of societal developments. The initial establishment of this country demanded strong leadership and wise guidance. Learned men such as John Adams, Thomas Jefferson, and James Madison, who were well versed in history and the writings of the great thinkers, emerged as leaders. Emphasis in education was placed on the power of the human mind to strive for ideals and intellectual creativity.

During the period of westward expansion, the need for practical, common-sense education replaced the drive for higher intellectual development. Problem solving became a valued commodity—but

---

[1]From Mark Van Doren, *Liberal Education* (New York: Henry Holt and Company, 1942).

in a natural, everyday context, not in the context of some theoretical, intellectual challenge.

The industrial revolution combined practical problem-solving abilities with innovation and intellectual thinking. Dissemination of information accelerated. Keeping up meant staying informed. Thinkers who could build on yesterday's achievements became highly valued.

With Albert Einstein came education on a higher plane. Suddenly the world was presented with a whole new way of thinking. Traditional thought processes and beliefs were challenged or destroyed. Once again human intellectual ability became the focus of education.

Where Are We?
The Optical Illusion of U.S. Business and Education in the Late Twentieth Century

American education during the 1930s and 1940s was relegated to a secondary concern as the United States struggled first against the oppression of a collapsed economic system and then against the oppression of expanding worldwide political systems. By the end of World War II, public schools in the United States were ready for sweeping changes. During the nearly twenty years of economic depression and war, the country had lost sight of the importance of the educational system. Wartime testing programs, which revealed alarming absences of scientific and mathematical abilities among public elementary and secondary school graduates, indicated that something was seriously wrong with our public educational institutions.

Concern about the health of the public educational system was heightened significantly in the late 1950s as the Soviet Union, with the launching of Sputnik and subsequent successful missions to put men and women into space, made a bid for worldwide scientific and technological superiority. During the presidencies first of John F. Kennedy and then Lyndon B. Johnson, a new era in education was initiated as significant changes were introduced into the curricula of public schools. Emphasis began to be placed in areas such as mathematics, science, and foreign languages. President Johnson's Great Society program viewed rapid advances in these areas as essential to the nation's strength and success in world affairs.

With all of the attention that was focused on education, one might reasonably conclude that American students would have prospered. Paradoxically, however, it appears that the educational "innovations" introduced during the 1960s failed to have their desired effect. *A Nation at Risk*,[2] the national report on the status of U.S. public education released in 1983, was one of the first comprehensive attempts to study the effectiveness of our educational system. It found that instead of producing students who were at the forefront of educational development, U.S. schools were producing students who could not read and could not think and who were woefully unprepared for facing the challenges of modern society. Subsequent innovations—such as increased emphasis on test scores and implementation of teacher evaluation programs—introduced in response to the concerns raised by *A Nation at Risk* were really nothing more than the same old medicine. Total spending on education increased by almost 30 percent. Forty-seven states passed major educational reform bills. Most of these bills accepted as their basis the old model but commanded it to speed up and be more effective. Hence, we had numerous requirements to teach more courses, give more tests, and spend more time in school. Like most command-and-control strategies, the reform bills failed. By the late 1980s, most educational reformers had given up on "traditional" reforms.

So what has happened? How can our schools be failing in the face of the current emphasis on and attempts to improve the process? We believe that the U.S. system of public education is failing primarily because of a fundamental weakness in the system's organizational structure. To understand more fully the meaning of this statement, we believe it is instructive to review the experience of American business in the last fifty years.

Unlike the educational system, American business in the years following World War II exploded with success. Facing an unparalleled demand for products and encountering virtually no competition from a world of nations devastated by war, U.S. businesses churned out a myriad of goods in record numbers. Production could hardly keep pace as a generation of prosperous Americans, inhabiting mushrooming suburbs, demanded more and more products and services.

[2]National Commission on Excellence in Education, *A Nation at Risk: The Imperative for Educational Reform* (Washington, DC: Government Printing Office, 1983).

In the face of this tremendous demand, U.S. business marched forward under the banner of "scientific management," the theory of industrial organization originally advanced by Frederick Winslow Taylor and others in the early 1900s. Scientific management is based on the assumption that human performance can be defined and controlled through work standards and rules. Concomitantly, it assumes that production can be increased by breaking down jobs into simple, separate steps to be performed on a rote basis without deviation. Efficiency is maximized by minimizing complexity.

Thriving business conditions led to increasing emphasis on the theories of scientific management. After all, success breeds success. American businesses evolved a rule-bound, top-heavy form of corporate structure, complete with a cadre of professional managers— benign dictators who were presumed to have all of the intelligence and information necessary to make accurate and successful decisions about a company's present and future production strategies.

In the late 1970s and early 1980s, however, American business learned some bitter lessons. Faced with accelerated global competition—particularly from Japan and Germany—business leaders were forced to confront the fact that U.S. business and industry were simply not good enough to compete in a global economy. It became clear that American businesses had the following weaknesses:

1. Their products were inferior in quality to those produced by other nations.
2. Their customer service was poor.
3. They were too slow in bringing new products and services to the marketplace.

In the years prior to the mid-1970s American businesses attributed much of their success to their organizational structure and management style. The experiences of the 1970s and early 1980s, however, clearly demonstrated the fallacy of this belief. American businesses began to discover that the successes they had achieved had occurred *despite*, not *because of*, the top-heavy management style. In fact, it was the inflexible and inefficient bureaucratic structure of U.S. companies that caused them to lose their competitive positions.

Faced with the possibility of extinction and elimination through the competitive process, American businesses—including major industrial corporations such as Xerox and Motorola—were forced to rethink their reliance on the top-down organizational structure. What American businesses discovered was that the new industrial powers had replaced the traditional top-down structure with a system more dependent on employee involvement and participation.

Traditional thinking about what kind of management approach is best was further shaken by several books that appeared during the 1980s and early 1990s. Among these were *Rebirth of the Corporation*,[3] *In Search of Excellence*,[4] *The Ultimate Advantage*,[5] *Deming Management at Work*,[6] and *The Wisdom of Teams*.[7] These books argued that competitive advantage can best be achieved *not* by doing the old management better but by adopting new and innovative management approaches that are more effective at organizing and managing people. While they vary in the specific details of the new practices they recommend, all of these sources state that to be competitive organizations have to move away from a top-down management structure. Such a structure is simply too mechanistic and bureaucratic to survive in today's world.

Employing the techniques of increased employee participation, many American businesses have begun to experience a resurgence. By becoming leaders rather than bosses, corporate managers have learned to reap the benefits of employee involvement.

American schools have a great deal to learn from the experiences of business. The Japanese and other successful industrial nations taught U.S. business the importance of employee involvement and of emphasis on product quality.

At present, most schools in the United Staes are organized as top-down, hierarchical, bureaucratic institutions that can probably best be described as control-oriented organizations. As control-oriented institutions, most school districts employ strict hierarchical and bureaucratic management practices. Virtually all decisions relating to the operation of the schools are handed down by the chosen

[3]D. Quinn Mills, *Rebirth of the Corporation* (New York: John Wiley & Sons, 1991).
[4]Thomas J. Peters and Robert H. Waterman, *In Search of Excellence* (New York: Warner Books, 1982).
[5]Edward E. Lawler III, *The Ultimate Advantage* (San Francisco: Jossey-Bass Publishers, 1992).
[6]Mary Walton, *Deming Management at Work* (New York: Perigee/Putnam, 1991).
[7]Jon R. Katzenback and Douglas K. Smith, *The Wisdom of Teams* (Boston: Harvard Business School Press, 1993).

few at the top. Frequently the decisions are accompanied by detailed rules and regulations, which in most cases prohibit or restrain the flexibility of individual schools within the district to apply the decisions in the manner deemed most appropriate for them.

What we see in education is a repeat of the mistakes made in the business world. Following World War II U.S. businesses thrived *despite*, not *because of*, their organizational structure. In fact, they thrived primarily because they were the only game in town—the other industrial countries had been ravaged by the war. When those countries finally recovered, they succeeded in overtaking the markets of U.S. companies because of the strengths derived from their collaborative management strategies and the tremendous weaknesses inherent in American business organizations. Bureaucratic organizations destroy employee morale and create significant barriers to the communication of information. Thus they tend to be unresponsive to changing times and the pressures of the marketplace.

American schools are now experiencing the kind of failure that characterized U.S. business in the 1970s. Our students are failing, and many do not graduate. Of those that do graduate, many lack the skills necessary to obtain employment. Even our "good" students are finding it difficult to obtain jobs in the face of competition from students educated in other areas of the world.

We believe that the reason for the crisis in U.S. education is organizational and management failure. We need a management miracle, not simply a minor tweaking of the current system. Major changes are required in how we organize and run our schools. Business as usual is unacceptable. What we need is a new sense of collaboration and teamwork that is designed to serve not only the students in each school but also the best interests of our teachers, parents, community members, and business leaders.

What must we do? We must create a total involvement-oriented approach at both the school and school system level. We must implement the same types of principles that underlie the successes achieved by U.S. businesses. We must have parents, teachers, community members, business leaders, principals, administrators, and students—collectively referred to as the Stakeholders—who care more, think more, know more, and do more. We need a community of Stakeholders at each school who are empowered to act and who are integrally involved in the success or failure of that school. In other words, we need Self-Directed Schools.

Part I

The Leadership Paradigm Shift

1

Rethinking Leadership
Responsibilities in Schools

*A pool table, don't you understand? Friends, either you
are closing your eyes to a situation you do not wish to
acknowledge, or you are unaware of the caliber of disaster indicated by the presence of a pool table in your
community.*

Meredith Wilson, *The Music Man*
Act I, scene 2

Why Change?

This book is about change—fundamental, revolutionary change in
the organizational structure of our educational institutions. We
believe that change is not only advisable but absolutely essential to
our continued existence as a free and democratic society. As with
any call for change, however, discussion must begin with an analysis
of the current situation. Are we, in fact, in trouble? Is there a figurative pool table in our educational community to which we may be
closing our eyes and which, if not confronted, will lead to disaster?
We believe the answer is a resounding yes.

Most U.S. schools today are organized like late-nineteenth-century factories: top down, hierarchical, and bureaucratic. This management approach, referred to as the control-oriented approach, is based on the assumption that hierarchical relationships are the most effective way to ensure that work gets done in a productive manner. The underlying principle is that productivity is maximized when the work of those at the bottom of the organization chart is specialized, standardized, and simplified.

In this system of control-oriented management (which we shall refer to as the centralized power model) school systems cling rigidly to well-defined rules established by traditional management theories. Decisions are passed down, and educational practices and attitudes are dictated by the chosen few who occupy the top spots in the pyramidal structure. The procedures imposed from the top are frequently accompanied by detailed rules and regulations that in many cases constrain flexibility and discourage or prohibit creativity.

Each participant in the system, ranging from the high-ranking administrators to the "lowly" teachers, perceives that the individuals occupying higher positions in the organizational structure are more educated and more informed and hence should be followed and obeyed with what may border, in some cases, on blind obedience. This sluggish structure exists at all levels of educational management—from the U.S. Department of Education to state education agencies to local school boards to school principals to individual classroom teachers.

School boards, superintendents, and other school administrators typically emphasize standardization and uniformity as a means of maintaining control. Specific educational programs and guidelines are frequently established by high-ranking administrators without any significant input from principals, teachers, or parents (that is, the individuals who work most closely with the students—the individuals who are in the best position to know the needs and abilities of the students).

In the centralized power model, teachers are viewed, in general, as not being very insightful. Teachers are closely supervised and are required to follow the methods advocated by the administration. Curriculum guides and the quest for teacher-proof materials dominate the thinking of state and central office administrators. Daily lesson plans are checked to make certain that all teachers are following the approved guides. Above all, teachers are evaluated by the use of standardized tests to ensure that the curriculum is being implemented and that the centralized power model is working.

But is the centralized power model working? Evidence strongly indicates that the system is *not* working:

- Approximately one out of every two students fails. About 25 percent of students drop out of school and never graduate from high school. Of the students that receive high school diplomas, approximately 25 percent are functionally ill equipped and lack the skills to secure and hold the types of jobs necessary to support themselves.[1]
- There is a wide gulf between the educational accomplishments of children of different socioeconomic and racial backgrounds.
- Students see schooling as confining and boring. For many it is seen as compulsory—something they are not attracted to or desire.
- Students acquire knowledge and skills as a result of rote learning or memorization of abstractions rather than through the presentation of material that has meaning for them.

Yes, we are in trouble. And while many educators and national leaders have written about the need for reform, we do not believe that the plans and programs offered to date go far enough to solve the problem. The vast majority of the programs that have been proposed focus on specific aspects of the current educational system— that is, the quality of teachers, new curriculum designs, new student grouping patterns, and so on. We believe the fundamental flaw in the work that has already been done is the failure to acknowledge that the centralized power model is outdated, arcane, and woefully inadequate.

American business has had to learn the hard way that centralized, bureaucratic organizations do not work in today's world. American businesses suffered dramatic losses in the 1970s and 1980s, not because the Europeans and the Asians are superior workers but because the U.S. businesses were committed to outdated, hierarchical organizational structures. Reliance on traditional theories of

---

[1]David T. Kearns and Denis P. Doyle, *Winning the Brain Race* (San Francisco: Institute for Contemporary Studies, 1989).

administrative, control-oriented management created organizational structures that were sluggish and incapable of adapting quickly to changing market conditions. The companies that have been successful during the last decade have not just updated or modified their traditional thinking about management processes, they have adopted a completely new way of thinking.

Revolutionary change is occurring in U.S. business simply because companies have *had* to change in order to survive. The companies that have regained world-class ranking have done so by relaxing traditional rules and procedures, delegating responsibility to employees, and involving individuals at all levels in the management and operation of the business. Successful companies have done away with the discredited traditional administrative practices that are still in place in most U.S. schools.

As long as we support the type of bureaucratic structure that is prevalent in education today, our students will continue to suffer. The centralized power model engenders an educational hierarchy that enfeebles all participants in the system—administrators, teachers, parents, community members, business leaders, and students. Most important, the centralized power model deprives individual schools and classroom teachers of the necessary strength, flexibility, and creativity to provide quality education.

As with U.S. business, the shrinking of the global economy and the coming of the information-processing age have created enormous pressures on education to adapt quickly to subtle—and sometimes not so subtle—changes in social, cultural, political, and economic conditions. The simple truth is that we cannot preserve the quality of life that we have long enjoyed in this country, nor can we continue to have a world-class economy, without a world-class work force. And we cannot have a world-class work force without world-class students.

The logical solution to the educational crisis in the United States is to debureaucratize the present system—to implement the same types of collaborative, cooperative management techniques that many U.S. businesses have successfully adopted to remain viable competitors in today's global economy. Educators and administrators at the district, state, and national levels, like senior managers in business, are in positions to facilitate, to provide leadership, resources, and inspiration, but they do not actually have a direct involvement with the product (in the case of education, the student). If we are truly going to serve the educational needs of our children, we must transfer authority and control of the educational process to the individuals who are most directly involved in, and who can have the greatest effect on, determining the quality of our schools—teachers, parents, business leaders, community members, and students.

Who Are the Stakeholders?

Before continuing, let us consider a term we will be using throughout this book: "Stakeholder." *Webster's New School and Office Dictionary* defines "stakeholder" as "the one who holds the money on a wager, to be turned over to the winner." Our usage of the term encompasses a much broader idea. We define "Stakeholder" as anyone who holds a stake or an interest in something—in other words, a person who has something to win or lose as a result of, or relating to, an idea or practice. In the case of education, we include in the term "Stakeholder" all of the individuals who are directly involved or interested in the educational process. This obviously could include every person in the world, since we all are affected in some sense by the quality of the world's educational process. To give specific meaning to the term "Stakeholder," we limit its usage to Stakeholders of a specific school. We include as Stakeholders only those persons who are directly involved or interested in the quality and performance of a particular school—the principal, the teachers, the parents of the students, the business leaders and members of the community in which the school is located, and, perhaps most importantly, the students themselves.

The superintendent and board members of the district in which a school is located can be considered secondary Stakeholders, for while they may have a stake in the performance of the individual school in question, their attention cannot be focused entirely on that school given the demands, needs, and interests of the other schools in the district.

For ease of reference, we shall capitalize the term Stakeholder to indicate its special meaning as discussed above. We shall also specifically identify any additional individuals who may be considered Stakeholders when the context so warrants.

A Continuum of Involvement and Participation

If the centralized power model is to be replaced, it is important to determine what different Stakeholder involvement and participation models look like and who is to have the power in the different models. We suggest that there exists a continuum of involvement and participation, as illustrated in Figure 1–1.

The continuum of involvement and participation ranges from the least involved act of simply being an interested recipient of information about a school (conforming) to acts requiring the greatest level of participation, such as designing a new educational system (creating). In between conforming and creating are three moderate levels of Stakeholder involvement that might include, for example, helping to improve the existing system (contributing), attempting to change the existing system (challenging), or seeking to involve or support others who share the goal of changing the system (collaborating). As a Stakeholder proceeds across the continuum from conforming to creating, each successive stage places greater demands upon the Stakeholder. Exposure to risk increases, but at the same time so does the potential for rewards.

At present, involvement and participation in most schools typically reflect only the first two stages of the continuum—conforming and contributing. Teachers perform their jobs in the classroom, but few if any are actively involved in the management of the school or in the development of the academic curriculum. Parents may join the PTA or other parent-teacher organization and become passive participants in the educational process (conformers). Or they may strive for greater involvement as PTA officers or classroom volunteers (contributors), but rarely, if ever, are they asked for significant input in the operation of the school. Perhaps most telling is the complete lack of involvement and participation by students and by Stakehold-

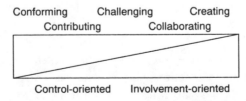

Figure 1–1. Continuum of Involvement and Participation.

ers outside the immediate realm of the school—that is, community members and business leaders.

Why is involvement so limited? Why are Stakeholders not playing a greater role? The first explanation is that education, perhaps more so than any other business endeavor, is strongly rooted in the past. Educational practices and ideas (such as the nine-month school year, rigid adherence to the grade-level approach, and the use of single-teacher classrooms) are frequently continued year after year for no better reason than "that's the way it has always been done." Most adults in the United States today were educated in school systems in which Stakeholders played a minimal role. Since "that's the way it has always been done," and because most Stakeholders (having been educated in a low Stakeholder-participation environment) probably conclude that greater Stakeholder participation is simply not permitted, there is a tendency to perpetuate a system of low Stakeholder participation.

More than inertia is at work here, though. As we explore in more detail later in this chapter, there are strong forces preventing Stakeholders from playing greater roles in the educational process. Simply stated, the centralized power model is sanctioned by the chosen few who are in power, and these individuals are typically reluctant to give up the power with which they have been entrusted. Consequently, the persons responsible for running centralized power model schools rarely invite or permit others to have a significant voice in the operation of the system or in the distribution of power within the system. Encouraging or even permitting Stakeholder involvement is viewed as a threat—as opposed to a benefit—to the educational system.

Exploring Systems with Greater Stakeholder Involvement

Although the array of models of educational systems utilizing greater Stakeholder involvement is virtually limitless, all have one thing in common: Stakeholders are given more autonomy and control over their schools. Since the range of this autonomy and control is rather broad, however, in each case it is up to the Stakeholders to determine how much and what types of involvement and participation they wish to have and the amount and type of power that will be retained by the superintendent and the school board.

To illustrate some of the differences between the centralized power model and a high-Stakeholder-involvement model (such as the Self-Directed School), we describe three models of school management that are presently in use or are in the process of being implemented in the United States today that rely on varying levels of Stakeholder involvement. Each model gives the Stakeholders different kinds and amounts of power. The models represent only the tip of the iceberg—there are hundreds of variations of these models.

The Principal Empowered Model

The first model is the principal empowered model, which gives the principal the final authority to make most of the decisions concerning the operation of the school. Under this model, a site council comprised of representatives of the teachers, parents, and community members serve in an advisory role to the principal. The principal, however, retains final decision-making authority. Some principals who use this model delegate certain initial decision-making power to committees, classroom teachers, and parent groups but retain veto power over all final decisions. The principal empowered model is relatively easy to implement and already exists in some schools. It is an easy model for a superintendent to monitor since all communication between the district office and the school is funneled directly through the principal, and the principal clearly has the power to stop decisions that the superintendent may oppose.

The principal empowered model, like the traditional hierarchical model, is still a control-oriented model and allows the Stakeholders only a limited amount of increased power. Many educators, parents, community members, and business leaders believe that implementation of the principal empowered model will not do much to change a school's performance. They argue that if decision-making power stops with the principal, then the benefits and advantages of Stakeholder empowerment and involvement will never be realized.

Power in the principal empowered model is merely transferred from one figurehead to another; no true dissemination of power or responsibility occurs. Stakeholders other than the principal, who assumes a position of great authority, are still left standing in the cold—with no real opportunity to voice their ideas, concerns, or suggestions. For these reasons, it is apparent that school systems which adopt this model and do not make plans for the subsequent transfer of the principal's power to all of the Stakeholders do so only as a cosmetic and largely symbolic response to the demands of critics. Reform of the system does not really occur.

The Local School Committee Empowered Model

The second organizational model is the local school committee empowered model, which is like having a school board at each school. This model is used successfully in many private schools. In most cases, the authority to control a private school is vested in a board of governors or trustees that has the legal right to make all decisions affecting the policy and structure of the school. These boards usually grant the principal or director of the school the discretion and resources necessary for positive leadership to take place. Under this kind of a system, the individual who runs the school has a strong incentive to please a clientele of parents and students through the decisions that are made. Some researchers believe that this responsiveness is one reason many private schools are successful.[2]

The local school committee empowered model is not reserved for private schools. In the fall of 1989 the Chicago public schools adopted this model with the Chicago School Reform Act creating local school councils at 542 attendance centers. Each council consists of six parents, two teachers, two community representatives, and the principal. Members are elected by constituent groups. A council, which has enormous power, hires the principal for its school and negotiates with the principal a four-year performance contract. A principal has only that power given to him or her by the council, with the power varying from council to council. The council drafts school improvement plans and is free of city-wide controls. Finally, the council controls the budget for its school and decides how to spend funds in order to best achieve the vision and plans for the school.

To date, the research that has been done on the local school committee empowered model is too incomplete to enable any definitive conclusions to be drawn about the effectiveness of the model in bringing about educational reform. We do know, however, that

---

[2]John E. Chubb and Terry M. Moe, *Politics, Markets and American Schools* (Washington, DC: The Brookings Institution, 1990).

problems relating to the formulation and execution of school policies have arisen between councils and principals. These problems are somewhat similar to those that presently exist between superintendents and school boards in traditionally organized school systems. In addition, teachers have said that there is too much parental control and that teachers are not treated as equal partners in the educational process.

The local school committee empowered model does give Stakeholders an opportunity to contribute and challenge the school and school system, but it allows only a limited number of Stakeholders to enter into the high-involvement-oriented mode of collaborating and creating.

The Self-Directed School Model

The Self-Directed School model reflects a completely new and different vision of school leadership. It is a model that is based on the collaboration of *all* of the Stakeholders of an individual school, it gives each school's Stakeholders the discretion and authority to design a new organization and to make key decisions affecting the teaching of students and the operation of the school. The Self-Directed School gives parents increased responsibility for their children's education and allows representatives of business and industry to have a say in the operation of the schools in their communities. It also gives students the right and responsibility to participate in forums in which the constitution of their classrooms and the content of their curriculum are forged.

The Self-Directed School not only *invites* participation, it *depends* on it. Without involvement of the highest order by all of the Stakeholders, the Self-Directed School is no more than a wolf in sheep's clothing—a control-oriented system run by the one or more Stakeholders who do choose to become involved.

Because the Self-Directed School provides the opportunity for all Stakeholders to become directly involved in developing and carrying out an effective curriculum, it is the model most likely to bring about significant improvements in school and student performance. Unfortunately, it is also the most difficult model to implement and many hours of training and retraining of staff members and community representatives are required before it can become truly effective. That is what the rest of this book is about.

Comparing the Centralized Power Model and the Self-Directed School Model

This book is designed primarily to serve as an aid for implementing the Self-Directed School model in an individual school or school system. Our intent is not to examine in detail the relative merits of each model or organizational structure—such a discussion is beyond the scope of this book. Suffice it to say here that we believe the Self-Directed School is the *best* model for administrative organization of our educational system and offers the most hope for effective school reform.

Notwithstanding what we just said, we believe it is irresponsible to delve into the intricacies of the Self-Directed School model without first pointing out some of the ways in which the Self-Directed School model differs—we believe for the better—from the traditional centralized power model that is prevalent in U.S. education today.

It is the complete redistribution and reallocation of leadership responsibilities that makes the Self-Directed School unique. In a Self-Directed School, everyone who desires to provide leadership or become involved in the operation of the school has an opportunity to do so. A Self-Directed School is guided by the belief that the sharing of responsibility throughout the organizational structure facilitates productivity, success, and leadership. By contrast, the centralized power model is guided by the principle that an organization functions most efficiently and effectively when a specific chain of command is in place and is clearly understood. Figure 1–2 (p. 22) compares some of the beliefs and values of the traditional centralized power model with the corresponding beliefs and values of the involvement-oriented Self-Directed School model.

Why Will the Self-Directed School Model Work?

We believe that an involvement-oriented approach is the best way to meet the educational needs of today's students. By relying on the same principles that underlie all democratic institutions (government of the people, by the people, and for the people), Self-Directed Schools offer to Stakeholders at all levels in the school system the power to influence and make decisions. The power to participate

TRADITIONAL ORGANIZATIONAL STRUCTURE (CENTRALIZED POWER MODEL)	SELF-DIRECTED ORGANIZATIONAL STRUCTURE (SELF-DIRECTED SCHOOL MODEL)
• Top of organization dictates goals and directions; control is key.	• Top of organization provides support and facilitates goal achievement.
• Solutions to problems are best solved by the administration.	• Solutions to problems are best solved by those who will implement them (i.e., the Stakeholders).
• Control remains at the top.	• Control is shared with those who influence operations and results.
• Decisions are made at the administrative level.	• Decisions are made by Stakeholders (site-based decision making).
• Information is restricted to school board and administration.	• Information is shared with Stakeholders.
• School board and district office know best.	• Stakeholders know best.
• Relationships between grade levels and schools need to be managed by administrators.	• Relationships between grade levels and schools should be managed by Stakeholders.
• Teachers in the school system exist to support the administration.	• The school system's administration exists to support the Stakeholders.
• Public input should be limited to selected board meetings.	• Constant input from *all* Stakeholders is *crucial* if schools are to succeed and remain abreast of changes in society.
• There is distrust of nonadministrators.	• All ideas merit discussion; solutions are found through collaboration, not individual experts.

Figure 1–2. Comparison of the Centralized Power Model and the Self-Directed School Model.

translates directly into increased feelings of responsibility for the performance of the system and a stronger faith in, and commitment to, the integrity of the system as an effective means of educating our youth.

Our confidence in the Self-Directed School model is based on four key assumptions:

- The Stakeholders of a school (the principal, teachers, parents, local business leaders, and community representatives) are the individuals most involved with the students of that school. As such, they are in the best position to understand the educational needs and potentials of the students and are, therefore, the individuals best suited to direct and create the school's educational environment.
- When people are actively involved in a collaborative effort to solve a problem, they develop a sense of ownership in, and commitment to, the proposed solution and are therefore more likely to accept responsibility for making the solution work.
- The collaborative effort of a school's staff and community members working together is far greater than the sum of their efforts made independently and in isolation.
- Treating school employees and community members as vital contributors to the educational enterprise, valuing their contributions and ideas, and involving them in decisions that affect them will increase their productivity and enthusiasm and thereby lead directly to significant increases in student learning and achievement.

The Self-Directed School depends on the sharing of authority and responsibility and on the complete and open dissemination of critical information. *Both* must occur if the Self-Directed School is to work. Organizational structures, procedures, and relationships must be changed and overhauled. How that can best be achieved is examined throughout this book.

Getting Started—The One Best Solution?

Whether you are a principal, teacher, parent, business person, school board member, or school administrator, you are aware of the need for school reform and have heard the exhortations to take the bureaucracy out of the educational system. Building upon the lessons learned in business and industry, educators and social commentators have argued convincingly that if we are going to experience any significant success in our educational system, we must open the system up—as business has done—and allow those who are the closest to the product (the students) to have a say in how the system is operated. Participatory management, shared decision making, and self-directed teams and clusters represent reforms that have been used successfully by businesses to bring decision-making authority as close to the product as possible. Unfortunately, visions of success based on similar reforms in school organization have not been accompanied by road maps on how to get there. We all want our schools to work better, and we all know that our schools have much unrealized potential. We just don't seem to know how to get things started.

Suppose your school was to try something really different. How would you go about it? What hassles would you meet along the way? How much leeway could you get from the school board and superintendent? Or, if you were given carte blanche, what would your school do?

This book provides a framework for answering such questions. The chapters that follow present a guide for implementing a collaborative working environment—the Self-Directed School—within an educational system. Included is a discussion of the various types of skills that will need to be developed by the participants in a Self-Directed School. We also explore a number of sample issues in order to illustrate how a collaborative decision-making model might deal with a particular problem.

This book is *not* a cookbook containing recipes for making the perfect Self-Directed School. There is no magic process or blueprint that a school can follow to become a Self-Directed School. The Self-Directed School is a concept based on principles of collaborative decision making. Each school that implements collaborative decision making will reflect the particular interests and strengths of its own participants. Like snowflakes and fingerprints, each Self-Directed School will be unique.

What we have done in this book is present a model of the Self-Directed School. For our purposes, a model does *not* mean a reproducible solution. The model discussed in this book cannot simply be duplicated and put into place. Instead, it must be modified to fit the specific needs of an individual school. We do believe, however, that our model can provide valuable guidance and assistance in establishing a Self-Directed School.

In keeping with the ideas expressed in this book, it is critical that school boards and educational administrators not seek to discover the perfect Self-Directed School format and then attempt to impose that format on all of the schools in the district. We realize that such restraint will take a herculean effort on the part of the administrators. Most administrators have been trained under traditional management theories. Under such theories, it is the specific responsibility of administrators (as the "trained thinkers") to develop solutions to management problems. It seems to be inherent in administrators to seek the one best solution to a problem and then attempt to duplicate its format across the board. Under this approach, every school in a given system would be expected to use the same format, regardless of the specific goals, objectives, and missions of the staff and community of each school. Nothing could be more damaging to the concept of Self-Directed Schools.

System-wide "solutions," while perhaps well intentioned, are counterproductive. For a Self-Directed School to be effective, it must have the freedom and authority to develop its own format. Each school should be set up essentially as a separate business in competition with itself (as well as with other schools in the district). By so doing, school systems can create the type of organizational structure that encourages individual schools to be entrepreneurial—to control their own destiny. Although there will obviously be similarities from school to school, each school will have modified the model to fit the needs and interests of its students. The particular form of the model that a school adopts will be determined by the school's Stakeholders—the individuals who are in the best position to assess the needs of the students.

The purpose of a Self-Directed School is to improve student performance by making those closest to the delivery of services (the principal, teachers, parents, business leaders, and community members) more independent and therefore more involved in, and responsible for, the results of the school's operation. When school boards and superintendents mandate formats for self-direction and add layers of administrative requirements, they make the circle back to conformity and debilitating hierarchy. Mandating a uniform Self-Directed School pattern contradicts the very assumptions underlying the rationale for moving to self-directedness in the first place.

We do not, of course, advocate the complete emasculation of school boards and central office administration. To the contrary, the central office will continue to serve several vital roles even after Self-Directed Schools are implemented. (We discuss the continued role of the central office in detail in Chapter 9.) For example, it will continue to make sense for school boards and central offices to establish certain goals and targets for school performance. It will not make sense, however, for school boards and/or superintendents to *tell* schools how to organize and operate in order to accomplish those goals and objectives. What is needed from the school board and superintendent is the necessary support to facilitate the implementation by individual schools of their own "personally created" Self-Directed School format.

School boards will also still need to be involved in establishing structures and procedures in many areas—such as in transportation, food service, purchasing, and payroll. Individual schools, however, must be given the freedom and authority to customize the model in ways that are deemed appropriate by the school's Stakeholders.

A Self-Directed School does not mean chaos, anarchy, or lack of central direction, nor does it mean the end of management. What it does mean is a new role for leaders and managers through the exercise of collaborative leadership.

Forces against Change

> *Those in power are the least likely to give it up.*
> Unknown

Changing the existing educational bureaucracy will not be easy. Leaders who decide to change radically the historical methods of doing business in our schools are taking on a major challenge.

For a number of reasons, bringing about change in the educational environment of U.S. schools will be unusually difficult. First, for any change to be effective, there must be a significant realignment and reallocation of power and control in the administration of our schools. As history tells us, any attempt to reallocate power in an organization is met with tremendous resistance by those who occupy positions of power or authority. Those who have achieved success or climbed to the top of the organization cannot be expected to embrace what they view as a usurpation of their position.

This type of oligarchical resistance to change is particularly characteristic of the field of education. Most school administrators have worked hard to become a part of their district's hierarchy. Much of their university and other training to receive administrative certification has focused on principles and methods of working within a traditional hierarchical management structure. As administrators in the "real" world, they have learned to succeed in the highly bureaucratized environment of most school systems. This kind of entrenchment—both academic and experiential—in hierarchical, control-oriented management systems will make it very difficult for them to rethink the fundamentals, which will be required in order to achieve success. In a traditional organization power cannot be delegated because position in the hierarchy would cease to have meaning. There cannot be complete openness because the authority of supervisors would be undermined. There cannot be full employee involvement because differences in status and rewards based on formal position would be erased. Prevailing theories of effective management also prohibit allowing differences among schools. Superintendents and school boards in traditional management systems prefer *conformity* and *predictability*. Conformity and predictability do not make for a better school system, but they make it easier for those in power to "manage" the system and to explain to their constituents what is going on in the system.

In addition to resistance by those at the top of the organizational pyramid, there is a second, less obvious factor working against the successful implementation of Self-Directed Schools. Education is replete with examples of failed attempts to slay the dragon of educational failure. People in school systems have been subjected to numerous innovative panaceas in an attempt to solve the problems of public education. Over the past several decades we have seen nongraded schools, new ways to teach mathematics, open classrooms, team teaching, and a variety of other programs designed to combat perceived weaknesses in our educational system. To make matters worse, most, if not all, of these programs were adopted at the district level and foisted upon all of the schools in the district. As each new program has failed, the disillusionment has increased. Therefore, it should come as no surprise if, at least initially, teachers and other educators fail to react enthusiastically to the Self-Directed School and instead see it as nothing more than the newest "flavor of the month"—rather than as a fundamental restructuring of the educational system. It is important to note that *none* of the new programs address the fundamental flaw in our educational system: that control is centered in the district office and in layers of administrative bureaucracy rather than at the individual school level.

A third factor operating against change is the rigidity of the hierarchical management structure of most school systems. It is in a school district's organizational structure that traditional managerial practices and decisions are most clearly reflected. In the vast majority of U.S. school districts today, each employee has a boss from whom he or she receives direction and by whom he or she is evaluated. The district organizational chart expressly defines the relationship of persons in the system and the degree of power each person can exercise. The typical chart concentrates power in the superintendent, with underlings having progressively less power until the chain of command reaches the teachers, who have little or no power. Parents and business people are excluded from the chart altogether and are left only with the power to elect the school board. They have virtually no opportunity to participate in the educational process or to interact with the real decision makers. Authority, decision making, individual responsibility, and personal status are all determined by the organization chart. Everyone knows his or her position in the chart. Change will require rethinking by everyone—a formidable challenge.

Has Anything Been Done Yet?

Many school systems have been trying to change, to streamline procedures, increase delegation of responsibility, refine methods of educational measurement, improve communication, and increase involvement. But for most school systems these efforts have been controlled at the district level. Each innovation has been accompanied by an administrator in charge. Some school systems have even appointed a director of site-based decision making. Of course, the terms "director" and "site-based" are mutually exclusive. For educational reform to be effective, important decisions must be made at the individual school level. By designing new programs at the district level, school administrators and school boards fail to understand that gains in education can be made only by rethinking who decides what will be changed at each school. A full transformation of managerial thinking is required. School district administrators must become *facilitators* of change rather than *deciders* of change. To make new programs work, there has to be a dramatic change in the structure of the organization—a change that gives the Stakeholders a voice in deciding what needs to be done and how it can be accomplished.

While many administrators have learned the language of educational reform, particularly the idea of decentralization, few have actually learned or have truly desired to implement the concept. Some school boards and superintendents believe that they are already changing their fundamental organizational structure, but most are fooling themselves. Some school systems embrace site-based decision making as a label for what they believe they are already doing, but discard the substance. They have adopted the rhetoric without seriously altering their organization or modes of operation. Bowing to increasing pressures to move toward site-based decision making, superintendents may announce that all has been transformed, without actually implementing crucial changes: "They talk the talk, but do not walk the walk."

In their attempts to increase participation, some school systems have created advisory committees as a way of involving staff and community. The problem is that these school systems have continued to retain control and veto authority at the district level. When school systems urge employees and the community to take greater risks, to take initiative, and to think for themselves rather than await direction while simultaneously maintaining the hierarchical structure, employees and community members quickly discover that the system's intentions are insincere at best or misguided at worst. As a result, the employees and community lose interest in the "experiment" and return more disheartened and disillusioned to their traditional roles as mere observers of the educational process.

Continuing reliance on hierarchical management is ironic because a careful examination of experiences with nontraditional structures in progressive school systems suggests that control need not be significantly sacrificed. In most of these systems, the school boards still establish goals that the district as a whole has to meet, and the superintendents still provide visionary leadership to give direction to the system. Part of that vision focuses on how to help each school achieve its own destiny.

Can We Succeed?

Many school board members, superintendents, administrators, and even some teachers doubt that substantive remodeling of the leadership responsibilities of schools can occur, and their skepticism may be well founded. The traditions of past decades will be difficult to change, but we must remember that our current centralized system is failing. Moreover, student learning will not improve significantly as long as we keep the present control-oriented organization structure. We simply cannot afford *not* to succeed. We cannot allow our students to be uneducated, unequipped, unprepared, and—ultimately—unemployed in the twenty-first century.

A key idea behind the Self-Directed School is that the overall improvement of American education depends on getting individual schools to operate more effectively. Today's school systems can be changed only by changing individual schools. System-wide change will occur by lodging greater responsibility with the Stakeholders of particular schools. Allowing individual schools a high degree of discretion in operating themselves is not inconsistent with the goals of the school system. System leadership and vision can align autonomous schools so that the results hoped for from the rigid controls in a hierarchy are achieved in alternative forms.

Success is possible. Progress will be slow, but change can occur—one school at a time. Fundamental leadership responsibilities can be reshaped and traditional hierarchy abandoned. We cannot afford not to change. It is time for a new and different form of administration. It is time for the Self-Directed School.

When given the authority to act independently to achieve stated goals, each school in a district will adopt individual programs and ideas that best fit the strengths of that school's community, staff, and students. With each school working with the fervor and enthusiasm engendered by autonomy and independence, the quality of the overall school system will become far greater than the sum of the quality of the individual schools. At that point, success will occur.

2

Clusters: The Heart of the Self-Directed School

We must all hang together, or assuredly we shall all hang separately.

Benjamin Franklin,
at the signing of the Declaration of Independence,
July 4, 1776

Traditional thinking in education has long maintained that the quality of an individual school is largely determined by the quality of the school's principal. In this light, schools begin to look very much like professional sports teams. The principal assumes the role of the coach and the teachers are the players. Taken one step further, the local school board can be viewed as the team's administrative office and the superintendent as the team's owner.

The analogy proceeds as follows: Just as professional sports players are hired and paid by the team owner, so are teachers hired and paid by the superintendent and school board. In essence, the principal/coach is simply provided by the board/owner with the teachers/players with whom he or she is to work. The board/owner sets the parameters within which the principal/coach is to work, and then the principal/coach is told to "go out there and win." The principal/coach works with the teachers/players, trying to prepare them for the game. When game time comes, the teachers/players become the participants, and the principal/coach is left as an observer. Strangely, however, the principal/coach receives an inordinate amount of praise for a successful team and the bulk of the blame for a losing team.

We believe that this traditional focus on the importance of the principal is myopic and hinders true improvement in our educational system. As Benjamin Franklin so sagely noted over two hundred years ago, true success depends more on cooperation than on individual heroics. It is time for a paradigm shift. We need to change the way we think about education and about the people who are responsible for the success or failure of our schools. In a Self-Directed School the quality of the educational process is not determined by the principal. Instead, quality is determined by the Stakeholders of the school working together collaboratively in clusters.

What Is a Cluster?

The key concept in the Self-Directed School—in fact, the *heart* of the Self-Directed School—is its cluster organization. A cluster is simply a group of people who work together, like a small team or a committee. Clusters are typically made up of a small number of Stakeholders who decide to become responsible for one or more issues affecting the operation of the Self-Directed School. A Self-Directed School may have many clusters operating at the same time. One cluster might be working to develop new science programs, while another works to solve discipline problems. A third cluster might be responsible for developing goals and plans for the school, and a fourth cluster for preparing methods to evaluate the success of particular school programs. While there might be some point at which the number of clusters operating at a given school could create such a state of chaos that their mere existence would prove detrimental to the school, it would certainly not be inconceivable for a school to have forty or fifty clusters in existence at any particular time.

Clusters require the participation of all Stakeholders. Instead of functioning as dictatorial units—or professional sports teams— schools become open democracies in which all Stakeholders have a say. Principals and district offices still exist, but their functions and responsibilities are drastically altered. (We examine the continued role of the principal and the district office in a Self-Directed School in Chapters 8 and 9, respectively.) Suffice it to say for now, however, that both the principal and the district office must abandon their well-established roles as *leaders* and assume new roles as *facilitators*. The principal, in particular, must become a skilled facilitator in order for the Self-Directed School to succeed.

As we stated in Chapter 1, there is no one correct form of Self-Directed School. Consequently, it is impossible for us to present here a definitive diagram of the organizational structure of a Self-Directed School. We can, however, offer examples that illustrate how some schools are using clusters as they move toward self-directedness. Figure 2–1 illustrates one example of a cluster organization. The chart represents the organizational structure that is currently in place at the Hillcrest Professional Development School in Waco, Texas. Instead of relying on the typical top-down organizational structure, the Self-Directed School relies on clusters of individuals working together. At Hillcrest Professional Development School, these clusters are arranged in almost random fashion, with no "top" or "bottom" on the chart, but all clusters are attached to a common vine. The common vine is the mission and vision of the school as developed and determined by the school's site council (a cluster in and of itself) and the governing school board. The clusters are determined by, and arranged in accordance with, the school's vision. The clusters work together to produce the programs and activities necessary to accomplish the mission and achieve the vision.

The clusters are responsible for numerous and diverse activities, ranging from planning curriculum to performing administrative functions. Each cluster develops its own expertise, pushes decision making toward the point of action, shares information broadly, and accepts accountability for its actions.

Figure 2–2 presents an alternative depiction of the type of non-hierarchical organizational structure present in a Self-Directed School. In the figure, the mission, goals, and vision of the school form the center of the school's "universe." The various clusters established by the school's Stakeholders exist in close orbit, their purposes and actions being ever drawn toward the center of the universe by the gravity of the school's goals, mission, and vision.

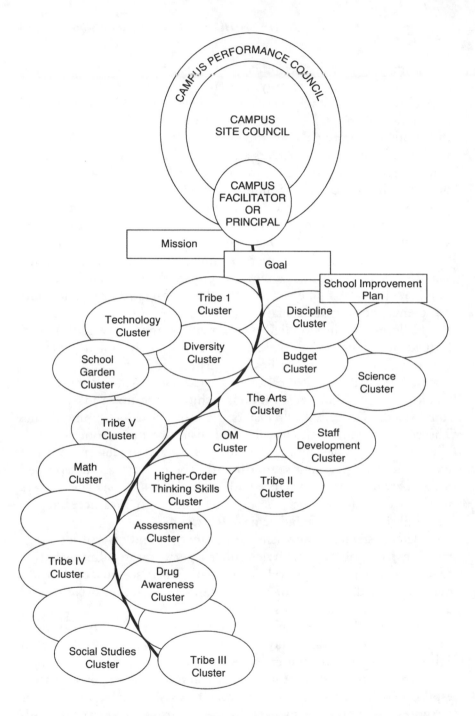

Figure 2–1. The Self-Directed School as Adapted by Hillcrest Professional Development School, Waco, Texas.

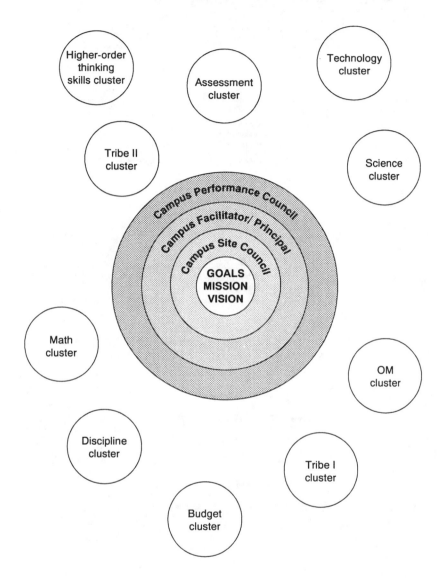

Figure 2–2. The Self-Directed School, an Alternative Adaptation.

Figure 2–3 shows the Self-Directed School model used by the Littleton High School in Littleton, Colorado. This model is quite different from the models depicted in Figures 2–1 and 2–2. However, all of the models are based on the same philosophical belief in the

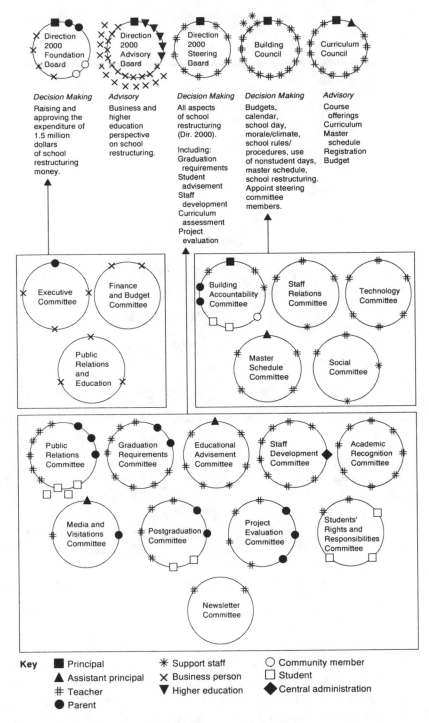

Figure 2–3. The Self-Directed School, as Adapted by Littleton High School, Littleton, Colorado.

strengths and advantages of collaborative decision making and total Stakeholder involvement. As we have stressed, no two models adapted by individual schools will ever look the same. Instead, each school's vision of the Self-Directed School will reflect the opinions, views, and beliefs of the Stakeholders of that particular school.

The Self-Directed School model reflects a new and different vision of school leadership and management. It is based on the participation and cooperation of *all* of the responsible parties at the individual school level. The Self-Directed School model gives each school's Stakeholders the authority to make key decisions affecting the teaching of students and the operation of the school. In a Self-Directed School, parents are given increased responsibility for their children's education. Business leaders and community representatives are provided with an opportunity to become active participants in influencing what schools are doing. Perhaps most important, the Self-Directed School model encourages student participation, allowing students the right and responsibility to participate in forums where the constitution and content of their classrooms are forged.

What Do Clusters Do?

Before discussing the administrative and organizational issues raised by cluster management, let us examine the types of activities in which clusters can be involved. By getting a better feel for the kinds of activities in which clusters will be engaged and the sheer magnitude of the decisions they will be making, the reader will better understand the managerial challenges presented by a cluster organization.

Several types of clusters are represented in Figures 2–1, 2–2, and 2–3. These are probably not the only types of clusters that will exist. Clearly, the specific types, sizes, and purposes of the clusters in existence at any particular school will be determined by the needs and circumstances of the school. However, the clusters represented in Figures 2–1, 2–2, and 2–3 illustrate the three general categories or types of clusters that will be present in most Self-Directed Schools:

Site council
Campus performance council
Project clusters, consisting of standing clusters, articulation
    clusters, and special interest clusters

The Site Council

Typically, the site council is comprised of parents, teachers, community members, business leaders, and the principal/facilitator. The primary responsibility of the site council is to make policy decisions concerning the school's curriculum, budget, staffing, and organization. The site council functions as a decision-making body that actually sets school policy. The principal/facilitator's role is to aid the functioning of the site council—especially in the initial phases—and to provide the necessary guidance and expertise to ensure that the decisions of the site council are consistent with school board policy, applicable regulations, and state and federal laws. The role of the principal/facilitator is further explored in Chapter 8.

The Campus Performance Council

In a Self-Directed School, responsibility for evaluating the performance of the school and its students and reporting the results of such evaluations to the superintendent and the board of trustees of the school district rests with what is known as the campus performance council. This cluster typically consists of the principal/facilitator, business leaders, parents, community leaders, and teachers. Again, the principal/facilitator's primary responsibility is to act as a facilitator for the group. The campus performance council, through the cooperation and participation of the school's Stakeholders, develops the school's overall mission statement and establishes goals that are consistent with that mission.

The campus performance council is also responsible for the final approval of the school improvement plan before it is sent to the superintendent and board. The school improvement plan is a collection of goals established by the campus performance council regarding student performance. The council is responsible for meeting with the school board to receive the board's input on the plan. During this consultation period, members of the school board should have ample opportunity to discuss with the campus performance council the goals established by the board for the schools in the district.

The campus performance council is also responsible for conducting studies, and reporting the results to the board and superintendent, to determine whether the goals outlined in the campus improvement plan have been met.

Project Clusters

Project clusters are the heart and soul of the Self-Directed School. At Hillcrest Professional Development School, project clusters take three forms: standing clusters, also referred to as tribes; articulation clusters; and special interest clusters. All of the clusters consist of small groups of Stakeholders who work together to solve problems or complete projects. Some clusters include parents and business leaders as members (such as clusters to develop and run homework clubs, care for school gardens, or develop science labs). Other clusters consist primarily of teachers and staff members (such as tribes, which are discussed below). The cluster groups emerge from two different motivations. The first is *proactive*—how can the school meet its mission and goals? The second is *reactive*—how can the school solve problems that may have been identified? The goal, of course, is to work toward a situation in which *most* of the clusters are functioning in a proactive mode.

Standing clusters, or tribes, are groups of teachers or staff members who work together for an extended or indefinite period of time. Tribes typically have representatives from all grade levels or departments. In that way, each tribe constitutes a cross section of the school. The diversity present in each tribe helps to produce high-quality programs that receive total school support. Effective teamwork in each tribe is based upon an effective mix of people who exhibit a variety of working styles or approaches to teamwork. (The various personal styles of individuals are explored in Chapter 3.)

Tribes are involved in school management in a variety of ways. At times tribes function as vehicles for developing the self-esteem and esprit de corps of the teachers and staff members. During such periods, the tribes focus mainly on group dynamics and individual self-reflections. At other times tribes are assigned or volunteer to review or modify broad aspects of the school's activities. Examples of tribes' involvement include formulating ideas to reduce unnecessary paperwork, developing an overall school discipline plan, and making plans for teacher inservice presentations.

Articulation clusters are created for the specific purpose of increasing the sharing of information among curricular areas, grade levels, and/or interdisciplinary teams. Grade-level, learning environments, and department teams are also articulation clusters. As we discuss later in this chapter, communication of information is one of the most important aspects of a cluster organization. If information is not readily available to all clusters and Stakeholders, then a school that is trying to implement cluster management will fail. Hence, articulation clusters are vital to the eventual success of the Self-Directed School.

Special interest clusters are created for the purpose of developing or refining special areas or programs in the school. Examples include technology clusters, greenhouse clusters, science lab clusters, and clusters responsible for developing specialized curricula (for example, a curriculum to provide instruction in building computerized robots).

Advantages of Clusters

Having briefly reviewed some functions of clusters, we can now turn to the advantages—and some of the perceived disadvantages—of cluster organization. Management by clusters offers two major advantages to schools. First, clusters empower the Stakeholders, resulting in greater Stakeholder participation, involvement, and commitment and in more creative plans for the future and more effective solutions to problems. Second, clusters help to eliminate the feelings of isolation teachers have traditionally experienced. We will examine each of these benefits in turn.

Clusters Empower Stakeholders

Cluster groups are based on the old saying, "Two heads are better than one." In the human embodiment of the German gestalt theory—which states that the whole is greater than the sum of its parts—cluster groups produce better, more creative, and more imaginative ideas than would be generated by individuals working separately. When individual Stakeholders are encouraged to work together, to share ideas, and to build upon one another's suggestions, the results will naturally be greater than the results produced by individuals working independently.

But the production of ideas through collective thought is only one step along the path of empowerment. The mere existence of an idea or proposal is useless unless it can be effectively implemented. This is where the real power of clusters comes in.

Clusters flourish because individuals are more likely to accept an idea and to be committed to making an idea work if they themselves are involved in the creation of the idea. Thus, Stakeholders who are actively involved in solving a problem or proposing a plan or program are more likely to accept and be committed to the successful implementation of the solution, plan, or program than if it had been handed down to them by imperial decree from the principal, superintendent, or other bureaucrat.

Empowerment of Stakeholders is one of the key concepts underlying the Self-Directed School. American businesses have, through self-directed teams, employee management groups, and other means of encouraging employee participation and involvement, begun to reap the benefits of employee empowerment. Empowered employees are more productive, more involved, and more committed to the success of the enterprise in which they are engaged than are nonempowered employees. Empowered employees have also proved to be more creative and imaginative in their ideas and proposals than upper-level managers, who are frequently trapped in their own traditional ways of thinking. The same type of empowerment is needed in the field of education. Empowered Stakeholders, when freed from bureaucratic restraints, will develop the new programs and implement the new ideas that are necessary to create world-class schools—schools that produce students able to deal with the challenges of today's rapidly changing world.

Many educators today spend a lot of time complaining about the lack of parent involvement in the educational process. They also bemoan the fact that they cannot get any significant input or assistance from business leaders or community members. What these educators don't seem to realize is that the hierarchical management structure that is present in most schools today actually precludes any real participation by these interested Stakeholders. The top-down management structure simply doesn't afford opportunities for involvement by anyone other than high-ranking management officials.

Clusters make possible the full empowerment of Stakeholders, providing an atmosphere in which individuals feel both the freedom and the support to act. Using clusters as a way of organizing a school rather than relying on the traditional hierarchical organization form provides the conditions necessary to make individual initiative possible.

Clusters Eliminate Teacher Isolation

Traditionally, teachers have been forced to work in virtual isolation. Armed with district policies, curriculum guides, and state requirements, teachers have been sent off to do battle—alone and behind the closed door of the classroom.

Functioning as an island, an individual teacher can only do so much. After all, an individual's time and resources are limited. As part of a team, however, a teacher can be provided with support and ideas that he or she may never have realized existed.

What is unique about clusters is that they combine individual initiative and teamwork. In fact, the teamwork that is such an important aspect of cluster activity serves to reinforce and enhance the individual. Clusters provide an opportunity for teachers to learn and grow, to share ideas, to meet new people, to develop new contacts, and to take advantage of the talents and energies of Stakeholders other than other teachers. In short, clusters offer much needed relief to what is otherwise the unrelenting, unappreciated, and isolated work of individual teachers.

A specific example illustrates the types of benefits that can result from cluster activity. A cluster group in a high school was given the responsibility of developing a performance-based evaluation system for the physics class. As a first step, the cluster requested help from a local steel company that had recently developed a performance-based employee evaluation system.

Not only were the representatives of the steel company helpful in developing a workable evaluation system, but they also suggested several ways in which they could contribute to the physics class by supplying materials and assisting in the teaching of the physics curriculum. The direct beneficiaries, of course, were both the teachers (who now were able to tap into and take advantage of resources that previously had been unavailable) *and* the students (who were now provided with insights and experiences that had not been offered by the teachers working in isolation).

While it is certainly conceivable that a teacher working individually could have gone to the steel company and enlisted its aid, it is a sad fact of reality that most teachers do not have the time, resources, or support necessary to accomplish such projects on a regular basis. By providing support, assistance, and encouragement, clusters make it possible for teachers to explore avenues and utilize teaching resources they may never have known existed.

Each participant in a cluster plays an important role. By communicating ideas in an environment of mutual support and respect, cluster members work together to accomplish tasks and achieve goals. Individual teachers are no longer forced to work in isolation under the direct supervision of a principal or department head. Instead, groups of teachers can work together to solve problems and develop school programs and activities. In many cases, clusters also include parents, business leaders, community members, and students, who add their support and cooperation for the collective good of the group. Cluster groups successfully harness the collaborative and cooperative drives of the Stakeholders into a very powerful mechanism for accomplishing goals and achieving objectives.

In short, clusters present a new way of tapping the full potential of a school's community and at the same time of breaking down the traditional hierarchy that prevents true change and reform. By empowering the Stakeholders and breaking down the traditional barriers leading to teacher isolation, clusters allow for the skills and aspirations of all of a school's Stakeholders to be utilized and maximized for the full benefit of the school and its students.

Cluster Empowerment: Is There Such a Thing as Too Much?

Educators have been talking about Stakeholder or employee empowerment for some time, but achieving such liberation of people from the "system" has proved difficult in traditional organizations. Chapter 1 considered some of the problems school boards and administrators typically experience in letting go of the authority with which they have always been entrusted. Even when school boards and administrators do attempt to let go, they frequently encounter problems in implementing the empowerment concept. This failure is probably due to a lack of understanding on the part of the school board and superintendent of the key elements of the concept of empowerment. At the same time, administrators have received insufficient training in the skills required to work in the new roles created by an empowered organization. (We will discuss the issue of training in Chapter 4.)

What are the key elements that make empowerment possible? An example will help identify them.

Suppose the superintendent of a medium-sized school district tells one of his principals (we will call him Principal Paul) that he can implement a plan to develop a Self-Directed School. The superintendent isn't quite sure what a Self-Directed School is, but since some of the innovative superintendents in the state have been giving their principals more freedom and authority to implement changes, he feels it is his duty to transfer more authority and freedom to his principals. Principal Paul, instead of retaining his newly acquired authority, immediately proceeds to transfer all of this authority to the Stakeholders of his school, who work in clusters as collaborative groups.

The foregoing example is more than hypothetical; it has actually happened—probably a number of times. And in districts in which it hasn't happened, it probably will happen in the near future as districts begin to decentralize and implement the reforms necessary to save the educational system in the United States. The example serves, however, as a means of identifying some of the issues and questions that may be raised in connection with attempts to delegate power and authority to individual schools.

The first question is, How can the superintendent or the board maintain control over the performance of a school if the school is free to make its own decisions and to substitute its judgment for that of the superintendent and/or the board? After all, if each school in the district is completely empowered to "do its own thing," won't the result be unstructured anarchy and chaos? Moreover, given the ever-growing number of state and federal laws, rules, and regulations governing the operation of schools, how can the superintendent and/or the board be comfortable that the individually empowered schools have the expertise necessary to ensure that their decisions and policies will comply with all of these laws, rules, and regulations? In the past, school districts have monitored compliance with applicable laws through the promulgation of detailed policy manuals that dictated the procedures to be followed by each school and provided guidance intended to reduce or eliminate divergent thinking by individual schools. In preparing these policy manuals, school districts have relied on legions of lawyers to sort through the maze of legal mumbo jumbo and to provide assistance in avoiding major pitfalls. Won't delegation of decision-making authority to individual schools undermine these attempts to comply with the law and remain abreast of the ever-changing legal environment?

The types of questions identified in the preceding paragraph are the questions most administrators will probably have as they think about the logistics of implementing Self-Directed Schools in their districts. The problem with the questions, however, is that they are overly simplistic and fail to take into account the realities of collaborative management and the Self-Directed School.

As proponents of Self-Directed Schools, we do not advocate the *complete* delegation of authority and control to individual schools. Rather, Self-Directed Schools *depend* on the existence of strong and effective school boards—albeit in a substantially different form than what we currently see. Suffice it to say for now, however, that the school board in a Self-Directed School system will still be responsible for providing valuable support functions, such as establishing the overall mission of the district, providing administrative assistance, coordinating the dissemination of important information, and facilitating the achievement of the district's objectives. With respect to the minefield of legal regulations governing the operation of schools, the board, together with the superintendent, will still be responsible—as a partner—for reviewing decisions made by individual schools to ensure compliance with all applicable rules.

The net result is that in a Self-Directed School system the superintendent and the board are facilitators rather than dictators. The central office continues to provide leadership and support, but it ceases to be involved in the active operation of individual schools. All decisions that relate to the actual operation of a school are delegated to that school. Only decisions that are specifically covered by federal and state laws and regulations remain the province of the central office. As we shall see in Chapter 7, this delegation of authority to individual schools actually gives the schools a great deal of flexibility in accomplishing their objectives and goals.

The delegation of authority to individual schools makes a great deal of sense. After all, the Stakeholders of a particular school are the individuals who are in the best position to know the strengths and weaknesses of both the staff and the students of the school. Central office administrators, regardless of their intentions, experience, or academic qualifications, are simply not in a position to know the ins and outs of each school in their district. Administrators, then, should assume the roles for which they are best qualified—providing input in establishing the overall educational mission and goals of the district and dedicating their administrative talents to helping individual schools accomplish their objectives and goals, which have been developed in accordance with the district's objectives and goals.

Under the current system of hierarchical management, decisions affecting critical aspects of our children's education are frequently slow in coming or simply never made as they are shuffled from layer to layer in the pyramid structure. When administrators become facilitators as opposed to dictators, however, the cluster groups at each school can assume responsibility and make much-needed decisions quickly and on a timely basis—resulting in direct and immediate benefits to our students and to the educational process.

Cluster Groups as Leaders: Determining the Degree of Delegation

Even assuming the proper structure is in place to ensure that administrators function as facilitators and that individual schools understand the scope of their decision-making authority (i.e., that decisions must be made in accordance with the overall mission of the district and must comply with all applicable laws, rules, and regulations), questions still arise concerning the ability of cluster groups to assume leadership roles at the individual school level. For instance, some educators wonder how a superintendent or school board can trust a school's cluster groups to function without specific guidance from "above." We believe a better and more constructive way to pose the question is: In what circumstances can school boards and superintendents feel comfortable about the delegation of decision-making authority to the Stakeholders at the individual school level?

The success of a Self-Directed School depends on the ability of its cluster groups to assume responsibility and accept the delegation of power and authority to the fullest extent possible. Five factors need to be considered in determining the degree to which the Stakeholders are prepared to accept the delegation of power and authority to operate the school:

1. The competence of the Stakeholders.
2. The Stakeholders' understanding of the mission.
3. The Stakeholders' ability to obtain and communicate information.
4. The Stakeholders' willingness to accept accountability.
5. Stakeholder trust.

1. The Competence of the Stakeholders

As with any human endeavor, if Self-Directed Schools are to succeed, then the individuals who run the schools must be competent. They must know what is expected of them, and they must know how to go about satisfying those expectations. It is not enough that the Stakeholders of a school want to make the school better; they must know how to take steps to get there.

Competence actually begins with the superintendent and the local school board. It is critical that the board prepare a comprehensive and understandable manual of district policies and regulations. The manual should state the educational mission and objectives of the district and should incorporate all applicable federal and state laws and regulations pertaining to the operation of schools. The manual should also contain a detailed explanation of the district's business and accounting procedures. The manual needs to be updated on a regular basis to keep up with developments in the legal and accounting fields.

It is the responsibility of a school's principal to know the limits of the school's power. The principal must be familiar with all aspects of the district manual and must be able to apply its provisions in a variety of settings. The principal's primary role is to provide guidance to the Stakeholders and clusters to ensure that all decisions made by them comply with applicable laws and regulations. The principal must therefore have a working understanding of the legal system and applicable accounting procedures. In addition, the principal must be able to see the "big" picture—that is, to understand the operation of the overall school system. The role of the principal in a Self-Directed School is discussed in more detail in Chapter 8.

Lastly, the Stakeholders of the school must be competent. They must be able to work together to reach agreement in teams, using conflict-resolution strategies and problem-solving techniques. Most Stakeholders will not have had any formal training in developing these skills. Such skills are generally not taught as part of any university teacher-training program, and they are not even included in most administrative certification programs. Consequently, Stakeholders will need to be taught these skills. It is simply a matter of fact that high-involvement programs like the Self-Directed School require continuing investment in the education and development of the people in leadership positions.

With cluster groups, all participants serve as leaders. Therefore, all Stakeholders need to receive training. Clusters depend on the competency of all of their members. There is no one person serving as the boss or leader. In order for clusters to experience the kind of commitment and creativity that can be achieved through collaborative activity, a Self-Directed School needs to make the investment in human capital that is necessary to provide its Stakeholders with the skills required to function successfully. More about the training of Stakeholders is contained in Chapter 5.

2. The Stakeholders' Understanding of the Mission

Each Stakeholder must understand the mission of the school system, of the school, and of his or her cluster. Moreover, since the cluster is only part of a much bigger whole (that is, the school system and the school), each Stakeholder must understand where his or her cluster fits in.

For example, the school district might have as its main emphasis the development of productive citizens who can be adaptable and successful in a global economy. It is then the responsibility of each school in the district to implement that mission in the manner in which the school's Stakeholders deem appropriate. As part of its implementation plan, an individual school will need to emphasize the development of collaboration skills, since that is one of the skills businesses have stressed is needed by employees in a globally competitive environment. One of the clusters in that school may then take on the responsibility of developing a program to teach students how to collaborate and work together.

The translation of the district's mission into real educational programs is something that the school board and superintendent must feel comfortable is happening in each school in the district. This will require coordination and communication. Only if each school and all of its respective Stakeholders know the overall mission of the district and what it means to them can they act in accordance with it. It is therefore imperative that the school board and superintendent work diligently to ensure that the mission of the district is clearly articulated and is understood by all of the Stakeholders in the district.

In addition to the district's mission statement, each school in the district needs to have its own mission statements which are compatible with the district mission and which take into consideration the needs of the particular school's population and community. Similarly, each cluster group in each school needs to have a mission statement clearly defining the purposes and goals of that cluster. Where collaborative or group activity fails, it is frequently the result of a lack of understanding of the mission or objective of the group. Nothing can disrupt group activity faster than a failure by the members of the group to remain focused on the objectives of the group. To avoid this kind of unfocused paralysis, specific mission statements should be prepared by each cluster.

All mission statements should be clearly written, understandable, and highly visible. Many school systems today go to a great deal of trouble to involve the community in developing a comprehensive mission statement only to put the statement away and not mention it again until a need arises for community support (for example, for a bond election or to resolve a sticky political situation). Hidden mission statements, just like hidden agendas, are not benignly invisible: They are inherently destructive to any attempt to organize individuals to work together in a positive and effective manner. Hence, it is imperative that all Stakeholders, including district administrators, engage in a continuing dialogue about the missions of the school district, of the individual schools, and of the various clusters in each school. Each Stakeholder must understand the meaning of each mission statement and how the mission statements fit together. The mission statements of each entity should be conspicuously present at each meeting of that entity and should be referred to on a regular basis.

3. The Stakeholders' Ability to Obtain and Communicate Information

Information is power, and power is control. If we are going to succeed in reforming our schools to become self-directed, then we must rethink, reorganize, and completely revamp the information and communication networks currently in place in most schools.

It is axiomatic that in order for people to make thoughtful and informed decisions, they must have access to all relevant information. If Self-Directed Schools are to be effective, then the Stakeholders operating in each of the clusters of the school must be able quickly and easily to obtain all needed information relating to the matters on which they are acting. This means that school systems will need to open up their data bases and implement sophisticated information-processing systems that will allow the people who need information to obtain it in an expeditious manner.

In today's world, the technology for such a free information school system is clearly available. Networked computer systems could be installed at the district office and in each school that would allow free and complete exchange of information between the school district and each individual school.

Traditionally, hierarchical organizations have maintained a tight grip on information. Either information has been denied to those seeking it or the individuals requesting information have been required to go through numerous levels of command in the organization to obtain the information. And information that finally has been obtained has frequently been "filtered" through each applicable level of command and is therefore either useless or subject to misinterpretation.

Hierarchical organizations have long maintained that it is necessary to retain information "at the top" (for reasons of security, confidentiality, or, simply, complexity). In the field of education, where the "products" of the enterprise are our children and where the Stakeholders are parents, teachers, community members, and other individuals who have a direct interest in the success and future of these children, we simply do not believe that the arguments for retaining information "at the top" outweigh the benefits of making information available to the Stakeholders. Information *must* be made available to Stakeholders. Otherwise, any attempt to reform our school systems through increasing involvement and participation by Stakeholders will be illusory.

The responsibility for sharing information is a two-way street, of course. Not only does the central office have a responsibility to make information available to Stakeholders, but the Stakeholders have a responsibility to share information with the central office and with other Stakeholders. In the Self-Directed School, lateral communication, or communication among clusters, is just as important as vertical communication between the central office and a cluster. To quote an old saying: "The left hand must know what the right hand is doing."

4. The Stakeholders' Willingness to Accept Accountability

Self-Directed Schools, with their emphasis on delegation of authority and increased Stakeholder participation, might appear on the surface to result in decreased, or at least diluted, accountability. After all, with responsibility for action spread among so many people, how can anyone remain accountable? The answer is that no one person remains accountable. Instead, *everyone* must accept accountability.

Each cluster member must accept accountability for the success or failure of the group. The more that individuals in a cluster accept this accountability, the more responsibility can be delegated to the cluster.

Clusters involve a philosophy of work and human behavior that requires a new way of thinking. When people are told exactly what to do, as in a hierarchy, they do exactly what they are told and little or no more. Clusters create a mechanism that permits each Stakeholder to go beyond the routine of the past, to make a total commitment to the cluster. The Stakeholder actually takes a personal interest in the cluster's objectives and accepts accountability for the overall results. It is the essence of a cluster that those individuals who have the power to do something also have the obligation to do it. Successful action comes from the freedom to act.

The increase in accountability engendered by clusters constitutes a fundamental departure from the mindset of hierarchical management and must be understood by those who wish to take advantage of the opportunities that empowered clusters offer. No longer is one person (like the coach of a sports team) solely responsible for success or failure. Instead, each person involved in the process is accountable for the results. As the willingness of Stakeholders to accept accountability increases—which will happen as the Stakeholders increase their involvement—so too will the effectiveness of cluster management as more and more responsibility is delegated to the clusters.

5. Stakeholder Trust

Stakeholders need to know that they are trusted and that they will not be penalized unfairly for the mistakes that will naturally accompany the exercise of their initiative. Mistakes occur in any human endeavor. Provided that the mistake of a Stakeholder is within the scope of discretion that has been accorded to that Stakeholder, then the mistake should be accepted. School boards, superintendents, principals, and district administrators must not sit in judgment over cluster decisions. If this happens, the clusters will fear being made scapegoats for errors and will cease to exercise their own initiative. The result will be the reinstatement of the hierarchical system.

To put this concept into proper perspective, we must remember that school boards and school administrators frequently make mistakes; some are noticed but many are "swept under the carpet." The following is a short list of mistakes that have been made by school boards and school administrators:

> Buying for a new school site property that later was placed in the federal marshland program, thereby preventing construction on the property.
> Allowing school board members attending conventions to use first class air travel and hotel accommodations at taxpayers' expense.
> Paying a search company $50,000 to assist in finding a new super-intendent and then firing the superintendent two years later.

All of these decisions clearly appear in retrospect to be mistakes. However, all of these mistakes—and many others—were dealt with and put into the past by the school districts. The same kind of acceptance of, and willingness to deal with, mistakes will need to be accorded to decisions made by cluster groups.

Just as a football quarterback must feel confident that he will not be benched for making a bad call, so too must Stakeholders feel that they have been entrusted to use their judgment and to "play the game." If they feel insecure about their authority, they will have a tendency to do nothing and to revert to traditional thinking by letting the principal or another "higher up" make the decisions.

Cluster Leadership: Summary

We have recounted briefly the conditions necessary for cluster group management to succeed. Unless all of these conditions are met, true empowerment of Stakeholders can be achieved only partially.

Developing competence, understanding the mission, getting and receiving information, accepting accountability, and developing trust are difficult conditions to create in a conventional, hierarchical organization. School administrators are often too busy "directing" to actually work with and listen to their constituents to develop a vision and communicate missions. They are too busy looking for means to obtain short-term gains on standardized tests to take the time and to budget the funds necessary to develop the competence needed by the Stakeholders to work in a high-involvement organization. Administrators often guard information closely as a key to power in the organization, and they don't trust the Stakeholders to exercise independent discretion and authority.

True empowerment of Stakeholders can be achieved, but it will require a drastic overhaul of the system. It can be accomplished only by developing and communicating the missions of the school system and of each individual school; by investing in the training of Stakeholders to establish competence in collaborative skills; by making needed information readily and immediately available to Stakeholders; by allowing Stakeholders to accept accountability for their actions; and by creating an atmosphere of trust between administrators and other Stakeholders. Only in this way can empowerment become a reality and the Self-Directed School succeed.

Questions and Issues About Clusters

Why clusters now?

As we've already discussed, the current system of public education in the United States is failing. Just as American businesses have discovered, educators are beginning to realize that top-down, hierarchical man- agement structures are too inflexible to respond to the ever-changing face of today's world.

Educators are beginning to see that survival depends on the commitment, the energies, and the skills of Stakeholders. The concept of the Self-Directed School, with its use of the cluster organization, is a way of involving and taking advantage of the talents and energies of Stakeholders. Failure to reform U.S. schools will lead directly to the failure of American society. To quote the late George Allen, "The future is now!"

In a cluster, who's in charge?

In well-trained, experienced clusters no one is in charge in the traditional sense. No one person is designated as a supervisor by higher-level management to whom individuals in the cluster must report. No individual has the authority to discipline, direct, or dismiss others. In highly trained and motivated clusters, everybody is, by virtue of his or her participation in the cluster, naturally committed to the success of the cluster (and of the school).

Will there be more mistakes made by clusters than by trained administrators?

The lack of a formal type of supervisory structure in a cluster organization does not mean that the organization lacks standards for performance or that the participants' performance will not be subject to observation and review. Actually, the contrary is true. Since all of the Stakeholders are responsible for the development of the goals and methods for achieving those goals, there will actually be more time and energy invested by people in observing performance. In clusters, where each member depends on the efforts of others, people will be quick to notice and evaluate errors.

There is no reason to believe that Stakeholders, working in groups, will make more errors than trained administrators. American businesses have learned that in most cases employee groups, although not formally trained, are actually better at solving problems than trained supervisors. Our legal system is also based on the belief that untrained individuals, working in groups (like a jury), are actually better at evaluating evidence and making critical observations than formally trained "experts." In clusters, errors will be made—just as errors are made in hierarchies or in any other form of human endeavor. Putting trust in clusters does not mean that no errors will be made. What it does mean is that, provided a cluster acts in good faith, the principal or the district office will not take away responsibility from the cluster if things don't turn out exactly as expected.

Having acknowledged that mistakes are going to happen, we feel it is important to distinguish between permissible mistakes and mistakes that should raise warning flags about possible flaws in the system which should be corrected. We believe that a mistake is permissible under the following four conditions:

1. The mistake is made in *pursuit of the applicable mission.* Obviously, things may not always turn out as anticipated. However, if the action leading to the mistake was undertaken

in pursuit of the group's mission, then the resulting mistake should be excused. By contrast, if the mistake occurs as a result of an action undertaken for some personal agenda or for any other reason not directly related to the group's mission, then the mistake should not be excused.

2. The mistake serves as *a learning experience.* Most mistakes satisfy this condition. In fact, most of what we learn occurs as a result of failure or mistake. That is why well-run organizations encourage initiative and risk taking by their employees. These organizations realize that we learn more from doing things wrong than from doing things right. Some organizations have even adopted the philosophy that we need to be making mistakes faster so that we can learn more.

3. The error is *not part of a pattern.* This is the condition that prevents condition 2 from being taken to a ridiculous extreme by an employee or participant who makes mistakes haphazardly or carelessly just to be making mistakes. This condition also serves as a check on participants who are simply following the wrong mission or plan. While individuals may be well intentioned, if their mistakes reflect a repetitive pattern, they may be misunderstanding the actual mission of the group. Repetitive mistakes may also signal a need for additional training. It may be that the group's members are simply not yet competent enough to handle the responsibilities with which they have been entrusted.

4. The error was made *within the scope of the group's discretion.* This condition is closely related to condition 1. It is imperative that individuals working in groups have a clear understanding of the scope of the group's discretion. Any action taken within the scope of that discretion should be accepted, even if the result is not what was hoped for. Actions taken outside the scope of the group's discretion reflect a problem—either in the group's intentions or in the group's understanding of the scope of its discretion.

In summary, a mistake is permissible when:

• It is made in pursuit of the applicable mission.
• It serves as a learning experience.
• It is not part of a repetitive pattern.
• It is made within the scope of the discretion accorded the action taker.

Mistakes that do not meet the four conditions outlined above reflect flaws in the system. Such mistakes should be investigated and the causes remedied. Blind punishment of the action takers is unproductive. Instead, the initial decision-making process which led to the mistake should be examined to determine whether it reflects a misunderstanding or an improper motive.

Of course, the foregoing discussion about permissible mistakes applies to mistakes made by any organization, hierarchical or otherwise. We include it here only to stress the importance of investigating the nature of a mistake. We understand that traditional educators are going to feel some reluctance in delegating authority to cluster groups. These educators will tend to look for Stakeholder mistakes and seize upon these mistakes as justifications to return to the old system. Yes, Stakeholders will make mistakes. In the vast majority of instances, however, we believe that these mistakes will be permissible. Even the "impermissible" mistakes, we believe, will be attributable in most cases to a failure in the system—for example, insuf- ficient training— as opposed to an improper motivation on the part of a Stakeholder.

Can all people work well in a cluster?

The short answer to this question is yes—provided two essential elements are fulfilled. To work well in clusters, people need both *ability* and *willingness*. Ability in this sense refers to an individual's level of competence in working in a group. In other words, does the individual possess the knowledge and social skills necessary to function in a group environment? Willingness, on the other hand, refers to a person's commitment to doing his or her job. Is the person motivated to succeed?

In order to be effective, clusters require that group members possess basic collaboration skills and a reasonable degree of motivation. A school that has a staff which is either unmotivated or poorly trained in group problem-solving skills will not reap the benefits attainable through a cluster organization simply by allowing the staff members to work together in clusters.

High-involvement organizations like Self-Directed Schools typically have a nonconformist flavor. They tend to attract highly motivated individuals seeking a forum that will allow them to express their ideas and share their initiative. Unfortunately, many schools in the United States today have driven out highly creative educators who are motivated to implement new ideas. Low pay combined with poor working conditions have forced many qualified individuals out of the education profession. The result in many cases is that our public schools are left with educators who are quite content to preserve the status quo ("Don't rock the boat") and who are not motivated to initiate significant change and reform. In schools in which the staff is either poorly trained or poorly motivated, or both, it is doubtful that cluster management will succeed. Clusters in and of themselves do not produce miracles.

The good news, however, is that miracles can be attained. A school needs only two conditions to experience the benefits of cluster management. First, the school needs to attract a sufficient number of Stakeholders who are motivated to become involved and who wish to implement changes. Second, the school needs to provide training to those Stakeholders in group mechanics and group problem solving.

Today, many U.S. schools probably lack enough motivated Stakeholders to implement cluster management. The vast majority of educators are both the products and victims of an educational system that for many years has discouraged creativity and innovation in the name of uniformity and control. Cluster management will not work unless a school has achieved some minimum percentage of motivated Stakeholders. A school does not need all of its Stakeholders to be motivated in order to commence cluster management. As long as there are a number of motivated Stakeholders, a school can take steps to implement cluster management. The motivated Stakeholders can then serve as inspirations to the other, less motivated individuals, energizing them to become involved. Gradually the school will increase its number of highly motivated Stakeholders, either by converting existing Stakeholders or by attracting new ones.

The minimum percentage of motivated Stakeholders needed by a school to commence cluster management will differ from school to school. It will depend, among other things, on the sophistication of the motivated Stakeholders: In addition to wanting to become involved, do they really understand their role as cluster members? It will also depend on the level of resistance to cluster management present in the "unmotivated" Stakeholders.

As we have indicated, having a fairly large number of motivated Stakeholders is not enough. A school wishing to implement cluster management must invest in training programs to provide its Stakeholders with the competence necessary to function effectively in clusters. (The training of Stakeholders is examined in Chapter 5.)

Societal pressures are driving schools toward cluster management. Americans are becoming increasingly concerned about the apparent inability of their schools to produce students who can successfully compete in the world marketplace. As this problem has become more acute, and more publicized, many individuals, including educators, parents, community members, and business leaders, are demanding more opportunities to participate in the operation and management of public schools. One indication of this heightened interest is the rapidly growing number of people who are enlisting in alternative teacher certification programs. Alternative teacher certification programs offer individuals who have obtained noneducation degrees, and who frequently have been working in careers outside education, the opportunity to become immediately involved as teachers in the classroom (without spending two or more years in a university certification program receiving an education degree). These new teachers bring with them the practical experience gained from working in the "real" world as well as new thinking about a teacher's role in the development of curriculum and in the management of the educational environment.

Increased interest in education is the first step toward successful cluster management. Training is the second. With the proper support and training, anyone who enjoys working with people and who is eager and willing to learn can be an effective cluster member.

What is needed for success?

We have discussed some of the elements that need to be present in order for cluster management and Self-Directed Schools to succeed. One of the most critical elements is the support of the local school board and superintendent. In their rhetoric many school boards and superintendents sound sincere about giving schools more authority and discretion. Many school administrators have learned the language of decentralization and site-based decision making; few, however, have actually learned to implement the concept. Some school boards and superintendents express the belief that they are already changing fundamentals and allowing more freedom at the school level. Unfortunately, most of them are fooling themselves.

If we are to make true progress in the area of school reform, school board meetings must change from the agenda of "administrivia" that is typical today to an agenda that centers on the plans, promises, and products of each of the schools in the district. Boards and superintendents need to be strong enough to be weak. They must be confident enough in their own mission and in their own training programs to allow the Stakeholders of each school to take control of their own destiny. Boards and superintendents need to be patient. Mistakes will occur. Progress will be slow. Changing decades of tradition takes time. But positive results will be forthcoming if superintendents and board members remain committed to the concept of the Self-Directed School. (Chapter 9 discusses the type of support that will be needed from the district office as well as the changing roles of the superintendent and the school board in a Self-Directed School system.)

How long does it take to implement successful clusters?

Clusters are composed of individuals with diverse attitudes, values, and backgrounds. Because of this diversity, learning to work together requires time, effort, and patience. Effective clusters and the Self-Directed School concept can develop only over time. We believe that a period of three to five years is required for clusters to become effective. Before high performance and efficiency can be achieved, certain predictable stages will evolve.

Stage 1: Getting Started (Years One to Two) Since no one knows quite what to expect in a cluster, there is confusion at first. The diverse collection of individuals who are members of the cluster are not yet clearly linked by any discernible goals, roles, or relationships. They are uncertain about what to expect and are not yet totally willing to commit themselves to the process, since they are not yet able to grasp the full power and scope of cluster organization. In essence, a cluster that is just starting out is not really a team, even though everyone might call it one. As with any "team," the individuals who are members of a cluster must go through a period of getting to know each other, of building camaraderie, of establishing roles, and of creating a cohesive feeling. (This start-up process is considered in more detail in Chapter 3.) Getting through stage 1 requires that Stakeholders learn new skills, develop the ability to tolerate mistakes, and react with patience as the cluster experiences the frustration of growing pains.

Stage 2: Getting on Course (Years Two to Four) During stage 2, clusters are becoming united. Members are starting to have a sense of belonging and are beginning to become comfortable with one another and with the objectives of the group. The cluster becomes increasingly more goal oriented and develops routines for handling new situations as well as internal disputes and problems. Cluster members begin to sort out responsibilities and start to rely on one another's talents. The principal can begin to give up control of the cluster because the cluster has sprouted the roots of stability necessary to support its growth to its full capability. Decisions previously made by the principal begin to be made by the cluster as cluster members demand greater control over their own environment.

Stage 3: Full Speed Ahead (Years Four to Five) At stage 3, clusters have achieved the level of maturity necessary to support true cluster management. Cluster members are committed to and take full ownership of both the cluster and its actions and decisions. In addition to being effective at reacting to school problems, stage 3 clusters consistently strive to be proactive by anticipating demands, identifying areas in which additional training may be necessary, and moving into new areas of responsibility. Clusters that have successfully attained the level of stage 3 demand the right to participate. They push for a greater voice in hiring decisions, they actively pursue the information necessary to make informed and reasoned decisions (even if that information has traditionally been viewed as confidential), and they assume roles traditionally reserved for the principal or other educational administrator. In short, they will not tolerate autocratic supervision and management. Instead, they demand democracy.

Stage 3 clusters are comfortable with the concept of self-directedness and can experience the true power of empowerment. Schools that develop stage 3 clusters can successfully challenge the sacred cow of hierarchical management and reap the benefits of the Self-Directed School.

None of the foregoing can happen, however, until the Stakeholders understand what it means to be a member of a team—that is, a collaborative cluster—and it is to that subject we turn next.

3

Teamwork and Team Players

When a team outgrows individual performance and
learns team confidence, excellence becomes a reality.
Joe Paterno
Head Football Coach
Pennsylvania State University

The use of clusters and the teamwork concept is increasing dramatically as school leaders begin to see that the hierarchical school organization, with its traditional top-down administration, is ineffective. Forward-thinking educational leaders are starting to understand the bottom-line value of team play. What has become clear is that the school with a principal at the top, teachers in box-type classrooms, faculty meetings in which teachers do not work with each other, Parent-Teacher Associations whose sole function is to provide student parties or booster clubs to raise funds, and business leaders who complain about the school's product (the students) but are afforded no opportunity to become involved in making changes is ineffective and unsuccessful.

Teamwork is needed to develop and operate new schools for the twenty-first century. The sheer complexity of today's global environment means that no one person can be an expert in all areas. With information expanding at an exponential rate, the rapidly increasing importance of technology, and the imperative of developing a world-class educational system, it is essential that our educational system develop and maintain cross-functional groups made up of teachers, business people, community leaders, parents, and district facilitators. If schools are going to have any chance of educating our young people, then Stakeholders must take steps to draw from as many resources as possible. Stakeholders need to learn to work as a team, sharing one another's strengths and drawing insight from one another's viewpoints and experiences.

As team members, Stakeholders will be required to work with other Stakeholders, many of whose backgrounds and personal styles may be quite different from their own. The challenge facing the Self-Directed School will be to build effective clusters composed of effective team players.

Based on reports of the benefits and advantages of clusters and cooperative teams in business and industry, it seems clear that cluster management and collaborative activity will result in similar benefits for education. Individual Stakeholders will, by having the opportunity to work with others in clusters to exchange ideas and creatively solve problems, become members of a team. The feelings of security and confidence and the sense of belonging engendered by team membership will foster the personal self-esteem of the Stakeholders. Growth in the self-esteem of the Stakeholders will, in turn, directly benefit the school and the students as the Stakeholders become more effective communicators and more enthusiastic and creative participants in the educational process.

The Stakeholders, working in clusters, will be involved in a meaningful way in the creation of their own work environment and in the formulation and articulation of the school's mission. Not only will the ideas that will be generated be more creative than would be the case under traditional top-down management styles (after all, two heads are better than one), but the Stakeholders—the actual managers of the school—will be much more enthusiastic about and committed to implementing those ideas since they themselves originated the ideas. Employee morale will improve since the employees will now "run the shop" and there will be no managerial figure to blame. With a growing esprit de corps, Stakeholders will move from feelings of helplessness and resignation to feelings of confidence and trust.

The challenge facing the Self-Directed School, of course, will be to make it all work—to successfully implement cluster management.

Clusters Are Teams

Although a great deal has been written about how teams work, most educators have neither worked in groups, teams, or other collaborative arrangements, nor have they received any training to develop collaborative skills. As a result, most educators who wish to implement cluster-style management will face significant obstacles in getting clusters started. With no academic training or real-life experience in working with teams and without the collaborative skills necessary to make teamwork effective, many administrators may shy away from implementing cluster management. In this chapter we examine the characteristics of effective clusters and present a skeletal blueprint for implementation of cluster management.

A cluster is a team. While this may seem like a patently obvious and overly simplistic statement, we believe it is the basis of any discussion of effective cluster activity. Like any sports team, a cluster is made up of a collection of individuals, each with his or her own special skills, strengths, weaknesses, and talents.

In a cluster, as on a team, it is imperative that each member understand his or her role in accomplishing the objectives of the group. The success of the cluster, like the success of a sports team, will then depend on the ability of the members to subjugate their individual interests to the overriding interests of the group and to work together to achieve the established goals of the cluster. Success will depend on the ability of cluster members to become team players.

In analyzing the characteristics of effective clusters, we have identified the following questions as the key issues that need to be addressed in connection with any attempt to ensure cluster success:

- What makes an effective team player?
- How do effective team players contribute to the success of the cluster?
- What can be done about ineffective team players?
- What are the roles of team players as leaders?
- What can a principal/administrator/facilitator do to create an environment that supports cluster activity, teamwork, and team players?

Each of these questions is addressed in this chapter.

Effective Teamwork:
The Chemistry of Personal Styles

Teamwork requires team players. As any coach knows, a good team is more than just a collection of talented individuals. For a team to be successful, all of its members must work together in synchronization and harmony. Each player must be aware not only of his own strengths and weaknesses but also of the strengths and weaknesses of every other member of the team. A successful coach is someone who can put together a diverse collection of individuals in such a way that the respective strengths and weaknesses of the various athletes complement each other and work together to create a unified whole.

The same approach must be present in a school cluster if the cluster is to be a viable entity. But whereas teamwork in sports involves primarily the combining of athletic skills, teamwork in clusters requires the combining of far less tangible characteristics. In a cluster, teamwork depends on the combining of personality styles.

A well-knit and effective cluster isn't the result of luck or the proper alignment of the stars. To the contrary, it's the result of chemistry. While we may not yet fully understand all of the complex reactions that take place in a functioning cluster, we do know that a good cluster is made up of a blend of individuals, each of whom contributes his or her own special talents. The cluster members depend on openness, trust, and excellent communication skills in working together to accomplish the objectives of the group. Effective teamwork is based upon an effective mix of members who exhibit a variety of *personal styles*, or approaches to problem solving.

The term "personal style" refers to the predisposition of a person to think or act in a particular way in a given situation. This predisposition is then manifested in particular behavioral patterns that can be observed by those with whom the person works.

The diversity of personal styles can be seen by watching any number of people react to a given situation—say a canceled flight on the day before Thanksgiving. Some people become angry and belligerent; others resort to reason and tenacity; and still others seem to resign themselves to quiet acceptance of the situation. There is something programmed in each of us that causes us to interpret and interact with the world in particular ways. Our interpretations and interactions then determine which of the broad range of behaviors available to us we will select for dealing with a situation that is presented to us.

Most of us are flexible enough to slightly modify our behaviors to meet the needs of particular situations. Undeniably, however, we tend to be more comfortable with some sets of behaviors than with others. That is why in certain situations we may feel helpless or frustrated. In many cases, our helplessness or frustration can be attributed to our inability to adjust our personal style to meet the needs of the situation. Personal style, then, can be defined as the set of preferred behavior patterns that we exercise most of the time, in most situations, and with most people. While we certainly have the power to *adjust* our personal style, few of us can effectively *change* our personal style to any significant degree.

An individual's personal style is evident in nearly every aspect of his or her life. Teachers know that in the classroom different groups of students will exhibit different learning styles, each requiring a slightly different teaching style in order to maximize educational growth. Parents with multiple children are reminded on a daily basis that their children are unique individuals, each exhibiting a particular personal style. Effective parenting requires handling each child differently in an attempt to best respond to his or her personal style. Successful marriages reflect the ability of a husband and wife to combine their individual personal styles in a complementary fashion.

Personal style is as important in our business and professional interactions as it is in our personal relationships. Each of us exhibits our personal style whenever we interact or work with others. Most of the time we are successful in achieving our goals. Sometimes, however, our personal style gets in the way of our goals and actually prevents us from achieving success. We will talk about how we can overcome these types of failures later in this chapter. For now, what is important to understand is that an individual's personal style can at times *promote* the effectiveness of a group, while at other times it can *interfere* with group effectiveness and threaten its chances for success.

Before proceeding, we believe it is critical to point out that there is no good or bad or right or wrong personal style. As we are using it, the term "personal style" is merely a descriptive term, not an evaluative one. An individual's personal style simply describes certain behavior patterns that predominate in that person's social interactions.

Although an individual's personal style carries with it neither positive nor negative connotations, all personal styles have both strengths and limitations when it comes to working with others. As we shall see, effective cluster members are those individuals who recognize not only the strengths and limitations of their own personal styles but the strengths and limitations of the personal styles of the other group members. Successful cluster participants work with other group members to maximize the strengths and minimize the limitations of all members of the group.

No one personal style has proved to be more effective than any other when it comes to working in groups. In fact, it is the process of checks and balances among cluster members with different personal styles that provides for an effective cluster. Each personal style contributes in its own way to the overall success of the cluster.

An example may serve to illustrate how diverse personal styles can interact in a cluster to accomplish a task. Suppose a cluster is given the responsibility for developing a discipline plan for a Self-Directed School. Previous attempts by the principal to implement an effective plan have failed, so the teachers and staff have turned to a cluster to develop "a better way." In order to get the ball rolling, one cluster member may take on the role of defining the nature of the cluster's mission and keeping the cluster focused on the objectives of the group. Another member may be the one to get the cluster to arrive at consensus on the big issues without getting bogged down on little issues. Still another member may act as the devil's advocate, seemingly slowing the group down but all the while making sure that all possible alternatives have been considered. Yet another member may feel responsible for making sure that all members have had a chance to express their ideas. If all of these group members work together and respect each other, the group should work quite effectively to develop a workable solution to the discipline problem.

Perhaps the most critical aspect of understanding how individuals work effectively in groups is the fact that certain discernible patterns of personal styles occur over and over again in the general population. This consistency of pattern helps us to understand personal style and allows us to make predictions about how one's personal style will fit particular situations. Most researchers who have studied personal style have identified four basic styles. Glenn Parker[1] uses contributor, collaborator, communicator, and challenger. Robert and Nancy Burgee[2] use precisive, directive, emotive, and responsive. Our categories of the *taskmaster*, the *process person,* the *analyzer*, and the *action person* are adapted from the works of Parker, the Burgees, and others who have

---

[1]Glen M. Parker, *Team Players and Teamwork* (San Francisco: Jossey-Bass Publishers, 1991).

[2]Robert Burgee and Nancy Burgee, *Effective Leaders—Effective Teams* (Estacada, OR: Stylemetrics Systems, Inc., 1981).

studied personal styles. These four styles define a conceptual frame-work for classifying the way people think and behave and provide valuable insights into how individuals work together in groups.

Each personal style is summarized briefly below. We then examine how these personal styles can interact to form an effective cluster.

The Taskmaster

The taskmaster is characterized by action, decisiveness, efficiency, and results. Taskmasters put a premium on accuracy, order, and structure. They typically maintain objectivity and emotional control in critical situations and take rational and logical approaches to problem solving. Because of their strong task orientation, taskmasters tend to maintain a serious and persistent approach in working through the problems presented to the cluster. Obviously, taskmasters can play an important role in getting a cluster to focus on the particular problem to be confronted and in motivating the cluster to develop solutions.

The limitations of taskmasters, from the point of view of group mechanics, are that they may become judgmental and overly critical at times and may discount or ignore feelings or emotional issues that may relate to the decision-making process. Taskmasters can sometimes be overly autocratic or controlling in their interactions with other cluster members.

In summary, taskmasters tend to be:

- Focused
- Accurate
- Action oriented
- Task oriented
- Result oriented
- Rational
- Disciplined
- Insistent
- Structured
- Serious

The Taskmaster

Strengths in Group Interactions	Limitations in Group Interactions
• Sets high standards for self and others	• Lacks tolerance for ambiguity or a free-flowing approach
• Puts a premium on accuracy and order	• Is insensitive to emotional aspects of communication
• Stays on target in discussions	• Is rigid, impersonal, and autocratic
• Remains focused on actions and results	• Discounts intuition as a reliable source

The Process Person

The process person is a people-oriented individual. People with this kind of personal style give primary emphasis to team *process*—that is, the way the team goes about completing its task and reaching its goal. The process person focuses on individuals and the social aspects of the work situation, acquiring information by sensing, listening, and interacting with others. Cluster members who are process persons are usually supportive, show warmth, will accept loose control, and prefer verbal interchanges to written reports. The process person is usually good at conflict resolution, consensus building, and supporting a relaxed climate within the group.

Unfortunately, other cluster members may see a process person as being too concerned about others, too wishy-washy, and too weak or indecisive to make hard decisions or to say no. A process person may discount facts and logic in favor of emotional appeals, especially when the issues being discussed involve strong moral or personal judgments. Process persons may lack discipline and structure in the use of time and may cause the last-minute syndrome in cluster meetings.

In summary, process persons tend to be:

- Supportive
- Informal
- Compassionate
- Good listeners
- Spontaneous
- Patient
- Praise givers
- Imaginative
- Encouraging
- Considerate

The Process Person

Strengths in Group Interactions	Limitations in Group Interactions
• Exercises and encourages creative approaches to problem solving	• Follows personal likes and dislikes in spite of concrete information to the contrary
• Relaxes others by warm and casual manner	• Loses sight of objectives and frustrates efforts to stay on target
• Introduces effective free association of ideas in brainstorming activities	• Lacks discipline and structure in the use of time
• Promotes a friendly, casual, and relaxed environment	• Praises indiscriminately and unspecifically

The Analyzer

The analyzer is characterized by the tendency to overanalyze a situation or overemphasize the need for a "perfect" solution. The analyzer has an unmitigated thirst for accurate and complete data to feed his or her thought processes and to evaluate multiple options. Analyzers generally try to gain the broadest possible perspective of a problem before attempting to develop a resolution. Such individuals tend to implement a rather formal decision-making process in solving the problem presented. The analyzer truly enjoys solving problems, searching for complete and accurate facts, and carefully studying the facts to see what possibilities exist. Generally, analyzers are good at detailed planning.

Sometimes group members see analyzers as being too rigid, too impersonal, and too cautious. The analyzer can sometimes overcomplicate issues and strive for perfection when perfection may be inappropriate. Analyzers procrastinate and take too long to make decisions, especially when complicated matters are involved. They may also drop out of heated debates, preferring the sound logic of facts and reason to what they may perceive as emotional whim and fancy.

In summary, analyzers tend to be:

- Problem solvers
- Cautious
- Reflective
- Thorough
- Precise
- Questioning
- Detailed planners
- Strategic thinkers
- Methodical

The Analyzer

Strengths in Group Interactions	Limitations in Group Interactions
• Sees the complexity of problems and looks at all sides of an issue	• Strives for perfection when inappropriate and lacks a realistic perspective
• Responds in a calm manner in working through issues	• Does not react to the need for immediate action
• Listens effectively, summarizes, and builds upon ideas	• Overlistens and does not know when to cut off discussion and act
• Provides an excellent damper against rash decision making	• Stays with one issue too long and overlooks others that demand attention

The Action Person

The style of the action person is characterized by a commitment to action and an emphasis on making decisions quickly. The action person promotes a sense of urgency in reaching goals. Such individuals are eager to take a stand on an issue and will clearly and demonstratively state their point of view. Action persons typically speak with certainty and directness and can effectively sell or push an idea through to the implementation stage. They usually grasp key issues quickly and can move through complex matters rapidly.

From the standpoint of the group, the action person can sometimes overwhelm others and force a fast-paced discussion when slow and careful deliberation would be more appropriate. At times, action persons use excessive persuasion to gain agreement and become argumentative and overly competitive in the face of resistance. The action person sometimes oversimplifies complex issues and may overlook possible alternatives in his or her drive to reach a solution.

In summary, action persons tend to be:

- Assertive
- Certain about their views
- Competitive
- Willing to confront issues
- Outspoken

- Driving
- Forceful
- Aggressive
- Dominant
- Eager to reach a solution

The Action Person

Strengths in Group Interactions	Limitations in Group Interactions
• Initiates discussion and keeps things moving	• Overstates position and at times does not listen
• Influences others toward consensus and promotes closure on issues	• Pushes others toward closure prematurely
• Promotes a sense of urgency in reaching goals	• Acts impulsively and without sufficient input or data
• Maintains a positive sense of timing for taking advantage of opportunities	• May become abrasive, pushy, and overbearing; may become arrogant at times

Analyzing Personal Style: Are We Monodimensional?

Few people exhibit just one personal style in their interactions with others. Most of us in our daily lives have one dominant personal style, with one or more backup styles that influence our behavior in particular settings. Some people are equally strong in two personal styles, whereas others may show a balance in all four personal styles.

Regardless of our preferred or dominant personal style, however, we all have the capacity to act within each of the four distinct style types. For instance, we are *process* oriented when we engage in intense relationships with members of our cluster; we are *task* oriented when we set priorities; we are *analytical* when we study things carefully; and we are *action* oriented when we need to get something done fast. While we may be better at some of these tasks than at others, at some point in our lives, we have all had to experience each one of these distinct personal styles.

Generally, research has found that a person tends to prefer one or two personal styles. With this in mind, consider the following questions and answers:

What if I am strong in both taskmaster and action person styles?

You take the lead in defining goals and objectives, are demanding of yourself and others, are effective in expediting action, and focus on results and achievement. Your limitations in group settings are that you tend to be autocratic and overbearing and may limit the perspective of the situation to your own view.

What if I am strong in both process person and action person styles?

Your strengths are that you can inspire and excite others with your ideas, you tend to use creative and novel approaches to issues, and you move into new situations quickly and optimistically. Unfortunately, you may overreact to limited information, and your excessive persuasiveness may appear manipulative and self-serving.

What if I am strong in both process person and analyzer styles?

In a group your strengths are that you have highly developed observation and listening skills that allow you to see both sides of an issue, you are an effective conciliator and negotiator in conflict settings, and you have the ability to conceptualize ideas. You are limited, however, in that you may take too much responsibility for others, may be overly cautious about hurting feelings, and may spend an excessive amount of time cultivating relationships.

What if I am strong in both taskmaster and analyzer styles?

You pay attention to detail, are accurate and dependable, and have highly developed logic and problem-solving skills. From the standpoint of the group, however, you may spend too much time analyzing issues and may get bogged down in details. Others may see you as a nit-picker and perfectionist.

What if I am equal in all styles?

This style carries the strengths and limitations of all four styles to some degree and from time to time. There are, however, some additional strengths and limitations that accompany the equally balanced personal style. People who are relatively balanced in all four personal styles have the ability to identify with and understand elements of all four basic styles. This makes the equally balanced person resourceful and effective in most situations. However, some group members may get mixed messages from the equally balanced person, viewing that individual as inconsistent and unpredictable.

Building Clusters: The Role of Personal Style

We have reviewed the four main types of personal styles. These personal styles will be used by Stakeholders as they interact in clusters to conduct the business of the Self-Directed School. In thinking about personal style, it is important to remember the following:

- No one personal style is more effective in a group setting than any other style.

- Being effective in a group does not require changing one's personal style.
- Any personal style can be effective as a chairperson, cluster member, problem solver, facilitator, or coach.
- Each personal style represents a valued component of the overall team.
- A *mix* of personal styles provides for team effectiveness through utilization of the strengths and counterbalancing of the limitations inherent in each personal style.

The last point may seem most surprising or anti-intuitive. At first glance, one might think that in order for a team to be effective all team members should have similar personal styles. That way members would be likely to understand each other and to function smoothly to solve problems. In reality, it has been found that successful clusters are composed of members with a diversity of personal styles. In these clusters group members take turns exercising their strengths as team members. Accordingly, some members (the action persons) set goals and define objectives; some members (the taskmasters) push the group to achieve the goals and implement solutions; some members (the process persons) make sure everyone participates and has a chance to be heard; and some members (the analyzers) make sure all of the alternatives have been considered before a decision is made. By recognizing the strengths and limitations of each member of the group, including themselves, members of diverse clusters can function effectively to ensure group success.

We will explore cluster effectiveness and the role of team player interactions within effective clusters in more detail shortly. Before we do, however, we need to consider *how* one goes about determining one's personal style. If we are going to be able to work effectively with others as a team, we need to be able to recognize both our own personal style and the personal styles of others. Being aware of the personal style of each group member will enable us to recognize the strengths and limitations of each person so that we can capitalize on the strengths and minimize the limitations.

Determining Personal Style

In order to determine personal style, we have developed the Cluster Style Inventory (see Appendix 3–1). This instrument, which is modeled on questionnaires developed by psychologists for determining general personality styles, is designed to provide an individual with insight into his or her personal style *in group situations*. In other words, the Cluster Style Inventory is limited to group interactions. It is not intended to serve as a comprehensive evaluation of an individual's personality. Rather, it is a mechanism for identifying certain behavioral tendencies exhibited when an individual works with others in a group. We believe that these behavioral tendencies, or "personal styles," are the key to understanding and evaluating effective group dynamics.

The Cluster Style Inventory consists of twenty questions, each with four responses, that relate to typical situations which arise when a person works in a group. Although each of the four responses to a particular question may appear equally desirable or undesirable, the instrument is designed to force individuals to rank or differentiate among the various responses. There are no right or wrong answers. The answers merely reflect an individual's preferences in particular situations.

After the Cluster Style Inventory has been completed, the numbers in each column are totaled. Column totals reflect the individual's personal style—the higher the total, the more dominant the personal style reflected by that column. The answers to each question have been arranged in such a way that column A reflects a process person, column B a taskmaster, column C an action person, and column D an analyzer.

As we have mentioned, the column totals of a completed Cluster Style Inventory may reflect a single dominant personal style, a dominant personal style with a secondary backup style, a combination of dominant personal styles and recessive styles, or a relatively balanced set of all four personal styles. Once an individual has determined his or her personal style, the person can use that information to become a better and more effective group member.

Personal Style: Self Profiles and Audience Profiles

There are two ways to gain information on your own personal style when working in clusters. First, you can complete the Cluster Style Inventory based on the way *you* see yourself when you work in clusters. This is called the self profile. The second way is to have the people with whom you work in a group complete a Cluster Style Inventory on you based on the way *they* see you work in the group. The composite of these responses represents how *others* see your personal style in clusters. This is known as the audience profile.

Whereas the self profile is certainly interesting (and sometimes quite revealing in a self-analytical way), it is far less valuable in terms of evaluating effectiveness in group situations than the audience profile. The reason for this is that the self profile only reflects the way we *think* we behave. Our inner thoughts, motives, and values may be so strong that we may be incapable in some situations of seeing how we *actually* behave. The audience profile provides valuable information about our actual behavior in a group setting. Behavior, of course, refers to those actions that are observable by others. Behavior in this sense has no inherent value judgment attached to it and does not necessarily reflect our inner thoughts and feelings. Our *behavior* is visible and audible to others. It provides others with the only frame of reference they have about us. Whereas we might *want* others to respond to our inner thoughts and feelings, we usually find that they are woefully bad at such a task. That is because they are responding to our *behavior*, not our inner thoughts. It is our behavior, then, not our inner thoughts, motives, or feelings, to which others respond and about which others make assumptions and draw conclusions. This distinction between outer behavior and inner thoughts and feelings is crucial to our understanding of group mechanics.

Comparing and contrasting the self profile and the audience profile results in what we call the perception check. By comparing the self profile with the audience profile, an individual can obtain valuable insight into his or her effectiveness as a cluster member. Individuals whose self profiles match their audience profiles can be confident that they are behaving the way they think they're behaving and that they are accurately communicating what they think they are communicating. Such individuals can then concentrate on acknowledging the strengths and accepting the limitations of their particular personal style and focus on applying those strengths and minimizing those limitations to become more effective group members.

For some individuals, however, the self profile will differ significantly from the audience profile. Significant variance between the audience profile and an individual's self profile is not a value statement about the individual, nor does it indicate that there is something wrong with the individual. Instead, it merely reflects a blind spot in the person's perception of his or her own behavior. Blind spots are not uncommon. Many of us *think* we are acting in a certain way when in reality we are not. In other words, we may not actually be communicating what we think we are communicating. This can obviously be quite debilitating to any attempt to work with others. The value of the audience profile (and the perception check) is that it allows individuals to identify exactly where their blind spots are. The audience profile permits individuals to identify *why* others are not responding to them in the way they might expect. Again, this information can then be used by the individual to become a more effective communicator and group member.

The Perception Check—An Illustrative Example

Principal Pamela is the principal of a mid-sized elementary school that is in the process of becoming a Self-Directed School. She is a firm believer in the power and benefits of cluster management and, as a result, has worked to downplay her position as principal of the school. As principal, she perceives herself more as a facilitator of cluster management than as a traditional direction-giving authority figure.

Most of the school's faculty members have worked with Pamela for three years. During that time, the teachers and staff have accumulated a great deal of experience working in clusters and have had ample opportunities to observe Pamela's behavior in cluster meetings and in "traditional" faculty meetings.

In an attempt to evaluate her effectiveness as a facilitator of cluster management, Pamela decided to prepare a perception check. Toward that end, she completed a Cluster Style Inventory to determine a self profile. Pamela simultaneously had the faculty members complete a Cluster Style Inventory on her to determine an audience profile. In order to make the data more manageable, she randomly selected five completed Cluster Style Inventory instruments from faculty members for compilation as the audience profile. The results of the self profile and audience profile for Pamela are summarized in Figure 3–1. It is clear, based on the summary, that Pamela's dominant personal style is that of an analyzer. Pamela's perception of herself as an analyzer coincides with the faculty's perception of her.

	PROCESS PERSON	TASKMASTER	ACTION PERSON	ANALYZER
Self profile	66	46	79	109
Audience profile	78	61	55	106

Figure 3–1. Summary of Principal Pamela's Self Profile and Audience Profile.

As an analyzer, both Pamela and the faculty can anticipate that Pamela will have certain strengths as a member of a cluster. For example, she can be expected not to be hurried into making a fast decision. Her other predictable strengths are:

- She will tend to recognize the potential adverse consequences of making a fast decision, even when pressured by a short deadline.
- She will look at all sides of an issue.
- She will ask good questions.
- She will listen well and summarize the issues.
- She will assist in getting mutual understanding of the issue and effectively utilize cluster resources in solving problems.

Along with her strengths, however, Pamela should be aware that as an analyzer she has several limitations as a group member. For instance:

- She may stay too long on one issue and overlook other issues that demand attention.
- She may overcomplicate issues and strive for perfection when perfection is inappropriate or impossible due to time constraints.
- She may not react to a need for immediate action.
- She may clash with action persons.

By knowing her dominant personal style, Pamela can be more cognizant of both her strengths and limitations as a group member. She can then use this awareness to capitalize on her strengths and minimize her limitations. In so doing, she will need to maintain a positive attitude and *not* view her limitations as weaknesses or criticisms. The fact that Pamela has limitations is *not* a moral judgment—we all have limitations. If Pamela gets bogged down with the idea that she must somehow "fix" her limitations, she will be focusing her energies in the wrong area. Instead, she should accept her limitations—by letting those who are strong in those areas assume responsibility—and focus on her strengths. The ability to focus on strengths and accept limitations is the *key* to being a good team player—an idea to which we will return shortly.

Although Pamela and the faculty agree on Pamela's dominant personal style, there is a significant blind spot in the area of Pamela's secondary personal style. Pamela perceives her backup style to be action person. By contrast, the audience profile reveals that the faculty perceives the action person to be Pamela's *weakest* personal style. With respect to backup style, the faculty perceives Pamela as a process person.

As revealed in her self profile, Pamela has a fairly strong need (her backup style) for action and for accomplishing objectives. The faculty, however, doesn't perceive this need. What they see (and hear) is an individual who seems to be more concerned about group consensus and having everyone feel good about decisions than she is about getting things done or implementing a decision. This blind spot in personal and group perceptions may be reflected in numerous situations. For example, Pamela may become confused or frustrated when she wants an issue to move along or get resolved and the rest of the cluster members are—in an attempt to fulfill Pamela's perceived needs and interests—more focused on establishing consensus and making sure everyone feels good about the decision.

The value to Pamela of knowing about her blind spot is that she can be aware of the group's perception and can make more of an effort to clearly and specifically communicate her true feelings and interests.

Again, if Pamela reacts negatively to the audience profile (by thinking, "How can the faculty possibly think that? How dare they?") or simply refuses to accept it (by saying, "The faculty is wrong, I'm not like that."), then she defeats the whole purpose of the exercise. We cannot emphasize enough that personal style is not a value judgment. There is no right or wrong involved. The purpose of determining an individual's personal style is to identify behavioral traits, not pass moral judgments. Each personal style does have strengths and limitations *from the point of view of group mechanics*, but those strengths and limitations do not have any inherent value, negative or positive, in an absolute sense. Accordingly, Pamela should accept the audience profile as an accurate perception of her behavior. She can then use that information to more clearly communicate her views, needs, and opinions, thereby becoming a more effective group member.

Team Players:
The Key to Cluster Success

We are now ready to return to the questions we posed at the beginning of this chapter:

- What makes an effective team player?
- What can be done about ineffective team players?
- What are the roles of team players as leaders?
- What can a principal/administrator/facilitator do to create an environment that supports clusters, teamwork, and team players?

What Makes an Effective Team Player?

An athlete is deemed to be a good team player if he or she has two things: athletic *ability* and the *willingness* to apply those abilities for the good of the team. The same two things must be present in a Stakeholder in order for him or her to be an effective team player. Therefore, it can be said that in a successful Self-Directed School, the Stakeholders have both the *ability* to function in clusters and the *willingness* to do so. Both must be present. Having one without the other will render a Stakeholder an ineffective team player and threaten the success of his or her cluster (and, ultimately, the success of the Self-Directed School).

Ability

In the sense we are using it here, ability refers to a Stakeholder's knowledge. Does the Stakeholder know how to function in a group and how to work with others? Many people assume that working in groups comes naturally to humans (like some sort of innate ability) and that no specific training or education is needed. Nothing could be farther from the truth. In reality, humans are actually quite poor at working with others. Interacting with others in a group setting does not come naturally to us—even to those who consider themselves social butterflies.

Working effectively in groups requires a variety of skills. In order for a Stakeholder to make a positive contribution to a group, he or she must have a working knowledge of each of the following:

- Ways to reach consensus in a group.
- Ways to resolve conflicts in a group.
- Ways to alternate leadership in a group without an appointed leader.

In addition, the Stakeholder should be aware of his or her own personal style as well as the personal style of the other group members.

In establishing a Self-Directed School it cannot be assumed that the Stakeholders have the ability to work in groups. The establishment of clusters and the transfer of decision-making authority to those clusters is not enough to achieve success. The Stakeholders must be educated in the skills that they will need as they work together in groups. A school system wishing to implement cluster management must be willing to make the commitment, in terms of both time and money, to train its Stakeholders. Failure to do so will almost certainly result in the disintegration of any attempt to make cluster management work. (The specific types of training activities that should be conducted for Stakeholders are discussed in Chapters 4 and 5.)

Willingness

It is not enough for a Stakeholder to know how to work with others in groups. The individual must be willing to do so. For Stakeholders who have traditionally been in charge of schools, such as principals and other administrators, this means a willingness to accept the fact that they are not the only experts in the education of our youth. These Stakeholders must be willing to take a step back and let others (parents, business leaders, community members, teachers, and students) play more active roles in creating and managing the educational environment. Concomitantly, it is imperative that Stakeholders who have heretofore not been involved in school management and decision making actually step up and take on more responsibility.

One of the most important aspects of a Stakeholder's willingness to work in groups is his or her attitude. To be an effective team player, a Stakeholder must maintain a positive and cooperative attitude. Each Stakeholder should realize that conflicts are inevitable whenever individuals band together in groups to exchange ideas. These conflicts should be viewed as crucial steps in the problem-solving process and not as personal criticisms or value judgments. If Stakeholders begin to feel personally affronted by these conflicts, they will have a tendency to drop out of discussions and cease to share their ideas. Each member of a cluster has an interest in protecting the feelings and supporting the attitudes of the other cluster members. (The principal/facilitator of the school can play a critical role in fostering the kind of supportive environment necessary for cluster success. The principal's role in this process is discussed in more detail in Chapter 8.)

Active involvement and participation by every member of a cluster is vital to the success of the cluster. Team players do not sit back and allow others to do the work. Rather, they cooperate, working proactively to achieve group goals and facilitate group cohesiveness and effectiveness. They take actions that demonstrate consideration for the feelings and needs of others and are acutely aware of the effect of their behavior and personal style on others. This means that cluster members who are effective team players make every effort to cooperate with and support one another.

Key behaviors of effective team players include the following:

- Recognize and consider others' ideas.
- Accept suggestions.
- Offer help without being asked.
- Ask for ideas.
- Take into consideration the needs and skills of other team members when offering help or advice.
- Work with other team members to solve a problem or implement a program.

The critical team player behaviors that are mentioned most frequently by cluster members are interpersonal in nature. Most cluster members prefer to work with someone with a good attitude who is willing to pitch in, support and encourage others, volunteer to work on problems, and remain positive and caring in resolving conflicts.

What Can Be Done About Ineffective Team Players?

The answer to this question depends on the reason a Stakeholder is an ineffective team player. Having just identified the characteristics of an effective team player, we know that ineffectiveness can be the result of a lack of *ability*, a lack of *willingness*, or both. During the initial phases of implementing cluster management, most, if not all, of the Stakeholders will be ineffective team players because they lack the ability to be team players. They simply have not yet had sufficient training in group mechanics to understand fully how to work with other Stakeholders in groups. As they receive training and gain experience, most Stakeholders will, provided they possess the willingness to cooperate and work together, develop into very effective team players.

A Stakeholder's lack of ability is a far easier issue to address than a lack of willingness. If a Stakeholder lacks the ability—that is, the knowledge—to be an effective team player, making training opportunities available to the individual should cure the problem. Working with a Stakeholder's attitude, or his or her willingness to work with others, is a much more complex matter. A lack of willingness may be caused by any one of a number of reasons, ranging from a refusal to take responsibility, a lack of self-esteem, a lack of confidence, or a general attitude of malaise or apathy.

Certainly training programs are available for building a Stakeholder's confidence or raising self-esteem. Sometimes an increase in confidence or a rise in self-esteem may be enough to shift the Stakeholder's attitude into one of cooperation and participation. In other cases, addressing the issue of a Stakeholder who appears to be unwilling to be a team player may be a much more complicated process. The principal/facilitator of the school, together with the other Stakeholders, must support Stakeholders whose attitudes make them ineffective team players by creating a comfortable and secure environment that fosters mutual communication, trust, and honesty. Creating such a setting can largely be accomplished by other Stakeholders serving as positive and enthusiastic role models. As the environment of mutual respect, trust, and security develops, most Stakeholders who originally experienced hesitancy in getting involved should achieve the comfort level necessary to support their full involvement and participation.

What Are the Roles of Team Players as Leaders?

Cluster management depends upon the sharing of authority among all the members of the cluster. If one or more members of a cluster are viewed as being in charge, then many of the benefits of working in a cluster will be lost. As long as cluster members feel that another cluster member is in a position of authority, then free, honest, and open communication and expression of ideas will be squelched or severely dampened.

Rather than leaders, clusters have facilitators. In fact, all members of a cluster are facilitators. At any one time, only one or two cluster members may be serving as the primary facilitator, or the person responsible for keeping the cluster on course and focused on its objective. But this mantle of responsibility will shift among members from meeting to meeting and, quite frequently, from issue to issue within a meeting. There is no formal designation of a cluster member as a primary facilitator—it simply happens. When all cluster members are effective team players, they will all recognize their own personal styles, with their corresponding strengths and limitations, as well as the personal styles of the other cluster members. Through mutual respect, it becomes quite obvious in any particular situation which cluster member should be serving as the unofficial primary facilitator.

Despite the movement away from traditional leadership positions in cluster management, there is a need during the initial implementation phases of cluster management for the Stakeholders who catch on most quickly to the concepts underlying the Self-Directed School to serve as leaders in a nonauthoritative way by modeling the types of behavior required of team players. As the other cluster members develop into effective team players, the initial "leaders" should be able to stop any conscious modeling behavior and simply function as participating members.

What Can a Principal/Administrator/Facilitator Do to Create an Environment That Supports Clusters, Teamwork, and Team Players?

We have talked so much about the need to eliminate the existing hierarchical structure in American schools and about the importance of transferring authority to the Stakeholders that it might appear there is nothing left for a principal to do. To the contrary, the principal is one of the most critical elements determining the success or failure of the Self-Directed School.

What we will not see in a Self-Directed School, however, is a principal functioning in the role that we currently attribute to the school administrator. Instead, the principal will be the main facilitator of cluster management. The principal will set the tone for Stakeholder participation, and it will be his or her responsibility to ensure that communication among clusters and cluster members is encouraged, supported, and protected. There is no room for gossip in a Self-Directed School. If Stakeholders are to engage in open and honest communication, then they must feel secure that what they say will be seriously considered on its merits and not be used against them. The principal can, through his or her actions, go a long way toward creating the kind of risk-free environment that is necessary for full exchange of information.

If cluster management is to succeed, then there must be a strong principal—a principal who is strong enough to be weak. Successful principals are strong enough mentally, emotionally, and administratively to let go of their authority and invite, encourage, and support participation by all Stakeholders. The image of the principal as the boss must be extinguished. In a Self-Directed School the bosses are the Stakeholders themselves. (The characteristics of successful principals in Self-Directed Schools are examined in Chapter 8.)

Team Players in Action—Illustrative Examples

Cluster organizations require intricate teamwork on the part of their members to be successful. For example, suppose a Self-Directed School wants to develop a new program for teaching the concepts of computer engineering and roboticized production in order to provide its students with the skills necessary to be employable in the twenty-first century. Given the rapidly increasing use of robots and computer-monitored production facilities in business and industry, many schools are, in fact, beginning to implement robotics and other types of computer applications in their curriculums. In the past, efforts to develop new curriculum areas may have focused on the "experts"—for example, the school district's curriculum administrator and one or two interested teachers. While such efforts may be well intentioned, they are not effective enough in this day and age to result in a challenging, applicable, and forward-looking curriculum.

Such a curriculum can be developed, however, through the efforts of a cluster of Stakeholders. The cluster developing a robotics curriculum might be made up of teachers, interested parents, engineers from local corporations, district facilitators who may be interested in using the curriculum in other schools in the district, and students. All of these diverse individuals must work together as team players, respecting one another's strengths and accepting one another's limitations. If they can function as team players, the resulting curriculum can be expected to be superb.

Schools definitely benefit from having Stakeholders who are effective team players. Some of the immediate benefits are increased productivity, more efficient use of resources, improved problem-solving abilities, increased creativity and innovation, and high-quality decisions. We know of a specific instance in which an elementary school was experiencing significant difficulties in its physical education, music, and computer classes. This school, together with all of the other schools in the district, had the physical education and music teachers working with fifty or more students at a time and the computer teacher relegated to twenty-minute classes which were largely unproductive because of the constant changing of classes. Dissatisfied with this schedule, the school decided to establish a cluster to look into the problem and develop a workable solution. The cluster succeeded. While all of the other schools in the district remained shackled to the old schedule with all of its problems, this school implemented a new schedule in which the physical education and music teachers worked with twenty-five or fewer students at a time and the computer teacher held regular fifty-minute classes. All of this was accomplished without significantly affecting any of the other teachers in the school. All it took was for the Stakeholders to work together as team players.

Effective Clusters

By now we know that effective clusters are made up of effective team players. Clusters that work well have members who understand personal style and who are aware of the strengths and limitations of each of the various types of personal styles. By understanding personal style, each member can focus on utilizing his or her strengths to best advance the interests of the cluster while at the same time minimizing any negative effect that his or her limitations may have upon the productivity of the cluster. In addition to acknowledging their own strengths and accepting their own limitations, effective cluster members acknowledge the strengths and accept the limitations of each of the other cluster members. By combining the willingness and the ability to work constructively in group situations, effective cluster members function as team players, thereby guaranteeing an effective and successful cluster.

One question we have not yet addressed is, How do we know if we have an effective cluster? While we might understand, conceptually, that an effective cluster is comprised of effective team players, how can we measure effectiveness? The following checklist, which contains numerous characteristics of an effective cluster, may be used as a rough mechanism for diagnosing the effectiveness of a cluster:

CHARACTERISTICS OF EFFECTIVE CLUSTERS

- An effective cluster from time to time independently stops to examine how it is doing and attempts to identify and eliminate any obstacles that might be interfering with its operation.
- All members of the cluster participate. Members work together to make sure the cluster stays on task during discussions.
- Cluster members are free to express their feelings as well as their ideas, and the articulation of problems is encouraged and supported.
- The climate tends to be informal, comfortable, and relaxed. There are no obvious signs of tension or boredom.
- Decisions are reached by consensus. Cluster members are able consistently to reach agreements that everyone in the cluster is willing to support.
- The cluster takes time to study an issue before reaching a consensus. By the time a decision is made all members are convinced that it is the best decision possible under the circumstances.

- There is disagreement. It is doubtful that any cluster doing serious work will be in agreement and harmony all the time. Conflict is understood as normal. Through open discussion cluster members resolve their disagreements.
- When cluster members disagree, other members step in to resolve conflicts and help establish a common ground.
- Cluster issues are handled by the cluster as a team, not by individual members in outside conferences.
- The cluster makes sure all information necessary for its effective functioning is provided to all members.
- Members of the cluster not only cooperate but collaborate. They don't go along just because someone tells them to do so. They willingly invest themselves in the cluster task and exercise their own judgment and thought processes.
- "Leadership" is passed from member to member within the cluster. Everyone in the cluster serves as a facilitator at some time or other.

Although not included in the checklist, an effective cluster is made up of a variety of personal styles. In fact, each type of personal style should be represented. Given the rather significant differences among personal styles, this may seem to contradict logic and reason. It certainly raises some questions.

What if a cluster does not have a balance of personal styles?

Having several members in a cluster with the same personal style can be counterproductive because these members will tend to reinforce one another's style characteristics. Where all personal styles are represented, a system of checks and balances is established. Each type of personal style serves as a check against the other style types. The net result of such a system is that no one personal style dominates the cluster, and the cluster can successfully draw from the different types of personal styles.

In contrast, a homogeneous cluster, or a cluster dominated by only one type of personal style, is unbalanced. The strengths of the dominant personal style will certainly be evident but so too will its limitations. For example, if a cluster is unbalanced with action persons, those members who are analyzers may not be well utilized. They may be discounted and even isolated. A cluster with many action persons may be the first cluster to complete a project, but the cluster members might not have considered all of the data. This cluster will then have earned the distinction of being the first to complete the task—incorrectly. It has been said that this type of cluster can go down the wrong road faster than any other group.

It is very likely that in each school there will be clusters that are unbalanced based on the personal styles of cluster members. Such clusters must recognize their limitations and must attempt to have members play the roles of the personal styles not present. In the cluster unbalanced with action persons, some members must stop the cluster from time to time to ask such questions as: What are the potential adverse consequences of our decision? Do we need to slow down and consider other alternatives? In other words, some cluster members must be willing to serve, at least temporarily, as analyzers. On decisions that have great importance to the school, a cluster unbalanced with action persons may want to ask an analyzer from another cluster to serve temporarily as a member.

Admittedly, having a cluster member play the role of another personal style is somewhat of a quick fix. Some cluster members are better at imitating unfamiliar personal styles than others. The best solution, of course, is to strive for an even balance of personal styles.

Don't differences in personal style conflict in the cluster?

Given individual differences, conflict within a cluster is inevitable. In fact, differences are desirable and useful. Once cluster members recognize the strengths and limitations of each type of personal style and accept the concept of style balance within a cluster, they will be able to see more clearly why they disagree or have conflicts. Then, rather than becoming angry about the conflict, they can focus on using their own strengths, together with the strengths of other cluster members, to resolve the conflict amicably and—in some cases, quite creatively—to the benefit of the cluster and the school. Recognition and productive use of the strengths that each person brings to the cluster increases the cluster's energy level, effectiveness, and credibility. Style checks and balances produce synergism. The total overall product of the cluster is greater than the sum of its individual parts.

With the knowledge of personal styles and some basic elements of process observation, a cluster can begin to analyze and critique its own interpersonal processes. This type of cluster awareness provides the mechanism for the shifting of responsibilities within the cluster to which we referred earlier. By supporting and accepting each other and by being constantly aware of the strengths and limitations of each member of the cluster, all cluster members can work together to achieve positive results. Conflicts will occur, but cluster effectiveness depends upon the ability of cluster members to orchestrate the resolution of these conflicts so that each cluster member operates on the strength side of his or her personal style ledger.

Conclusion:
Teamwork Improves the Quality of the School

Cluster management results in tremendous benefits for the Self-Directed School. By creating the opportunity for Stakeholders to become involved in the decision-making process, cluster management heightens both the interest and the enthusiasm of the Stakeholders. Stakeholders are more committed to the successful implementation of decisions made by clusters than they are of decisions made by hierarchical managers because they themselves have made those decisions.

Decisions made by clusters are also more creative, more practical, and more effective than decisions made by individual managers or administrators. As cluster members develop into effective team players, they learn to capitalize on the strengths and minimize the limitations of each cluster member.

The security and safety of the team atmosphere creates an environment in which ideas are shared freely and without reservation. Through open communication and positive encouragement and support, cluster members can, working as a team, consistently produce better and more innovative results than they could if they worked on their own. Better results translate directly and immediately into better educational programs and opportunities for students.

Appendix 3–1 Cluster Style Inventory

The Cluster Style Inventory consists of twenty questions, each with four responses, that describe typical situations facing cluster members when working in groups. Although each of the four responses to a question may appear equally desirable or undesirable, the instrument is designed to force you to rank or differentiate among them. There are no right or wrong answers. Each response is ranked either 1, 2, 4, or 8, with the highest number indicating the greatest degree of preference; thus, a ranking of 1 indicates the response that you least prefer, 2 indicates a response that you consider on occasion, 4 indicates a response that you might consider, and 8 indicates the response that you usually use. As you respond to the question, think about how you typically make decisions or how you usually work in clusters.

1. When our cluster is trying to get consensus, I:	Go with my intuition	Go with the facts and data	Make my decision quickly	Think the issue through completely
	_____	_____	_____	_____
2. When our cluster is discussing a problem, I:	Praise others for good ideas	Stay on target	Am able to grasp the key issues quickly	Look at all sides of the issue
	_____	_____	_____	_____
3. I work best with cluster members who:	Have a good imagination	Are logical problem solvers	Push an idea to the implementation stage	Strive for mutual understanding of the issue
	_____	_____	_____	_____
4. My biggest problem in helping my team is:	I resist structure and rules	I sometimes spend too much time on details	I sometimes interrupt another cluster member	I strive for perfection
	_____	_____	_____	_____
5. When the cluster deadline is close, I:	Help to relax others	Want our solution to be correct	Keep things moving	Recognize the potential adverse consequences of making a fast decision
	_____	_____	_____	_____
6. Other cluster members usually see me as:	Supportive and informal	Disciplined and rational	Assertive	Thorough and methodical
	_____	_____	_____	_____
7. I believe cluster decisions should be based on:	Creative approaches to solving the problem	Weight of the evidence	The solution that will solve the problem the fastest	A study and assessment of the issues
	_____	_____	_____	_____

8. I believe cluster problem solving requires:	That everyone participate	Good solid data	The ability to juggle many issues at once	Good listening skills
	_____	_____	_____	_____
9. Most of the time when I work on a cluster, I:	Show a personal interest in others	Am responsible and hardworking	Help get the discussion started	Am cautious and ask questions
	_____	_____	_____	_____
10. I expect the people in my cluster to:	Be patient and considerate	Be focused and serious	Confront the issue	Develop good plans
	_____	_____	_____	_____
11. Other members consider me:	Supportive	Task oriented	Forceful	The analyzer
	_____	_____	_____	_____
12. As a cluster member, I am usually most concerned about:	How well we are working together	Staying on target in discussion	Reaching our goals	Looking at all sides of the issue
	_____	_____	_____	_____
13. In working on teams, I am good at:	Getting support for our decisions	Keeping us on task	Initiating the discussion	Asking good questions
	_____	_____	_____	_____
14. Cluster members like working with me because I am:	Relaxed and friendly	Focused on results	Energetic	Methodical and precise
	_____	_____	_____	_____
15. When our team is trying to get consensus, I:	Want everyone to feel good about our decision	Set high standards	Promote closure so we can move on to the next issue	Want us to consider all the alternatives
	_____	_____	_____	_____
16. When two people in our cluster get into a debate, I:	Try to get them to see both sides	Try to get them to focus on the objective	Try to get closure on their debate	Listen and help summarize the issue
	_____	_____	_____	_____
17. Sometimes I wish the chairperson would:	Be more sensitive	Stay on target	Go to the next item on the agenda	Slow down
	_____	_____	_____	_____

19. When I am not sure what to do, I:	Look for suggestions from other members of the group	Search for more facts	Pick what seems to be the best solution and move on	Wait before making a decision—think about it
	_____	_____	_____	_____
20. When time is important, I:	Go with the group—consensus	Follow priorities	Decide and act quickly	Refuse to be pressured by time
	_____	_____	_____	_____
TOTAL	_____	_____	_____	_____

Part II

Skills for Collaboration

4

Training for
Self-Directed Schools

> *Training is everything. The peach was once a bitter*
> *almond; cauliflower is nothing but cabbage with a*
> *college education.*
>
> Mark Twain
> *Pudd'nhead Wilson* (1894)
> *Pudd'nhead Wilson's Calendar,* Chapter 1

When asked which factor most influences the success of people working in a Self-Directed School, researchers and experienced practitioners invariably cite training. Providing Stakeholders with sufficient training and adequate time for implementing such training is a key ingredient in developing a successful Self-Directed School. Inadequate funding and insufficient time for training will, on the flip side, be the biggest obstacles to developing an effective Self-Directed School. In a period when dollars are tight and school budgets are scrutinized as never before, finding the necessary funds and time for the training of Stakeholders is difficult—especially when time and training costs are perceived by most boards of education as superfluous expenses in already overstretched budgets.

These maxims are especially true when it comes to implementing the Self-Directed School. Changing from a hierarchical, highly bureaucratic school organization to a high-involvement, Self-Directed School costs money—sometimes a great deal. Stakeholders will need to be trained, new skills will need to be learned, and everyone involved in the operation of the school will need to be given the time to learn how to make things work.

The costs are not insignificant. School boards and superintendents wishing to implement Self-Directed Schools will be required to allocate a significant amount of time and money to training. When done correctly, this investment will be more than offset by higher student achievement, improved employee morale, and greater Stakeholder enthusiasm, commitment, and creativity.

If a school district cannot justify the costs of training, then the concept of having a Self-Directed School should not be part of that school district's plans.

Providing an Adequate Budget for Training

In making budgetary decisions about providing for the training of Stakeholders in the skills necessary to become effective participants in a Self-Directed School, school boards would be wise to acknowledge the current situation in American education. According to David Kearns and Dennis Doyle, the situation is alarming:

> One fourth of the nation's young people drop out before finishing high school. Another one fourth don't graduate with the skills necessary to find work, or they go on to post secondary education needing remedial help.[1]

The current system of U.S. public elementary and secondary education is *failing* about *half* of its students. Does this suggest a school system that works? Have the budget allocations for training that have been recommended by superintendents and approved by school boards been adequate to prepare the school staff and the school community to produce qualified, well-prepared students? *We think not.*

While a number of schools today are in the early stages of

---

[1]David T. Kearns and Dennis Doyle, *Winning the Brain Race* (San Francisco: Institute for Contemporary Studies, 1989).

implementing high-involvement organizations like the Self-Directed School, most have not put the necessary resources into the proper training of Stakeholders. As a result, it is difficult to identify any success stories in the field of public education—that is, schools that have been able to achieve significant improvement in the performance of their staff and students as a result of becoming a Self-Directed School. In American business and industry, however, numerous companies have, through the implementation of employee-involvement programs and the elimination of many unnecessary administrative positions (corporate "flattening") achieved remarkable success.[2]

Successful companies have discovered that in today's highly competitive and rapidly changing world economy it is not possible to remain afloat without the involvement of employees as equal and valued participants in every aspect of the company's operations. These companies have made the necessary budget allocations to train and develop their employees, and the allocations have paid off—often with astounding results.

Case 1: *Harley-Davidson* In 1973, Harley-Davidson had 75 percent of the super heavyweight motorcycle market in the United States. By 1983, the company was barely hanging on to 25 percent of the market. Harley had fallen from grace, and few industry experts gave it more than a minimum chance of surviving—but it did. By the late 1980s, Harley had recaptured much of the market it had lost in the late 1970s and early 1980s. How did this company save itself? It implemented new team systems and provided the budget to train and support the teams.

Case 2: *Motorola* In the early to mid-1980s, Motorola was in trouble. Once a leader in the field of electronic communications, including the manufacture of the microchips necessary to operate these communication devices, Motorola experienced a significant decline in market share. With the introduction of high-quality pagers and cellular phone equipment by the

---

[2]Joseph Boyett and Henry Conn, *Workplace 2000* (New York: Dutton Books, 1991).

Japanese to the U.S. market, Motorola suffered a rapid loss of market share in these product lines. In only a few years, Motorola went from being the second largest producer of microchips in the world to being an also-ran. But just five years later Motorola was back. By 1989, Motorola had become number one in semiconductor chip sales in the United States.

Much of Motorola's success resulted from significant improvements in quality, cost containment, and efficiency. For example, production time (order to shipment) for two-way radios was cut from thirty days to just three days. Product defects company-wide were cut from 3,000 per million units in 1983 to less than 200 per million units in 1989. In recognition of its impressive gains in performance, quality, and productivity, in 1988 Motorola received America's prestigious Malcolm Baldridge National Quality Award.

How did Motorola make its comeback? Simply stated, the company fundamentally changed the way it did business. To ensure that employees focused on quality, Motorola reduced managerial and supervisory layers and increased areas of employee control, encouraged teamwork and employee ownership, and changed the traditional style of company management from one of policing to one of coaching. To promote employee involvement, Motorola established teams throughout the company to strive for quality improvement. To ensure that the teams had the necessary skills, team members were trained in problem-solving, decision-making, conflict-resolution, consensus-building, and quality-improvement techniques. By 1990, Motorola had established a goal that each of its employees worldwide would participate in a minimum of forty hours of education and training each year.

Training costs are a significant part of Motorola's annual budget. It is obvious, however, that such costs have reaped enormous dividends.

Harley-Davidson and Motorola are only two of the U.S. corporations that have changed the way they do business. Xerox, Sara Lee, Wal-Mart, Corning, Digital Computer, Proctor and Gamble, and AT&T are just a few of the many other companies that have changed their way of doing business.[3] All of these companies have one thing in common—they have deemphasized the traditional, hierarchical corporate structure and have implemented procedures and opportunities for increased employee involvement and participation at all levels of operations. In most cases, the implementation of new, high-involvement policies has required the companies to allocate a much larger percentage of their budgets to the training and development of employees than had been allocated under the traditional management style. Had any of the companies we have mentioned attempted to save money on training costs and chosen, instead, to continue to do things as they always had, it is doubtful that they would have survived—or, if they survived, that they would have experienced the success that they have enjoyed.

It is a simple fact that high-involvement organizations require a significant commitment to training. At Corning, for instance, employees serving on employee management teams spend 15 to 20 percent of their time in training—approximately one day a week.

Training Is a Survival Issue

For companies like Harley-Davidson, Motorola, and numerous others, finding a new way to manage business was a matter of survival. Given their rapidly deteriorating market positions, these companies had little choice but to explore new and creative ways of doing business. What they found was that the key to their survival lay with their employees. And the key to tapping the full potential of their employees lay not only with increasing the opportunities for employee participation but also with providing the employees with the skills necessary to be successful in the new, high-involvement environment.

In business and industry, economic pressures have dictated the need for change. Corporations that have been willing to be creative and to explore new ways of doing business have survived and even prospered. Those that have clung to traditional ways of doing business have, in most cases, failed or are on their way to bankruptcy.

Schools today still operate and look like the many failing U.S. corporations that have refused to change their way of doing business. The majority of U.S. schools continue to operate under the

---

[3]Boyett and Conn, *Workplace 2000.*

same theory that has failed business and industry—that is, the science of industrial production.

For decades, U.S. educators have believed that schools should be managed like factories. Under this scenario, the teacher is the worker manning the production line, the student is the product being manufactured, the principal is the foreman making sure that the workers toe the company line, and the superintendent is the CEO responsible for the overall management and productivity of the factory. The school board functions as the corporate board of directors, and the citizens of the community represent the stockholders. Curriculum guides and lesson plans are developed by the central office just as employee manuals and company operating policies are developed by high-level managers in hierarchical business structures. Teachers are treated as doers rather than as independent and committed thinkers and are assigned specific work days and work hours, just as industrial workers have traditionally been. In short, schools operating under this kind of thinking function as small factories of learning—with all that that implies.

What is implied, primarily, is that, like many traditionally structured companies, schools are failing to produce quality products. The statistics bear this out. Approximately half of the students in public schools drop out or need remedial help upon the completion of their education. Even those that do "succeed" (based on such traditional measures of success as achievement tests, grades, and graduation) are finding it increasingly difficult to compete for jobs in what is rapidly becoming a world-wide economy. In industrial parlance, our schools have a defect rate of over *50 percent*—a truly appalling figure. In business, a company with a 50 percent defect rate would fail and would be held up as an example of how *not* to do business. But our schools just keep chugging along—hoping, perhaps miraculously, that things will somehow get better.

With alarming frequency the products of U.S. schools are finding themselves unqualified and unprepared for the challenges of today's competitive employment market. Even more disconcerting is the fact that a large percentage of school administrators and educators do not seem to see the problems that exist. They do not appear to comprehend the fundamental weaknesses of a system that *fails* 50 percent of the time. These administrators and educators, many of whom hold masters' and doctoral degrees and are thus well trained in traditional educational methods, continue to believe in and perpetuate an educational system that is structured to meet the educational needs of the grandparents of today's youths. It is truly a recipe for disaster.

In business and industry, economic pressures dictate when change and reform are necessary. Inefficiency and ineffectiveness in a company's organizational structure or work force are reflected, sooner or later, in the company's financial position. Failure to respond to problems or weaknesses leads inexorably to the death of the company.

Obviously, the same types of economic and financial pressures are not present in the field of education. In fact, schools are almost completely insulated from any external pressures to make adjustments or modifications. While achievement tests and other standardized assessment procedures do provide some measure of a school's effectiveness, they do not create the same kind of immediate and overwhelming pressure for change that falling profits create for a business.

We believe that U.S. schools are on the brink of bankruptcy (some are already in Chapter 7) and that fundamental change is needed. Just as businesses have achieved success by revamping their organizational structures to increase employee involvement and incorporate team approaches to problem solving and management, schools need to tap the abundant resources and talents of Stakeholders.

Stakeholders need to become involved in a meaningful way in every aspect of the operation of our schools. In order to implement such a fundamental change in organizational structure, it is essential that the Stakeholders—both the newly involved Stakeholders such as teachers, parents, and community members and the traditionally involved Stakeholders such as principals and administrators—be *trained* in the skills that will be required of them in the new, high-involvement environment. This training will require a heavy commitment of time and resources. We believe such a commitment will yield dividends many times greater than the actual investment.

Training—The Seven Principles for Success

Placing so much emphasis on training is understandable when one considers the many types of skills Stakeholders need to function effectively in a Self-Directed School. Traditional organizational structures really do not demand much in the way of individual contributions from their participants. What is demanded is an adherence to the hierarchical chain of command and a willingness to carry out orders. Participants do not work collectively to solve problems and produce results—they work individually to carry out instructions and follow orders. Training requirements are minimal because once a worker has been told what his or her job requires, little else is expected of that employee.

In a high-involvement organization, however, employees are expected to think, contribute, and work together. The ability to do a specific job or to carry out instructions is no longer the sole measure of the employee's effectiveness. Instead, to be successful employees need to know how to interact, how to work together to solve problems, how to reach a consensus in groups, how to communicate, how to collaborate, and how to evaluate ideas and suggestions. Training to develop these skills needs to be extensive and broad based.

It may seem difficult at first to get a handle on the type and extent of training required to develop and implement a Self-Directed School. We believe, however, that effective training can be achieved by following the seven principles for success:

1. Commence training by helping Stakeholders develop into a supportive and cohesive group.
2. Provide a core set of high-involvement group interaction skills.
3. While developing collaboration skills, continue to develop and refine the staff's skills in curriculum and instruction.
4. Provide time for training.
5. Provide training at the most teachable moment.
6. Have Stakeholders start working together as quickly as possible even if they do not have all of the necessary skills to do so.
7. Provide opportunities for Stakeholders to use new skills.

By following these principles a school can develop productive and effective Stakeholders who participate actively in, and make valuable and meaningful contributions to, the creation and operation of a Self-Directed School.

Training Principle 1:
Commence Training by Helping Stakeholders
Develop into a Supportive and Cohesive Group.

Perhaps the single most important skill required of Stakeholders in a Self-Directed School is the ability to work with other Stakeholders in groups. Accordingly, in implementing the concept of the Self-Directed School, it is essential to understand the stages that groups pass through as they develop and the major issues that arise as clusters learn to work together. Figure 4–1 illustrates the gradual evolution of a Stakeholder's role from working on an individual basis in an environment that provides a great deal of structure in the form of directive-type leadership (stage 1 of group development) to working as a team player and valuable cluster member in a Self-Directed

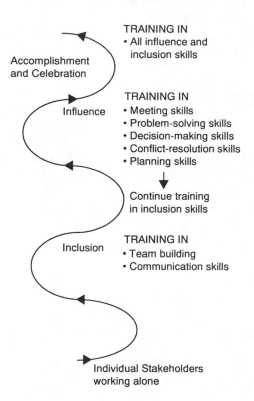

Figure 4–1. The Evolution of Group Development.

School (stage 3 of group development).[4] By the time they reach stage 3, the Stakeholders as a group will have moved from a traditional, hierarchical organizational structure to an organizational structure that supports cluster management and that depends on leadership not from the top but from within.

As the Stakeholders proceed along the path of group development, they gradually take increasing amounts of initiative and begin to play a more active role in influencing what is happening in the school. Eventually they assume leadership of the school through their clusters. The net effect is that the responsibility for the success of the school is transferred from the principal and district office to the Stakeholders themselves. This process of transference depends on the talents and resources of the Stakeholders. Once completed, it enables the Stakeholders to accomplish tasks through collaborative activity in satisfying and creative ways.

In order to more fully understand the evolution of group development depicted in Figure 4–1, we present the following short discussion of each of the three stages of group development.[5]

Stage 1—The Stage of Inclusion

We all experience from time to time the feeling of being uncomfortable with a new group of people or with people we do not know well. As we look around the group, we have many unspoken questions: Will the other members accept me? Do I want to work with this group? How can I contribute to this group? What will the other members of the group think of me? Am I good enough to be a member of this group? If people stay immersed in these initial anxieties, they will never learn how to work together and will never achieve the type of creativity and commitment that can be attained by working in teams or clusters.

In order to overcome the anxieties that all Stakeholders will experience when they start to work in clusters, a school looking toward becoming a Self-Directed School should, before forming clus-

---

[4]This idea is adapted from Jeanne Gibbs, *Tribes* (Santa Rosa, CA: Center Source Publications, 1987).

[5]The three stages of group development discussed here and depicted in Figure 4–1 correspond to the three stages of cluster development referred to in Chapter 2.

ters or beginning cluster work, have its entire staff participate in at least sixteen hours of inclusion activities. These activities, which frequently form the basis of seminars designed to build self-esteem, help to create and establish a sense of community among staff members.

All of the school's Stakeholders should participate in the inclusion activities. The greater the degree of Stakeholder participation, the stronger will be the school's basis for developing into a successful Self-Directed School.

Because the inclusion activities are critical to the development and future success of the school, they should be conducted by a trained facilitator. During these activities, the participating Stakeholders should get to know each other and should learn to incorporate the following norms, which will be crucial to their ability to work successfully in groups, into their behavior patterns and thought processes:[6]

Attentive Listening Attentive listening means that when a person is speaking, the listener acknowledges the speaker with full attention and eye contact. The listener does not interrupt but waits until the speaker has completed the thought at hand before commenting or asking questions.

Attentive listening may appear to be something that we all do naturally when we're engaged in conversation with others; in reality, it is a skill that must be learned. Many of us may be unwilling to admit it, but in most conversations we are actually doing more talking than listening. We are a nation of talkers, not listeners. Truly trained listeners—for example, psychiatrists and psychologists—are so valued in our society that many people pay them a great deal of money to listen. Our intent is not to denigrate the value of counseling and therapy or to reduce the role of the psychiatrist, psychologist, or therapist to that of an attentive listener. Obviously, therapists and counselors do much more than listen. The point is that truly attentive listening is a skill that must be developed.

Because it is crucial to the development of effective team players, attentive listening must be one of the first skills presented in the training of Stakeholders.

---

[6]From Gibbs, *Tribes.*

No Put-Downs It is important that all members of a cluster feel good about themselves and the group. Put-downs, even friendly ones, distract from the positive climate so essential to cluster interaction and introduce the possibility of misunderstandings and hurt feelings. There cannot be a positive climate unless the group prohibits put-downs and encourages members to exchange statements of appreciation and positive recognition. In order to foster good feelings among group members, some clusters enforce a rule of never ending a meeting without first giving each member positive reinforcement about how that individual helped the cluster work together in the meeting.

The Right to Pass The right to pass means that each person in a group has the right to determine the extent to which he or she will share in a group activity. If a member chooses not to contribute actively in a particular situation or at a particular time, then that person has the right to pass. Passing on an issue does not mean that the member is not participating. Being a silent observer is a form of participation and often leads to greater or more enhanced learning—especially if the issue being discussed is particularly complex or the person is a new member and is trying to understand the interactions of the group.

Confidentiality Confidentiality means exactly what it says. All interactions among cluster members during a meeting are to be held in confidence by the cluster members. At McQueeney Elementary School in McQueeney, Texas, one classroom of students working on developing collaborative problem-solving skills rephrased the confidentiality rule as, "What you say here, what you hear here, let it stay here when you leave here." If cluster members are ever going to be willing to share what they really think about an issue (which is the fundamental prerequisite of effective group activity), then they must feel secure in the knowledge that what they say will not be shared with others behind their backs. Gossip is an incredibly destructive practice and is the Achilles heal of cluster management. To be successful, cluster members must be willing and able to keep cluster discussions in confidence.

Keeping cluster discussions confidential does not mean that cluster decisions are to be kept a secret. In fact, quite the contrary is true. In order to preserve and maintain the legitimacy of clusters and the cluster decision-making process, all decisions and actions of a cluster should be recorded in the written minutes of meetings. Individual confidences, such as who said what and in what words, can be maintained without sacrificing the need for the cluster to be accountable for its decisions and actions. Every cluster in a Self-Directed School has both the right and the obligation to know what every other cluster in the school is doing. This can be accomplished only through the recording and publishing of minutes by each cluster. The minutes should reflect the decisions and actions of the cluster without compromising the confidentiality owed to individual members.

Like the right to pass, the norm of confidentiality protects and honors the integrity and security of each cluster member.

Stage 2—The Stage of Influence

As individuals become comfortable working in groups during the stage of inclusion, they will begin to feel ready to broaden the scope of their participation in group activity. As they start to feel empowered, they will look for opportunities to become involved. During the stage of influence cluster members begin to take more initiative and to make suggestions. As Stakeholders mature during this stage, they become more insistent on receiving answers to their questions and more critical of the traditional organizational structure. The trappings of hierarchical management begin to crumble, and collaboration starts to take over.

The stage of influence is a period of both tremendous growth and frustration for Stakeholders and is actually the most difficult stage for the Stakeholders to pass through. Having progressed through the stage of inclusion—in all likelihood relatively easily—the Stakeholders are more confident in their ability to work in groups. As a result, they will begin to seek projects to work on. No longer are they content to have issues spoonfed or assigned to them by the principal.

As clusters extend their spheres of influence, the issues that they must wrestle with will become increasingly more complex, more sensitive, and more volatile. Of course, this tendency for issues to become more and more difficult is reflected in all aspects of human endeavor and is not a special characteristic of school administration. It is natural to resolve the easy issues first. Like cream rising to the top of milk, easy issues surface and are handled first, leaving more difficult and complex issues to be confronted at a later time.

As the issues become more complicated, discussions among cluster members will probably become more heated and emotional, and conflicts will almost certainly arise. A number of questions are raised during the stage of influence, and the stakeholders need to develop new skills and techniques for effectively resolving the issues presented. Among the questions that arise are:

- How do cluster members know which problems to work on first?
- How can each cluster member influence the goals, tasks, and decision-making process of the group?
- How should cluster assignments be made—in other words, who should work on which clusters?
- How do clusters know which issues are the ones that clusters can decide?
- How can cluster members assert their individuality in the midst of the group?
- How can leadership be shared so that the resources and potential of each member are used?

These questions need to be answered by providing the Stakeholders with the necessary training at the correct moment (Training Principle 5—Provide Training at the Most Teachable Moment). Training should include instruction in

- Communication.
- Conflict resolution.
- Problem solving and decision making.
- Reaching a consensus.

Stage 3—The Stage of Accomplishment

When the Stakeholders reach the stage of accomplishment (after much struggle, a lot of frustration, and the growing pains experienced during stages 1 and 2), there will be a natural desire to celebrate and an insidious tendency for Stakeholders to want to rest on their laurels. The Stakeholders must resist this temptation at all costs. Training must be continued in all aspects of group collaborative activity. Those who have progressed through stages 1 and 2 may have a tendency to become intoxicated by their wealth of experience and begin to assume positions of power in "leading" others. If this happens, the Self-Directed School will simply revert back to the traditional hierarchical model, and the struggle of the Stakeholders will be for naught. Constant and continuing training will help to remind experienced Stakeholders of the importance of shared responsibility.

Stakeholders in this stage also need to realize that the Stakeholder base of a school is constantly changing. Staff members leave or retire, parents of graduating students resign, new parents join, and so on. As the Stakeholder membership evolves, new Stakeholders must be taught the skills needed to be effective participants.

Mere accomplishment is not enough. Stakeholders must continually strive to be more creative and more effective. The future of our youth is at stake. Fostering the commitment and creativity engendered by collaborative activity through ongoing training in group interaction skills will prepare the Stakeholders to develop the best educational environment possible.

Training Principle 2:
Provide a Core Set of High-Involvement
Group Interaction Skills.

To function effectively in a Self-Directed School, the Stakeholders must be equipped with a core set of group interaction skills. The skills comprising this core set include the following:

Cluster Facilitation Skills The proper facilitation of cluster activity is one of the most important skills for Stakeholders to learn. As we have stressed throughout this book, clusters do not have leaders—they have facilitators. This distinction between leadership and facilitation, while it may seem subtle, constitutes one of the fundamental differences between traditional, hierarchical organizations and high-involvement Self-Directed Schools.

Leadership implies an organizational structure in which one or more individuals, possessing special knowledge, education, or abilities, are responsible for making decisions and leading or motivating other individuals to carry out those decisions. By contrast, facilitation connotes an organizational structure based on equality of positions and absence of rank or levels of responsibility.

On the other hand, no organizational structure can exist in a condition of anarchy. At any particular time, someone must be in charge. The critical attribute of a Self-Directed School is that the person in charge at any given time is not responsible for leading. Instead, that person is responsible simply for facilitating the applicable activity. With respect to group discussions, the facilitator's job is to try to keep the discussion on track, to try to serve as a reminder of the group's norms, and to try to protect the interests of all group members. With respect to the implementation of group decisions, the facilitator's job is to serve as the coordinator of activities or programs designed and developed by the group. Each Stakeholder must learn the many subtle nuances of being a facilitator because each Stakeholder will, over the course of time, serve as a facilitator.

Problem-Solving and Decision-Making Skills Cluster members must be able to identify the problem that is presented to them, explore possible solutions, evaluate the pros and cons of each option, and reach agreement on how to proceed. In the process of problem solving, cluster members must develop respect and appreciation for both the strengths and the limitations of each member of the cluster. As we discussed in Chapter 3, each cluster member has his or her own personal style. It is up to each cluster member to maximize the strengths and minimize the limitations of each member of the cluster.

Interpersonal and Conflict-Resolution Skills Common understanding and unity of purpose are end results of good communication and interpersonal skills. Stakeholders must be effective communicators. Unfortunately, since our society does not value good communication skills, few of us have had much practice in developing these abilities.

One critical aspect of good communication is an appreciation of divergent points of view. If individuals are truly open and honest about their thoughts and ideas, which is the goal of collaborative activity, then *conflict will arise.* All too often people engaged in a discussion interpret conflict or disagreement as a rejection of or personal attack on whatever their own particular position may be. Stakeholders must overcome the tendency to view conflict as a problem and learn to accept the fact that conflict is natural and to be expected. Moreover, conflict is the one and only source of growth. If members never disagree, then the cluster is not forced to confront issues and wrestle with alternatives—alternatives which could often lead to creative, effective, and previously unimagined solutions.

Building Accountable Plans Plans provide clusters with blueprints for future activity. They are not etched in stone, but they provide direction for a cluster's efforts so that the resources of the cluster are used most effectively. Plans also provide a mechanism for monitoring cluster activity, both within the cluster and outside of it.

As we stated earlier, implementing cluster management and a Self-Directed School does not mean abandoning accountability for the performance of the school. Instead, accountability actually increases. The principal remains ultimately accountable for the performance of the school and its students. (This point is discussed in more detail in Chapter 8.) However, in addition to the principal, each cluster is accountable for its actions. Establishing plans forces each cluster to identify its goals and objectives for each issue it must resolve. The plan should identify specifically the means for determining whether a decision made by the cluster was a success or whether it should be rethought and reevaluated.

Training Principle 3:
Continue to Develop and Refine the
Staff's Skills in Curriculum and Instruction.

Training in group interaction and communication is not the only kind of training needed by Stakeholders of a Self-Directed School. In their desire to learn how to become effective team players in a collaborative work environment, Stakeholders must not forget about or downplay the importance of keeping the teachers well trained in and informed of the latest developments in their applicable curriculum areas.

Curriculum skills and cluster/interaction skills must be used in concert. A staff member of a Self-Directed School must be able to combine expertise in a particular curriculum area with interaction skills in order to be an effective participant in the overall process of the Self-Directed School.

A short example will illustrate the importance of using curriculum skills and cluster/interaction skills together. Imagine a cluster of Stakeholders who have assumed responsibility to develop a new science curriculum. Imagine further that the teachers who are members of this cluster have focused their energies on cluster/interaction skills and have failed to keep up with the latest developments in the field of science—say, laser disk technology. Under this scenario, the cluster members will probably be very effective at communicating ideas and reaching a consensus, but their solution or proposal is likely to be inappropriate, outdated, or just plain unacceptable. By contrast, imagine a cluster in which the teachers are well trained in the field of science but have had virtually no training in group interaction skills. (This is actually the situation in existence in most schools in the United States today.) Under this scenario, the Stakeholders are not likely to be effective at communicating the valuable insights and information they possess. Their weak group skills will probably be reflected in a wide array of adverse and unproductive reactions. The ultimate result is likely to be stagnation, frustration, and general apathy about whatever decision the cluster reaches. Without the sense of commitment and enthusiasm engendered by an open and honest exchange of ideas among members, the decision of the cluster is likely to be ignored and unsupported by the members. The teachers will simply return to their rooms, shut their doors, and do whatever they wanted to do in the first place.

In this hypothetical example, the Stakeholders lack a critical component of the overall skills needed to be effective cluster members. The result is ineffectiveness and, quite possibly, failure. Cluster members must be equipped with both curriculum skills *and* cluster/interaction skills.

Training Principle 4: Provide Time for Training.

Time for training represents the single largest investment and the single largest cost in implementing a Self-Directed School. Whereas it is fairly easy to quantify the dollar cost of other training expenses, such as the cost of consultants and the cost of materials, quantifying the cost of time is exceedingly difficult. In most cases, however, Stakeholders involved in creating a Self-Directed School will probably underestimate the amount of time that will need to be allocated to training.

In discussing the investment of time in training, we are not just talking about the amount of time spent attending training sessions. That is actually a fairly small percentage of the total amount of time that will need to be invested in training. To better understand the issue of time, consider the three different types of investments of time that will be needed as part of the training process for a Self-Directed School:

- The time spent by Stakeholders in attending training sessions (a relatively small portion of the overall time investment in training).
- The time devoted to providing opportunities for Stakeholders to build and sharpen their group interaction skills.
- The time involved in holding cluster meetings and addressing issues that would require less time if they were handled by an individual with designated authority or dictated by a policy manual.

The last type of investment represents the greatest investment of time in implementing a Self-Directed School.

Cluster meetings, where people use interaction skills to discuss issues and solve problems, are the lifeblood of the Self-Directed School. It is a fact of life, however, that cluster meetings are time consuming. In high-involvement scenarios, where many people share ideas and provide input, the decision-making process requires more time than it does in hierarchical, top-down management systems.

Is this tremendous investment of time in the collaborative decision-making process worth it? We believe it most definitely is, for two important reasons. First, cluster meetings provide an opportunity to explore new ideas and new ways of thinking. In hierarchical organizations, management often becomes predictable and unimaginative. Nagging problems tend to recur on a periodic basis, and solutions often seem to be impossible. What happens is that the managerial leaders become locked in, limited in their problem-solving abilities by their own ways of looking at things, their own personal styles, and their own strengths and limitations. The knowledge and experience needed to handle every situation that arises in an organization cannot reside in a single person. The necessary knowledge and experience can, however, be pieced together by combining the knowledge, experience, and insight of many people.

Second, in addition to providing an opportunity to combine knowledge and expand individuals' abilities to think in a variety ways, cluster meetings provide an opportunity to build consensus and commitment. In cluster meetings, Stakeholders can express their beliefs and argue their positions. Because they have been given a chance to be heard and have been included in the process of arriving at a decision, they are far more likely to be committed to implementing a decision than if the decision were decreed from above.

Cluster meetings take time. But that time is well spent because of the greater creativity of the solutions arrived at and the heightened commitment on the part of Stakeholders to making the solutions work.

Training Principle 5:
Provide Training at the Most Teachable Moment.

Most educators understand this principle well. Teaching of a concept will result in the greatest retention of knowledge when it is provided as closely in time as possible to an event that is relevant to the concept. This window of opportunity for learning is known as the teachable moment. The principle of providing training at the most teachable moment is just as true for adults working in clusters as it is for children working in classrooms. It is important that Stakeholders be provided with training in a particular skill as closely in time as possible to an opportunity for the Stakeholders to use that skill. A great deal of training can be rendered useless if the Stakeholders are not given an immediate opportunity to apply their new knowledge. Training without good timing usually results in one of a number of negative reactions from Stakeholders: "Why am I in this training?" "When is this training going to be over?" "Didn't we learn something about this last year?"

Based on this principle, it should be apparent that training in all of the skills that Stakeholders will need to be effective participants in a Self-Directed School should *not* be lumped together at the beginning of the implementation process. Providing training in the types of skills Stakeholders will need in stage 2 of the implementation process will do little good if the Stakeholders are still in the nascent phases of stage 1. Such training will in all likelihood be long forgotten by the time the Stakeholders make it to stage 2. The Stakeholders will then need to be retrained, resulting in wasted dollars and wasted time.

Group facilitation skills are a good example of the importance of providing training at the appropriate time. All cluster members will, at some point in time, serve as the facilitator of their cluster. In fact, even though there may be one cluster member who has informally assumed the role of the primary facilitator in a particular meeting, in mature clusters all cluster members serve as supportive facilitators, equally sharing the responsibility for facilitating the meeting. Accordingly, facilitation skills will need to be learned by all Stakeholders of a Self-Directed School. A school will make an enormous mistake, however, if it attempts to provide training in facilitation skills at the very beginning of the process of implementing a Self-Directed School. During stage 1, Stakeholders are more concerned about getting to know each other and learning to trust and believe in each other than they are in learning how to facilitate a cluster meeting. Stage 1 Stakeholders are content to simply let someone else, either the principal or an outside consultant, serve as facilitator.

As the Stakeholders achieve a sense of inclusion in stage 1 and gradually become more comfortable with the notion of working together, they will begin to take more of an interest in facilitating their own meetings. At that point they will be thirsty for training in facilitation skills. The result should be attentive and enthusiastic participation in facilitation training. Long-term learning will be achieved, and training effectiveness will be maximized.

Training Principle 6:
Have Stakeholders Start Working Together as Quickly as Possible Even If They Do Not Have All Necessary Skills to Do So.

Since Stakeholders need to receive training in group interaction skills in order to become effective participants in a Self-Directed School, then common sense would say that the Stakeholders need to receive all of the necessary training *before* they begin to work in clusters. In this particular case, however, common sense is wrong. It is impossible, given the enormity of the challenge and the length of time required to implement a Self-Directed School, to provide all of the necessary training before the Stakeholders begin to work in clusters. Moreover, as we discussed in connection with Principle 5, even if it were possible to provide all of the training in advance, much of the effectiveness of the training would be lost by the time the Stakeholders actually got a chance to apply the skills that were taught.

The key, then, is to start the Stakeholders down the road to self-directedness with the knowledge that they do not have all of the skills necessary to be effective participants in the process. The Stakeholders should be warned that frustrations will arise due to their lack of training in the skills they need. It is especially important during the early periods of experimentation by the Stakeholders for the principal to serve as facilitator and to emphasize his or her role as facilitator over the other roles played by the principal in a Self-Directed School. (See Chapter 8 for a discussion of the various roles played by a principal in a Self-Directed School.)

As Stakeholders experience the process of working together in clusters, they will become more aware of the skills they do not have. This will increase their interest in receiving training in those skills, creating, in turn, valuable teachable moments for providing such training.

Training Principle 7:
Provide Opportunities for Stakeholders to Use New Skills.

Maintaining newly learned skills is a must. The saying "we lose what we don't use" is as applicable to learning new collaborative skills as it is to any other area of human endeavor. Just as individuals who study a foreign language must have opportunities to use the language if they expect to maintain the ability to speak the language, so too must Stakeholders be given opportunities to use, practice, and develop the skills they have acquired. If opportunities to use new skills are not provided, the new skills will be quickly forgotten and the benefits of training will be lost.

Principle 7 is actually a corollary to Principle 5. In order for training to be effective, it must be presented at teachable moments. In addition, participants in the training must be given the chance to use and practice their new skills. In the case of Self-Directed Schools, there should be ample opportunities for Stakeholders to practice their newly acquired group interaction skills. Daily cluster meetings, Stakeholder-created professional development programs, and teacher-led faculty meetings all provide opportunities for Stakeholders to practice and develop their group interaction skills.

Evaluating Training Effectiveness

Although not stated as a separate principle above, it is imperative that a Self-Directed School periodically evaluate its current position and the effectiveness of its training programs. Has training been provided at the most teachable moments? Have the Stakeholders been given the opportunity to practice their skills? Do certain areas of training need to be revisited? Are there weaknesses that need to be addressed? If a school does not intend to invest the time, energy, and money to assess and maintain the skills and knowledge gained by Stakeholders in training programs, then it should not provide training in the first place.

Using Skills Presented in Training: Building the School's Professional Development Program

In most school systems today staff development programs are designed and implemented by people other than the individuals who will be expected to use the skills presented. In these school systems there is typically an individual or department who has the responsibility is to develop training programs for all staff members in the district. While some of the programs are successful, most fail to adequately address the needs of the staff. Because district-planned development programs are forced upon staff members, frequently without any consultation with staff members about their interests or needs, staff members fail to take an ownership interest in the content of the training programs and, as a result, fail to commit themselves to learning the skills being presented. In many districts, staff members report that their district-planned training programs are largely irrelevant and inappropriate for their school and for them as individuals.

In a Self-Directed School, most professional development programs are designed by the faculty and Stakeholders, not by the district office. The need to shift responsibility for creating and implementing professional development programs from the district office to the Stakeholders is based on the following set of beliefs:

- No two schools are alike in their professional development needs. District-planned inservice programs are usually mass produced and do not fit the needs and desires of an individual school's Stakeholders.
- Planning a school's development program is best accomplished by soliciting the input of the school's Stakeholders. This means that each school's program will be unique.
- People tend to resist what they're not involved in designing. Asking Stakeholders to participate in the planning and

implementation of the school's professional development program taps everyone's expertise and resources. It also gets everyone to commit to the success of the program.

- The Stakeholders of a school know best the needs and interests of the staff and the students of the school and are therefore in the best position to design and direct the professional development program for the school.

- The collaborative effort of a school's Stakeholders working together to plan a professional development program is far greater than the sum of the efforts of the principal and district administrators working independently and in isolation to design development programs for all schools in the district.

The Stakeholder-Directed Professional Development Model

The collaborative model described in Chapter 2 (see Figures 2–1, 2–2, and 2–3) represents a new and different vision of school management. It reflects the collaboration of all of the various Stakeholders of an individual school as they work together to shape their own destiny.

The professional development of a school's staff is one of the most important determinants of a school's destiny, and the program should be designed and implemented by the school's Stakeholders. One of the clusters in a Self-Directed School should be the professional development cluster. This cluster should assume the responsibility to develop, refine, and facilitate the total professional development program for the school and its Stakeholders. In planning and implementing the program, the cluster will have to confront all of the issues presented in the professional development guide illustrated in Figure 4–2.

As presented in the professional development guide, the professional development cluster will have to work through each of the following issues:

Needs Assessment The first step for the professional development cluster will be to identify and assess the existing skills and anticipated needs of the school's Stakeholders. The cluster will have to answer the question: Do the Stakeholders have the skills necessary to accomplish the mission of the school? The cluster will then need to determine the skills that are missing or need additional work, develop a performance assessment for each skill, and compare the

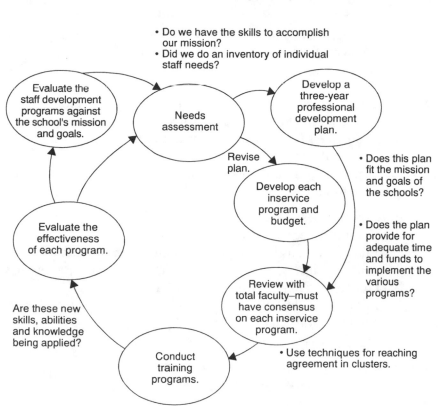

Figure 4–2. Professional Development Guide.

abilities of each Stakeholder with the performance assessment for each skill.

Develop a Three-Year Professional Development Program Many skills will need to be learned—many more than can be taught in one year. Training should be sequenced in a logical order so that the various sessions build on one another. Training should be presented at the most teachable moments possible (see Principle 5). Toward this end, the professional development cluster should prepare a comprehensive three-year plan for development training. When the draft of the plan is completed, two questions should be asked. First, will the three-year plan help the Stakeholders accomplish the mission and goals of the school? And second, does the plan provide for setting aside the time and funds necessary to implement all of the aspects of the plan? Answers to these questions may require revision or modification of the plan.

Develop Each Inservice Program Training programs should contribute to the overall three-year plan for the school. Each program should be scheduled for presentation at the most teachable moment possible and should address the specific needs and/or interests of the Stakeholders. In addition, each program should incorporate the following basic principles:

1. Activities designed to build teamwork and esprit de corps should be integrated into each training session.
2. Training sessions in interpersonal and group interaction skills should be interspersed to allow time between sessions for Stakeholders to practice what they have learned.
3. Training should be provided as close in time as possible to actual use of the skill.

Training can be rendered useless if it is not presented at a teachable moment or if the participants are not given an immediate opportunity to apply their newly learned skills.

Gain Faculty Support People tend to resist training programs that they are not involved in designing or do not get a chance to approve. Accordingly, the professional development cluster has two responsibilities. First, the cluster should act in a representative capacity to solicit ideas from all of the Stakeholders of the school regarding training. Second, after plans for a training program have been prepared but before they have been finalized, the cluster should have the Stakeholders approve the proposed training. By soliciting suggestions and obtaining the final approval of the Stakeholders, the professional development cluster will greatly increase both the enthusiasm of the Stakeholders for the planned program and the commitment of the Stakeholders to the successful implementation of the training.

As part of the process of gaining Stakeholder support, the professional development cluster will need to make sure it has addressed two issues: First, have the Stakeholders reached a consensus on the need for the program? And second, does each Stakeholder know what will happen in the training session and what he or she will be expected to learn? Making sure that these two questions are answered affirmatively will force the cluster to clarify ambiguities and will help to eliminate uncertainty among the Stakeholders concerning the objectives of a particular training session.

Conduct Training Programs Training programs must be of high quality. Nothing will kill training or the desire to undertake additional training faster than a poor presentation. This is especially true of professional development programs. Students at all levels of the educational process learn to accept and cope with a certain amount of boredom and/or inefficiency in the dissemination of information by the instructor. This is *not* true of teachers or any other group of adults who participate in professional development programs. Time is of the essence for busy professionals, and unless the presenter of information can capture the attention of the audience and disseminate timely and relevant information in an efficient and interesting way, the program will be a disaster. There will be tremendous pressure on the professional development cluster to plan and organize effective programs and locate qualified presenters.

Evaluate the Effectiveness of the Training Program Given the amount of time and money that will be invested in training, it is essential for the professional development cluster to undertake an evaluation of the effectiveness of the training programs that are held.

By effectiveness we do not mean whether the participants in a particular session or program liked the session or the presentation. Such "happiness" surveys taken immediately after training sessions are shallow and quite frequently useless in determining whether any skills were actually learned by the participants. What we mean by the "effectiveness" of a particular program is whether the skills taught in the program are actually used and practiced by the participants on an ongoing basis.

In order to determine the effectiveness of a training program, then, the professional development cluster will need to design and construct mechanisms for measuring the application over the long term of the skills taught. In other words, do the faculty members actually *apply* the skills? Have they incorporated the skills into their everyday behavior in clusters and/or in the classroom? Obviously, the mechanisms for measuring the effectiveness of training programs will vary from program to program. One of the unique and most challenging responsibilities facing the professional development cluster is to develop accurate means of evaluating the effectiveness of each training program.

Evaluate the Training Program Based on the School's Mission and Goals In addition to assessing the effectiveness of individual training programs, the professional development cluster will need to evaluate each training program to determine whether it helped the Stakeholders attain the goals and serve the mission of the school. While all programs should be evaluated in this light before they are held, they should also be reevaluated after completion to see whether and to what extent they satisfied the objective of assisting the Stakeholders to accomplish the mission of the school. In evaluating a program, the professional development cluster may discover new areas in which the Stakeholders need to receive training or identify issues that should have been addressed by the program but were not. Only through this constant process of evaluation can the professional development cluster ensure that the overall training plan is truly working to help the Stakeholders reach their goals and achieve the mission of the school.

Conclusion

As in any situation in which new skills, behaviors, or techniques must be learned and adopted by individuals in order to achieve a goal, training is the key to achieving success in a Self-Directed School. In order to become effective participants in a Self-Directed School, Stakeholders will need to learn new ways of interacting with others, new ways of solving problems, and new ways of communicating. The degree to which the Stakeholders learn and incorporate these new skills into their everyday interactions with others will be reflected directly in the success or failure of the attempt to implement a Self-Directed School. This chapter has focused primarily on the types of training needed by Stakeholders in order to successfully implement a Self-Directed School. In so doing, we have identified and discussed several principles that should serve as guidelines for the construction of specific training programs. In the following chapters we will examine in more detail the substantive content of the specific areas of training that will need to be provided to the Stakeholders of the Self-Directed School.

5

Group Interaction Skills: Communication, Coordination, and Conflict Resolution

It is well to remember that the entire population of the universe, with one trifling exception, is composed of others.

John Andrew Holmes

School-district staff development personnel typically address the issue of training in terms of the functional levels in the organizational structure of the school district. Under this kind of thinking, superintendents need one type of training, district office administrators another, principals another, and teachers still another in order for each person to best do the job expected of his or her position. Parents in these school districts might receive minimal training in child-rearing skills, but community members and other business representatives who volunteer time typically receive no training of any kind. This kind of segregated training program is inadequate and inappropriate for a Self-Directed School.

When cluster and team environments are introduced into schools and school systems, no longer are superintendents the strategists, principals the tacticians, teachers the "doers," and parents, community members, and business people the observers. Instead, all of the Stakeholders work together as team members to create the best educational environment possible. Although superintendents and principals in Self-Directed Schools retain some of their traditional administrative functions, a Self-Directed School requires a much greater overlap of responsibilities and functions among all of a school's Stakeholders than does a traditional system. In a Self-Directed School, power and responsibility are shared. Because of this overlap of functions, all Stakeholders must receive the same type of training in order to achieve consistency and ensure competency in critical skills.

For optimum results, a Self-Directed School requires cross-functional training—that is, all Stakeholders must be trained in all of the skills that must be used in order to function effectively in clusters. This is the only way to ensure that all Stakeholders are "on the same page" and are prepared to work as team players toward a common end: a world-class school.

Basic Team Player Skills: Communication, Coordination, and Conflict Resolution—"The Three C's"

Early in the process of implementing a Self-Directed School, the Stakeholders should receive training in what we call the three C's: *communication skills, coordination skills, and conflict-resolution skills.* All of these skills are crucial to the Stakeholders' ability to be productive team players. Because the skills tend to be used as an integrated package, it is often extremely difficult to identify the one skill being used in a particular situation. Most of the time, elements of all three skills are used simultaneously. For ease of discussion, however, we will discuss each skill separately.

Communication Skills: Listening and Information Sharing

> *A riot is the language of the unheard.*
> Martin Luther King, Jr.

Effective cluster management requires a high degree of communication both among cluster members and among the clusters themselves. For some people, this high degree of communication will be easy; for others, it is difficult. We are all different in our ability to communicate and in our style of communication. Some people are gregarious and outgoing whereas others are inhibited and introverted. Interestingly, though, effective communication skills are not related to a person's personality or predisposition. In other words, having a friendly and outgoing personality does not necessarily make a person an effective communicator. Similarly, being quiet or shy does not mean that a person is an ineffective communicator.

As we shall see in a moment, effective communication is not based on a person's ability to talk. Rather, it is a function of a person's ability to send accurate messages and to receive (or listen to) messages being sent by others. These are skills that must be learned and practiced. Regardless of a person's particular predisposition as talkative or quiet, everyone can learn to improve the quality of their communication skills.

People block communication in many ways. Some people have a compulsion to give advice. Others hardly hear what another person is saying because they are busy mentally rehearsing their response. In some cases, verbal barriers arise because of a person's inability to explain something clearly. Talking too fast or using slang, jargon, or "terms of art" can keep a person's message from getting through. Some people have such strong preconceptions or opinions about a matter that they seem to be incapable of hearing any other point of view. In all of these cases there is a common problem: The intended message does not get through.

In working in clusters it is critical that messages do get through. Cluster members must wrestle with very difficult issues about which they may have very divergent points of view. The question then, is, How can cluster members learn to communicate so that their messages get through?

Communication is the exchange of information, ideas, and feelings in order to get a message across. The key word in the preceding sentence is *exchange*. As we all know, but rarely seem to practice, communication is a two-way street. For communication to be effective, it must be both given and received. Having one without the other short-circuits the process. Effective communication works as follows: One person—the sender—delivers a message. Another person—the recceiver—hears the message. Upon receipt of the message, the receiver provides feedback concerning what he or she understands the

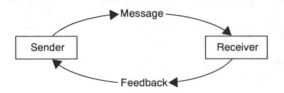

Figure 5–1. The Process of Communicating.

message to be. The sender then has a chance to clarify his or her message, check for understanding, and eliminate any ambiguity. Figure 5–1 illustrates this simple idea of effective communication—an idea that, for most of us, seems to be very difficult to put into practice.

Effective communication involves sending *and* receiving information. As individuals become better at sending and receiving information, they become better communicators. Moreover, there is a direct, positive correlation between effective communication and improved productivity, heightened problem-solving abilities, improved working relationships, and increased personal satisfaction. In short, as people become more effective communicators they become happier and more efficient employees.

How can Stakeholders become effective communicators? We believe that for the purpose of developing basic collaborative skills, training in effective communication skills should focus on two aspects of communication—*active listening* and *information sharing*. Both sets of skills are vital components of the stage of inclusion described in Chapter 4 and depicted in Figure 4–1. Such skills will continue to be used and improved on by the Stakeholders throughout their involvement in the Self-Directed School and for the rest of their lives.

Active Listening[1]

Active listening is a way of receiving information that encourages others to continue speaking while enabling the listener to be certain that he or she understands what the speaker is saying. In active listening, the listener pays attention not only to the content of what the speaker is saying but also to the feelings and emotions underlying

---

[1]Adapted from Ronald G. McIntire, *Active Listening* (Evanston, IL: Universal Dimensions, 1986).

what is being said. The goal in active listening is to help the speaker express clearly what he or she thinks or feels, that is, to transmit an accurate message, and to show that the listener understands the message that was intended.

Active listening involves the following behaviors:

Showing Interest The most important contribution a listener can make to effective communication is to show an interest in what the speaker is saying. Too often when we engage in conversation we are thinking about all of the things that are affecting our lives—meetings, deadlines, appointments, and so on—rather than about what the other person is saying. Since every person thinks differently and has different opinions and ideas, it actually requires an effort on the part of the listener to really understand what a speaker is saying. This cannot occur if the listener is busy thinking about all the things he or she must do. Showing an interest, then, requires the listener to try to block out extraneous worries or concerns and focus on the speaker's message. If there are aspects of the message that the listener does not understand or feels are ambiguous, the listener will then be in a position to ask questions. The speaker, buoyed by the attention being paid to his or her message, will be more motivated to be accurate and precise in conveying his or her message than he or she would be if the listener showed little interest in what is being said. Showing an interest improves both sides of the communication exchange: It enhances the listener's ability to receive a message, and it increases the speaker's motivation to transmit an accurate and understandable message.

Making Eye Contact Many people consider the eyes to be the most expressive part of the human body. Making eye contact is a prerequisite for successful interaction with another person. It is a powerful sign of respect and attention. It says to the other person, "I am more interested in you right now than I am in anything else." Making eye contact is one of the most visible signs that the listener is taking an interest in what the speaker is saying. Making eye contact also forces the listener to focus, at least in a visual way, upon the speaker, thereby making it very difficult for the listener to be thinking about other things.

Asking Open-Ended Questions Often it takes effort to express a point or to reveal honest feelings. When a listener asks open-ended questions, or questions that require more than a yes or no answer, about a speaker's message, the listener gives the speaker a chance to add to the message or to explore areas of the message not yet adequately addressed. Open-ended questions are like essay questions—they require the speaker to think about his or her message and to examine his or her views or feelings. By asking open-ended questions, the listener gives the speaker a chance to explain and elaborate on the message. In addition, the listener demonstrates to the speaker that he or she is interested in the message and that he or she wants to know more.

Paying Attention with the Whole Body Nonverbal signals convey powerful messages about what we think or feel about another person and about his or her message. A listener who does not face the speaker or who fidgets while the speaker is talking conveys a lack of interest in the message or a disrespect for the speaker. The speaker will then be less motivated to convey the message clearly, and the result will be a breakdown in communication. A relaxed and open body position on the part of the listener will enable the listener to focus on the speaker and will be interpreted by the speaker as a signal that the listener is interested in what the speaker is saying and is prepared to receive his or her message.

Listening to the Feelings behind the Message A speaker's true message is often somewhat hidden. Despite his or her best efforts, a speaker may not be able to convey all of his or her thoughts or feelings about a particular issue or matter. Therefore, in addition to listening to the actual words used by a speaker, a listener should be sensitive to discovering the speaker's true feelings. There may be many signals that a speaker's words do not reflect his or her true message. Although the signals may be difficult to identify or describe, most listeners know when they have a "gut" feeling that there is more to a speaker's message than the spoken words. In those situations, the listener should explore the unspoken area of the message by asking questions. In order to appear less threatening, the questions should begin with phrases such as, "I am sensing that . . ." or "It seems to me that you are concerned about . . ." or "What I am feeling is that you are worried about. . . ."

Confirming and Clarifying What Is Heard Before responding to a speaker's message, the listener should paraphrase what he or she believes the message to be. Although this practice may seem somewhat patronizing or even annoying at first, it is a valuable mechanism for making sure that a discussion is to the point and relates directly to the speaker's original message. In clusters, where discussions are sometimes emotionally charged, it can be easy to misinterpret a speaker's message. If the message is paraphrased, however, a great deal of misunderstanding, or possibly hurt feelings, can be avoided. Discussion can continue on the basis of what the actual message is, not on what one or two cluster members think the message is. In addition to serving the purpose of eliminating misunderstandings, paraphrasing a speaker's message tends to make the speaker more receptive to comments or suggestions about the message by providing assurance that the message was, in fact, received and understood by others. Frequently the mere fact that a speaker has had an opportunity to convey his or her views will make the speaker more amenable to discussing and considering changes to those views.

We believe that the ability to listen is the single most important communication skill that a cluster member can possess. Listening not only improves one's ability to understand a speaker's message, it also increases the speaker's self-esteem and confidence. Therefore, the speaker is more likely to offer suggestions, get involved, take risks, be creative, and speak openly. It is this ability on the part of the speaker to share information to which we turn next.

Information Sharing

The second aspect of communication that we believe needs to be addressed with Stakeholders is information sharing—the process of disclosing information to, and receiving feedback from, others. Teamwork requires good information sharing. Effective sharing of information, in turn, requires a high degree of trust. The key to creating effective information sharing is to create an environment of trust and security, an environment in which the participants feel safe to express their thoughts and ideas.

The process of establishing an environment of trust is the focus of the inclusion stage of cluster development. Inclusion itself is based on the premise that people tend to work best with people they know and trust. When strangers are forced to work together in a group, the barriers to effective communication and productive activity are, in most cases, too great to overcome, and the results of the group's efforts are often unsatisfying and unimaginative.

In order to foster effective information sharing in a Self-Directed School, Stakeholders must get to know one another. By this we mean far more than getting to know one another's names and sharing a little bit about one another's backgrounds. Getting to know a person for purposes of improving the ability to share information means getting to know the person's strengths and limitations, learning about the person's special talents and likes or dislikes, and getting some insight into what the person desires and expects from his or her job and from life. By getting to know one another, Stakeholders create an environment in which all of the Stakeholders feel safe enough to share their thoughts, ideas, and opinions. That is when effective information sharing can take place.

The problem with getting to know one another is that it does not happen naturally. If left to their own devices, people are simply not very good at getting to know one another—even if they are given clear instructions and ample time to do so. Some people disclose almost nothing about themselves and are perceived by others as being distant, remote, or unfriendly. Others have a tendency to talk incessantly—usually about themselves—and show little or no interest in others. The result is that no one really gets to know anyone else.

One way to combat this problem is through a series of organized activities designed to encourage and promote self-disclosure. One such activity is described below. During the course of these activities, the Stakeholders are given the opportunity to share on a one-on-one or small-group basis information about their special abilities, their interests, their expectations, and other matters relating to their inner thoughts or opinions. These self-disclosure activities are effective in promoting a sense of security among cluster members. Their structure ensures that self-disclosure among the Stakeholders remains symmetrical—that all Stakeholders are sharing the same type and roughly the same amount of information. No Stakeholder is asked to share more information than any other Stakeholder. Through these activities, Stakeholders learn to create a balance between disclosing information about themselves and listening to information about others.

Self-disclosure activities play a vital role in encouraging Stakeholders to get to know one another. As they become more familiar with each other, the Stakeholders will feel more secure. As trust develops, the Stakeholders will be ready to share their thoughts, ideas, and opinions about matters affecting the educational curriculum and environment as their clusters work to solve problems and make decisions.

In most American elementary and secondary schools faculty members, as well as the other Stakeholders, are virtual strangers to one another. The Stakeholders may know one another's names, may get along well together, and may even enjoy socializing from time to time; but few Stakeholders actually know much about the inner thoughts, opinions, or motivations of other Stakeholders. Having come from different backgrounds, different geographical areas, and/or different educational and professional experiences, most Stakeholders know very little about other Stakeholders. Box-shaped buildings, separated egg-crate classrooms, and isolated portables are architectural features of many schools that exacerbate the feelings of individualism which tend to exist among faculty members and other Stakeholders.

In a Self-Directed School it is critical that each Stakeholder feel included as a part of the team. Individual strengths are valued; individualistic actions are not. The importance of teamwork permeates every aspect of the Self-Directed School.

Self-disclosure activities can be very effective means of developing trust and familiarity among Stakeholders. This trust and familiarity, once established, slowly matures and blossoms into a sense of loyalty and commitment to the team—that is, the collection of Stakeholders.

Self-Disclosure Activity: An Example The following activity is an excellent exercise for having Stakeholders get to know one another. By taking thirty minutes periodically to conduct the activity, the Stakeholders can go a long way toward developing the feelings of mutual trust and security that form the basis of effective information sharing.

"Getting to Know You" Ask everyone to pair with a person in the group whom they do not know very well. After partners are found, each pair of Stakeholders should move to an area of

the room where they can sit down and have a semiprivate conversation. The partners should sit face to face. After everyone is sitting with a partner, the facilitator of the session asks one or more of the following suggested questions, one at a time. Each partner is given a specified period of time (usually one to two minutes) to answer the question. While one Stakeholder talks, the other Stakeholder simply listens, making eye contact, nodding attentively, and so on. At the end of the specified period, the Stakeholders switch roles and the initial speaker listens while the initial listener speaks. The exercise proceeds question by question until completed or until the time allocated to the exercise expires. It should be noted that the facilitator of the session should also be a participant in the session. A facilitator should never ask the participants in a session to do something he or she is not willing to do. The facilitator simply has the responsibility of watching the time and keeping things moving.

SUGGESTED QUESTIONS

- *What's the best team experience you've ever had?*
- *What are your favorite things to do?*
- *What's an issue you feel strongly about?*
- *What are some things you want to start doing at this point in your life?*
- *What was the most interesting period of your life?*
- *Who was or is the most important person in your life?*
- *What do you consider the turning point of your life?*

Self-disclosure activities, like the one described above, build familiarity, trust, security, and commitment. By getting to know one another, the Stakeholders become more sure of themselves and more tolerant and accepting of others. Instead of being offended or put off when another Stakeholder is having a bad day, Stakeholders who feel included as members of the team tend to take an interest and offer help ("What's wrong?" "What can I do to help?"). Inclusion occurs when the Stakeholders take the time to get to know one another and to understand one another's feelings and values. Mutual respect and consideration develops and trust—the basis of effective information sharing and communication—is the result.

Coordination Skills

Collaboration
The act of working jointly with others or together in an
intellectual endeavor.

In the Self-Directed School, where collaboration and interdependence of Stakeholders are inescapable requirements for success, meetings are a fact of life. If Stakeholders are to work together, then they must have the opportunity to meet. Meetings provide a forum for sharing, comparing, and distributing information as the Stakeholders work together to make decisions and solve problems.

Unfortunately, in most schools today teachers have little if any time to meet. They work full time with students most of the day, and when they are not in their classrooms teaching they are planning lessons, contacting parents, or gathering or preparing materials for upcoming classes. In the afternoon, many teachers are involved in extracurricular student activities or face pressures to get to a class they are taking or to another job that they have taken to try to make ends meet. One afternoon a week is usually taken by a faculty meeting lasting anywhere from a half hour to an hour and a half. With these kinds of restrictions on their time, it is often difficult to find even fifteen minutes either before, during, or after the school day in which Stakeholders can hold a hurried meeting.

In order to conduct the business of the Self-Directed School, it is imperative that teachers and other Stakeholders have more time to meet than is presently available in today's school environment. We believe that a Self-Directed School will need to devote a minimum of five full days and five half days each school year to Stakeholder inservice activities in order to provide adequate time for training sessions and cluster meetings. This amount of time should be sufficient and effective—but only if all of the meetings are planned and conducted in an efficient manner.

Ill-conceived, poorly planned, and poorly conducted meetings are the death knell of the Self-Directed School. Stakeholders will lose all motivation to work together if meetings they attend turn out to be boring, ineffective, irrelevant, or unproductive.

Since meetings are the backbone of the collaborative process, it is tragic, even frightening, that most meetings are poorly conceived and poorly conducted. What is most disturbing about many group sessions is the apparent lack of effort by the group leader to do anything about planning or conducting a productive meeting. In many cases, the meeting turns out to be an interaction in which the unwilling, selected from the uninformed, led by the unsuitable, discuss the unnecessary and are required to write a report on the unimportant. The Self-Directed School cannot afford this kind of wasted activity.

Poorly conceived and poorly conducted meetings do not have to be accepted as a way of life within the Self-Directed School. In fact, they *can't* be passively accepted. If they are, the Self-Directed School will stagnate, stumble, and ultimately self-destruct in a mire of confusion, frustration, annoyance, and misguided activity.

The good news is that effective meeting skills (what we call here coordination skills) are not innate—they can be learned. By adopting and implementing a few simple techniques, those conducting meetings and those attending meetings can ensure effective, productive, and perhaps most importantly, efficient group interaction, which will, in turn, ensure success. Effective meeting skills require knowledge and understanding of the following areas:

- The role of the meeting facilitator.
- The responsibilities of members of the group.
- The techniques for planning and holding a meeting.

The Role of the Meeting Facilitator

In most schools, the principal serves as the chairperson of most if not all meetings. As the duly appointed "leader" of the school, the principal typically "runs" the meetings with an iron fist—more often making announcements and dictating policy than actually soliciting or encouraging discussion. Information is transmitted but not exchanged.

Self-Directed Schools depend on an exchange of information. For the Self-Directed School to succeed, its Stakeholders must be able to communicate effectively and share their thoughts, ideas, and opinions. This means, among other things, that meetings must be facilitated, not led. Moreover, the Stakeholders must feel a sense of equality among themselves. Any apparent or implied "rank" among Stakeholders will resurrect feelings of hierarchical management and will tend to dampen or destroy the free exchange of information as certain Stakeholders begin to fear repercussions from "higher-ranking" Stakeholders. For this reason, all Stakeholders at one time or another serve as meeting facilitators. Accordingly, every Stakeholder needs to have the skills necessary to plan and facilitate effective meetings.

Simply stated, a facilitator is a person who helps a group, such as a cluster, free itself from internal obstacles and difficulties so that the group can more effectively pursue the achievement of the desired outcomes of group meetings. To offer yet another sports analogy, the facilitator is not so much a player or a coach as a referee. It is the facilitator's role to start the meeting on time and to make sure that the rules of the group are enforced throughout the meeting, protecting the interests of all of the group members. When a discussion gets out of hand, for example, runs too long, gets too personal, or stalemates, it is the facilitator's job to "throw the flag" and step in to restore order. In the purest sense, a facilitator acts as a neutral servant of the people who are meeting.[2]

Every meeting should have a primary facilitator who performs the following functions:

- Focuses the energies of the group on defining and accomplishing the group's objectives.
- Respects and employs group decision-making processes at every opportunity to earn each member's support for the final decision, thus gaining each member's commitment to implement the decision.
- Takes primary responsibility for establishing and maintaining a supportive atmosphere throughout the group and encourages every member to participate.
- Protects group members and their ideas from attack, so that members feel secure in sharing and exploring proposals, ideas, thoughts, and opinions.

To achieve success, facilitation philosophy and behaviors must be shared by all group members. The facilitation role cannot evolve into the exclusive domain of a few Stakeholders on whom clusters

---

[2]*Note:* Experience has shown that if the primary facilitator actively participates in the content of the meeting, he or she invariably gets swept up in the discussion and tends to forget about facilitation. Accordingly, it is important for the primary facilitator to remain as neutral as possible. If the primary facilitator wishes to enter the debate, he or she should ask another group member to serve temporarily as the primary facilitator.

depend for facilitation services. Any type of formal or informal establishment of certain Stakeholders as permanent leaders or facilitators will hearken back to a hierarchy. To avoid this trap, clusters should rotate the role of primary facilitator, giving every member the opportunity to serve as the primary facilitator. For the sake of continuity, certain large clusters—for example, the site council—may find it useful for the primary facilitator to serve for a relatively extended period of time rather than change at every meeting. Such clusters will need to be extremely careful to avoid the establishment of a pecking order among members, however. In no case do we believe it is advisable for a primary facilitator to serve for a period longer than two or three months.

The Responsibilities of Members of the Group

Facilitation of a group meeting is not the sole responsibility of the primary facilitator. Although one group member will always have the formal responsibility of being the primary facilitator for a particular meeting, facilitation must be shared by everyone in attendance if the meeting is to be successful and the group's productivity maximized. Whenever a cluster comes together to exchange information, solve problems, and/or make decisions, every member of the group must share the responsibility for making the session as successful as possible. By recognizing that facilitation is a group function to which all members can contribute, group members help to develop a sense of teamwork and group cohesion. This sense of shared responsibility ensures that all group members will participate in the meeting, even if they don't say anything, and that all of the resources of the group will be used efficiently and productively.

How do members of the group contribute to the facilitation of an effective meeting? Among other things, every member of a group has the following responsibilities:

- To be at group meetings on time. Time is a priceless and remarkably scarce commodity. There never seems to be enough of it. Arriving at meetings on time and being prepared to address the issues to be discussed shows respect for other members of the group.
- To help all group members stay within the time limit allotted for each issue.

- To understand each issue discussed at the meeting. Any ambiguity or confusion should be clarified through questioning and requests for further explanation or discussion.
- To be prepared if he or she has the responsibility to present an issue to the group for discussion and to make an efficient and informative presentation. This includes having any necessary or applicable written information prepared in advance of the meeting for review by members of the group prior to their arrival at the meeting.
- To listen attentively to other group members to ensure that speakers' messages are interpreted accurately. This includes the responsibility to ask questions whenever appropriate to clarify meaning or determine intent.
- To avoid the tendency to dominate the discussion or talk excessively. While it is important for each member of the group to communicate and share thoughts, ideas, and opinions, it is equally important that no one member of the group dominate the discussion or assume an inflated sense of responsibility for the development of the group's thought processes. Collaboration requires the participation of everyone—and the dominance of no one.

In short, effective meetings require participation. Each group member must understand that he or she plays an important role in the group process of exchanging and sharing information. Passively sitting back and receiving or accepting group information will not suffice. A meeting requires the involvement of each group member. If group members are not actively involved in a meeting, either by verbally sharing information or by nonverbally providing supportive facilitation, then what is disguised as a meeting is really a presentation—and the true power and creativity of the group will not be realized.

The Techniques for Planning and Holding a Meeting

Group sessions, or meetings, offer results that cannot be obtained in any other way. By harnessing the collective talents, energies, and resources of a group of people working together for a unified purpose, meetings create opportunities for developing plans, strategies, and solutions that are far more creative and more effective than those developed by individuals working separately. The key to achieving such success, however, is the holding of an efficient and productive meeting.

Efficient and productive meetings don't just happen—they are planned. Planning a successful meeting requires that each of the following questions be carefully considered and answered in the affirmative:

- Have the Stakeholders established an effective structure for holding and conducting meetings?
- Have the objectives of the meeting been identified and specified prior to the meeting?
- Is a meeting necessary?

Establishing an Effective Meeting Structure

The Stakeholders of a Self-Directed School must be willing to adopt and accept a structure for the holding of meetings. An effective structure simply establishes an understandable and predictable system for the consideration of issues by group members. All too often in today's schools, the principal arrives at a meeting that he or she has called and proceeds to conduct the meeting based on an agenda that only he or she knows about. The teachers (or other "participants" in the meeting) are completely in the dark about the issues to be discussed—or presented—and the amount of time to be devoted to each issue.

The key to establishing an effective structure for holding meetings is the preparation of a *written agenda* prior to the meeting. The agenda should consist of the following:

- A statement of the time the meeting is to start and the time the meeting is to end. If Stakeholders are to commit themselves to enthusiastic participation in a meeting, then they must be able to plan. Establishing the beginning and ending times of the meeting allows Stakeholders to plan their schedules accordingly and to devote their full attention to the issues being discussed at the meeting (without having to worry about how long the meeting will last or whether the meeting will infringe upon their other obligations or commitments).

- A listing of each issue or topic to be discussed, together with a succinct statement of the group's objective for each topic or issue. In order to be effective participants in a meeting, the Stakeholders must understand the purposes and goals of the meeting. The importance of establishing the objectives is actually the subject of the second question posed above and will be discussed in more detail shortly.

- A statement of the estimated amount of time to be spent on each issue or topic to be discussed. Again, the purpose of establishing time constraints is to assist the Stakeholders in planning. By knowing the amount of time to be spent on each issue, the Stakeholders can better plan the extent and scope of their comments. Establishing time constraints also helps to provide group discipline and reflects at least an initial estimate of the degree of importance of each issue. A sample agenda is presented in Appendix 5–1.

Setting time constraints both for the overall meeting and for each issue or topic to be discussed is a critical aspect of establishing an effective structure for meetings. The institution of time constraints does not mean, however, that discussion must be limited to that amount of time. It does mean that discussion *at that meeting* must be limited to that amount of time. If at the expiration of the allotted time the group members have not arrived at a consensus or have not completed their discussion of the issue or topic, then the issue or topic should be rescheduled for further discussion at a later meeting. Exceptions to this rule should be made only in very special circumstances—for example, the existence of a pressing deadline for a particular matter. Where exceptions are necessary, corresponding offsets to the amount of time allocated to other issues should be made so as to maintain the overall meeting schedule as much as possible.

While a written agenda goes a long way toward providing the kind of operational structure necessary to conduct an efficient and productive meeting, an agenda is not by itself sufficient to ensure success. In addition to supporting the concept of having an agenda, the Stakeholders must commit to the preeminence of the meeting process. That is, the Stakeholders must recognize the importance of the meeting as a forum for exchanging information and ideas and must be willing to make the sacrifices necessary to make the meeting work. In terms of real-life examples, this means, among other things, that the Stakeholders must respect the concept of sticking to the agenda and its time constraints for discussions. In addition, Stakeholders must, during the time period allocated to the meeting, devote their full attention to the issues under discussion.

We have all attended meetings in which the principles outlined here have been violated. For example, a discussion may seem to be proceeding well when all of a sudden it gets sidetracked onto a tangential issue, and soon the meeting turns into an aimless exploration of irrelevant topics. Alternatively, a meeting may seem to be progressing productively when one or two group members receive messages that they have important phone calls. The members leave to take the calls, which for some reason are deemed more important than the meeting, and immediately the continuity and effectiveness of the meeting are broken.

In both of the examples just given, what could have been a productive meeting turns into a morass of frustration and unproductivity because group members have failed to respect the importance of *structure*. If meetings at a Self-Directed School are to be efficient and productive, then the Stakeholders must develop an acceptable structure for holding and conducting meetings and they must commit to respecting that structure. This structure, once developed and fully adopted, will facilitate the collaborative process, ensure Stakeholder participation, and greatly increase the chances of having productive and efficient meetings.

Defining the Objectives of the Meeting

It is critically important that the specific goals and objectives of a meeting be identified and defined in the agenda. A clear understanding of what is to be accomplished at a particular meeting is the foundation on which the entire meeting rests. If the purposes and objectives cannot be defined and specified prior to bringing the group together, then the meeting should not be held. Without a clear purpose and succinctly defined objectives, the meeting will meander aimlessly with confused and irritated participants. Participants will either tune out completely or fail to contribute their best efforts. The meeting will then have the proverbial two chances of being a success: slim and none.

As stated earlier, each issue to be discussed at a meeting,

together with a specific objective statement on each issue, should appear on the agenda of the meeting (see Appendix 5–1). The objective statements are short and specific statements identifying what the group hopes to accomplish in the meeting. The statements create common expectations among the group members. They also provide focus for the meeting and a benchmark against which the actual outcomes of the meeting can be compared to gain a sense of the meeting's effectiveness or success.

The preparation of the objective statements, together with the rest of the agenda, is the responsibility of the primary facilitator. Information regarding the issues to be discussed, as well as the objective statements on each issue, are obtained by the primary facilitator from a variety of sources: past meetings, interested Stakeholders, other group members, and so on. The objective statements do not need to be perfectly drafted and etched in stone prior to a meeting. After all, they can always be changed by the consensus of the group. What is important is that there be written objective statements for each issue on the agenda prior to the meeting. Group members will then at least have a common point from which to begin discussing the issue in question.

Determining the Necessity of a Meeting

After the first two questions noted above have been addressed, the most fundamental question must be asked: Is a meeting really necessary? In many cases in schools today, meetings (faculty meetings, administrator meetings, principal meetings, and so on) are scheduled weeks or even months in advance. When the time comes for the meeting, the meeting is held—even if there is nothing important to decide or discuss. The attitude seems to be, "Well, we've decided to hold a meeting, now we better figure out a reason for holding it." This kind of thinking will almost always result in a poorly run and unproductive meeting. The participants sense the unimportance of the meeting and develop resentment over the waste of their time. We believe that two maxims should govern the holding of meetings.

Regularly scheduled meetings should be held irregularly.

Regularly scheduled meetings are the bane of group organizations. Because regularly scheduled meetings are held even if there is nothing important to talk about, group members tend to develop a certain amount of apathy about participating. As a result, group members do not come to the meetings with the concentration and commitment necessary to deal with complex issues. When something important does come up, the group members are simply not prepared to deal with it, and the meeting turns into a disaster.

> *When it is not absolutely necessary to hold a meeting, it is absolutely necessary NOT to hold a meeting.*

The initial planning for a meeting involves two steps. First, identify the objectives for each issue. Second, determine if there are ways to accomplish the objectives without holding a meeting. If the objectives can be achieved through some means other than holding a meeting, then a meeting should not be called.

Many meetings seem to be called for the sole purpose of making announcements or detailing future schedules. Dissemination of general information about schedules or plans does not require a meeting. Instead, the following possibilities should be considered:

- Faculty bulletins.
- Communications via computers—for example, E-mail.
- Faculty bulletin boards in high-traffic areas.

Other meetings seem to be called for the purpose of gathering initial information about an issue or obtaining the initial reaction of certain group members to a subject. A meeting is a very inefficient way of accomplishing either of these objectives. Some group members may not even be aware of the issue or may have such a lack of information about the issue that they feel uninvolved or ignored and so they tune out. It is better to gather reactions or background information in ways other than group meetings. After the issue has been initially developed and explored, then a meeting should be called for group action. As an alternative to calling a meeting to gather information, the following approaches can be considered:

- Make telephone calls to individuals who are informed or who are close to the issue at hand.
- Hold informal conversations with group members.

Sometimes having a meeting is the only way to proceed. For example, if the issue fits any one of the following conditions, then a meeting is probably required:

- Complicated information requiring oral explanation needs to be communicated for immediate action by group members.
- After initial information has been obtained, an issue has been identified as needing the attention of the group for problem solving or decision making. (This should be the most common reason for calling a meeting.)
- Group consensus or acceptance of an idea is needed.

Evaluating the Effectiveness of a Meeting

To obtain feedback and to provide a constant incentive to plan and hold productive meetings, the Stakeholders of a Self-Directed School should prepare a meeting evaluation guide. A sample meeting evaluation guide is given in Appendix 5–2. The meeting evaluation guide should be used to assess the effectiveness of every meeting held by the Stakeholders.

As with virtually every aspect of the Self-Directed School, there is no one correct form for a meeting evaluation guide. Different people have different opinions about what constitutes an effective meeting. The Stakeholders of each Self-Directed School will have to share their ideas in order to develop a guide that works and is relevant to them. On some issues, however, there seems to be almost universal consensus about the characteristics of an effective meeting. For example, it seems that almost everyone agrees that

- An effective meeting starts and ends on time.
- Each issue or topic to be discussed at the meeting has an allocated time period to ensure maximum productivity and participant attention.
- The issues to be discussed, together with their corresponding objective statements, have been clearly stated prior to the meeting.
- Discussion of an issue does not begin until it has been established that every participant understands the issue as well as the proposed objective statement for the issue.
- Information that is needed by or that might be useful to group members in discussing an issue or in attempting to generate solutions is distributed to group members prior to the meeting.

Since much of the work in a Self-Directed School is accomplished by Stakeholders working together in meetings, it is critical that meetings be run efficiently. Effective meetings require careful planning and coordination in order to ensure that productivity is maximized and that the time spent in the meeting is worthwhile. By utilizing the skills and techniques discussed here, the Stakeholders can significantly increase their ability to plan and conduct meetings that are relevant, efficient, and productive.

Conflict-Resolution Skills

The situation is common and quite predictable: During the course of a meeting, two or more group members who are engaged in a discussion disagree in some form or fashion and a conflict arises. In some cases the conflict is relatively minor and is easily resolved. In other cases the conflict persists, and the group members do not resolve their differences. The conflict then turns into a problem that affects the entire group. If it is not handled correctly, the conflict becomes so severe that irreparable damage is done to the group and its productivity.

Conflict is often cited as one of the main reasons people dislike working in groups. This presents an interesting dilemma for the Self-Directed School because conflict is bound to arise among Stakeholders. Whenever individuals work together in groups, *conflict is going to occur*. It is as predictable as death and taxes.

How, then, can a Self-Directed School succeed when it is inevitable that conflict is going to arise and it is well established that people do not like conflict? The answer lies in a complete rethinking of the way Stakeholders view the issue of conflict. Stakeholders need to accept the fact that conflict is the natural by-product of the group decision-making process. Moreover, conflict is a positive, not a negative, occurrence. Through conflict the group is forced to confront difficult issues and resolve what can often be very emotional situations. This process, in turn, creates an opportunity for the group members to use their creativity to come up with new and innovative ways of dealing with the issue that gave rise to the conflict. It is then that the group realizes the full power of the collaborative process. It's like the old phrase used by athletes in training: "No pain, no gain." If a group is not presented with a conflict (that is, the "pain"), it is not challenged to apply its resources and skills to arrive at creative solutions (that is, the "gain").

Accepting that conflict is natural and that it creates the opportunity for creative solutions is one thing. Actually dealing with the conflict is another. Most people by nature are conflict avoiders. Rather than create or confront a conflict, they simply choose to keep their opinions to themselves. This kind of antiparticipation is extremely detrimental to the kind of group interaction upon which the Self-Directed School depends. To be successful, the Stakeholders must learn to deal with conflict. By following the techniques and suggestions discussed in this section, the Stakeholders can greatly improve their ability to confront and resolve the conflicts that are inevitably going to occur.

Before addressing the resolution of conflict in group situations, however, we need to consider how conflict is resolved in hierarchical organizations. Most people in traditional educational systems do not have to deal with conflict. When conflict does arise, it is typically resolved based on position within the system. The administrator in charge simply makes the decision and the conflict is eliminated. This is not to say, however, that the problem goes away. In many cases the problem simply gets worse. The real weakness of the boss approach to resolving conflict is that most of the time the person making the decision does not possess all of the knowledge necessary to address adequately the concerns of the individuals affected by the decision; nor does the decision maker take the time to acquire such knowledge. Instead, the decision maker "hides" behind his or her position, training, and experience as an "expert" administrator and decrees a solution.

The reliance on position or power to make a decision, especially when coupled with a failure to permit those who are most affected by the decision to have a say in constructing the decision, creates a fertile environment for the emergence of resentment and the ultimate disintegration of the relationship between the decision makers and the affected participants in the system. Many people believe that this is the major cause of the cold war that presently exists in most school systems in the United States between district-level administrators and school-site personnel. This cold war has had a devastating effect on the ability of educators—teachers, principals, administrators—to work together to create a positive and productive educational environment.

In the Self-Directed School, every attempt should be made to avoid the temptation to resolve conflict by relying on positions of authority. The costs of such an approach, in terms of resentment and alienation, are too great.

Turning conflict into a positive opportunity for growth and creative problem solving involves concentrating efforts in the following three areas:

- Creating a positive atmosphere for resolving conflict.
- Clarifying perceptions about the conflict that arises.
- Establishing ground rules for dealing with conflict.

By developing their abilities in each of these areas, Stakeholders can become very effective at confronting conflict and using the conflicts that do arise as opportunities to reap the benefits of collaborative problem solving.

Creating a Positive Atmosphere

The atmosphere within which Stakeholders attempt to resolve conflict is a key determinant of the Stakeholders' ability to handle successfully situations involving conflict. It is extremely difficult for effective conflict resolution to occur in an atmosphere that obstructs rather than promotes positive interaction. Accordingly, the Stakeholders must work together to create a positive atmosphere of mutual trust and support.

In part, the creation of a positive atmosphere for resolving conflict depends upon the overall ability of the Stakeholders to develop their communication skills and their feelings of inclusion, trust, security, and interdependence. In addition to developing their interpersonal skills, however, the Stakeholders will discover that selecting an appropriate time and place for attempting to resolve a conflict plays an important role in maintaining the type of positive atmosphere required to achieve a resolution of the conflict.

Although some conflicts erupt so suddenly that Stakeholders have no choice but to deal with them immediately, most conflicts offer an opportunity to choose when the conflict-resolution process will begin. Several criteria can help the Stakeholders make the best possible choice of timing:

- *Choose a time that is long enough and free enough from outside distractions to allow for effective interaction.* This can be difficult in a school in which large blocks of uninterrupted time are hard to find. In an attempt to address this problem, some schools now allocate a half day a week without students to allow Stakeholders to work in clusters. When a block of time is allocated for a meeting, the Stakeholders should devote their full attention during that time to the resolution of the conflict. Allowing outside distractions such as telephone calls or other "important" messages to interrupt the meeting will destroy the group's chances of achieving success.

- *Choose a time that maximizes concentration and communication.* Many school meetings are held for short periods of time just before school starts or lets out. It is difficult for teachers to concentrate on a topic when they must teach a class in ten minutes or when they have just survived the rigors of a day's work. Conflict resolution takes time. If a cluster has a conflict to resolve, it should not attempt to squeeze in a meeting if the only times that are available are just before or just after school. Instead, the cluster should wait for an opportunity when all of the cluster members can get together for an extended period of time and concentrate on resolving the conflict. Sometimes this means that other teachers, with the assistance of community and business people, will need to double up or volunteer to teach the classes of Stakeholders who must attend a conflict-resolution meeting. The amount of time allocated for the meeting should be sufficient to permit complete exploration of all relevant issues, but should not be so great as to exhaust the participants. Usually working on one conflict for more than an hour at a time diminishes effectiveness. If more than an hour is required to achieve resolution, it is advisable to meet in several sessions.
- *Choose a time that maximizes the positive skills of all members of the cluster.* Conflict resolution works best when all parties are functioning at effective levels of cooperation, concentration, and communication. Therefore, it is best to allow cluster members to choose a time that everyone agrees on as conducive to effective performance. The ability to reach a consensus on time is, in turn, a function of the Stakeholders' ability to interact and communicate effectively.

Determining where a conflict will be worked on should be consciously thought out by the Stakeholders. Far too often group members do not think about the place in which conflict resolution will occur. The location can have either a negative or positive influence.

Although each situation is unique, it is helpful to keep in mind the following guidelines in selecting the location of the meeting:

- *Choose a place that is nonthreatening to all parties.* For example, if one of the parties is the principal, it would not be wise to hold the meeting in the principal's office. It is important to take great care to locate the conflict-resolution process in a physical environment that makes all group members feel as secure as possible. If a group member feels threatened by the location or the location supports feelings of power by one member over another, then the members of the group will not feel positive about working together on the conflict.

- *Choose a place that promotes a relationship of being connected in a partnership rather than being divided.* If possible, a circular seating arrangement should be used rather than seating at rectangular tables where participants face one another. Circular seating, with or without tables, promotes a sense of unity and equality. There is no head of a circle as there is a head of a rectangular table. Circles also allow every group member to establish eye contact with every other member of the group. The location of the meeting should be devoid of distractions or diversions. It is preferable that there not be a telephone in the room and that there be no windows overlooking areas of activity that might distract or capture the attention of group members.

Although Stakeholders may experience initial difficulty in acknowledging the importance of setting a time and place for holding meetings, it should become quickly apparent that selecting the appropriate time and place for a conflict-resolution meeting can have a tremendous effect on creating the positive atmosphere necessary to support the process of arriving at a satisfactory resolution.

Clarifying Perceptions

One of the most critical aspects of dealing with a conflict in a group is to make sure that what is perceived as a conflict actually is a conflict. Alternatively, it is possible that some group members perceive an existing conflict one way, while other group members perceive the conflict entirely differently. In either case, if the group initiates the process of resolving the conflict before taking the time to clarify and crystallize the conflict in the minds of the group members, the result will probably be a great deal of wasted time and, in all likelihood, an unsatisfactory or ineffective resolution.

Although there are many models on how to clarify perceptions, it is preferable, whenever possible, to have a relatively neutral cluster member help the disputants work together to resolve the conflict. This kind of internal mediation has proven to be effective with both students and adults. For Stakeholders to perform in this role, they need to receive training in mediation skills. If cluster members can work together to resolve conflicts without the assistance of an outside mediator, the cluster will be more autonomous, more independent, and ultimately more effective at arriving at creative resolutions than it would be if it has to depend on an outside mediator.

The process of clarifying perceptions involves helping the "disputing" cluster members ask and gain answers to the following important questions:

- *Is the conflict over an isolated event, or is it simply the latest in a series of disagreements revealing underlying problems within the group as a whole?* As the first step in evaluating how to resolve a conflict between group members, a Stakeholder must attempt to determine whether the conflict relates to a particular event or issue or whether the conflict is symptomatic of a much deeper and ongoing personality rift between the parties involved. If the disputing members maintain a fairly positive relationship in other aspects of their interactions, and the conflict appears to be only a difference of opinion on a specific issue or topic, then the supporting Stakeholder can probably help the disputing group members reach a resolution. If, on the other hand, the conflict is but the latest in a series of disagreements between the disputing parties, then the conflict may reflect a serious problem in the relationship between the disputing parties that will require outside intervention.

- *Is the conflict over goals or methods?* Activity in a cluster involves a two-step process of first establishing a goal or objective and then developing a method for achieving that goal or objective. If a conflict arises during the process of reaching a consensus on a goal or objective, it is fairly easy to identify that conflict as one that centers on the appropriateness or applicability of the goal or objective itself. A conflict that arises after a goal or objective has been established, for example, during the process of agreeing on one or more methods for achieving the goal or objective or during the process of implementing methods intended to achieve the goal or objective, may relate either to the goal itself or to the method for accomplishing the goal. For example, some group members may, during the course of discussions on methods for achieving a particular goal, reevaluate their original position on the goal itself. Alternatively, they may continue to support the goal, but disagree with the course the discussion is taking with respect to methods. If the conflict is over the goal, then the group will need to go back and gain a new consensus on the goal or develop a revised or modified goal. If the conflict relates to how a goal is to be accomplished, then the group should focus its efforts on evaluating methods for achieving the goal, but should not reevaluate the goal itself.

- *Can the components of the conflict be prioritized?* Although a conflict may appear to be one huge entity without discernible points of entry, most conflicts are comprised of discrete components that can be identified. Once the components of the conflict have been identified, it is usually possible to classify or prioritize them so they can be dealt with more effectively. In a given conflict, for example, it may be possible for a cluster to identify three separate components. After the components have been identified, the cluster may realize that one component is based on misperception or hearsay, one is outside the power of the cluster, and the third is an actual disagreement or difference of opinion between members of the cluster. By going through the process of breaking the conflict down into its components, the cluster is able to deal quickly with the aspects of the conflict by clarifying the misperception and separating the component that is outside the control of the cluster. The cluster can then focus on the remaining component. By first confronting components that can be easily resolved, the cluster experiences initial success. The good feelings and confidence generated by this success can then be used to help the cluster resolve the more difficult components. A cluster that is able successfully to identify, classify, and prioritize the components of a conflict greatly increases its chances of achieving a resolution that is acceptable to all members.

- *Do the cluster members understand what the parties involved in the conflict are saying and meaning?* Many people try to deal with conflict by talking more and listening less. It is as if the parties involved believe that the conflict will disintegrate and crumble in the onslaught of words. Nothing could be farther from the truth. In fact, incessant talking about a conflict, without listening, can often make the conflict worse. The parties involved become more stubborn, more ensconced in their positions, and less willing to compromise or make adjustments. Although it is important for the cluster members involved in a conflict, as well as the other members of the cluster, to state their concerns, needs, goals, values, and feelings as clearly and straightforwardly as possible, it is equally important for *all* of the members of the cluster to be active listeners. As part of the process of being active listeners, cluster members who are listening to a speaker should ask questions whenever there appears to be ambiguity in the speaker's message or whenever there seems to be a "hidden" message behind the speaker's actual words. Cluster members can greatly assist the process of clarifying the speaker's message by asking such questions as, "I think I hear you saying . . . , is that correct?" or "It seems to me that you're saying . . . , is that what you mean?" Asking these types of questions can help the conflict-resolution process in several ways.

First, the questions demonstrate to the speaker that the members of the cluster are interested in what the speaker is saying. A person involved in a conflict may need only the opportunity to be heard. Once the individual has spoken and the person is convinced that others have listened, he or she may be amenable to making compromises or supporting an alternative position.

Second, clarifying the speaker's message through questioning allows the cluster members to delve more deeply into the speaker's message. As a result, cluster members, as well as the speaker, may discover that what the speaker thought was a concern over the particular issue under consideration may actually be a concern over an unrelated issue, thereby allowing the cluster to resolve quickly the conflict at hand. Alternatively, the cluster may uncover a concern regarding the process of decision making used by the cluster. Again, the cluster should then be able successfully to resolve the conflict at hand and turn to the larger issue in question.

Third, and perhaps most obviously, asking questions about the speaker's message enables the cluster members to identify the scope and nature of the conflict so that the cluster members can respond to the real issues at hand, and not to a misinterpretation or misconstruction of what the issues are perceived to be.

At the first sign of a conflict, cluster members should rally around the persons who are involved and work in a supportive way to clarify the perceptions of all of the members of the cluster. Many people shy away from a conflict, probably in the hope that if the conflict is ignored it will go away. Unfortunately, as we all know, conflicts do not simply go away. If not addressed and dealt with when they arise, conflicts will continue to fester, like cancerous growths, only to resurface at a later time, probably in a much more insidious way. By working together to clarify perceptions when conflicts arise, cluster members can go a long way toward enabling the cluster members to successfully resolve conflicts on a consistent basis, thereby making for a creative, effective, and productive cluster.

Establishing Ground Rules for Dealing with Conflicts

Too often people develop the attitude that conflicts have to have winners and losers and that in the resolution of a conflict someone is going to win and someone is going to lose. Such an attitude is inconsistent with the principles underlying the Self-Directed School, which are based on the ability of people to work together to solve problems and to achieve solutions that are acceptable to all members of the group.

The collaborative process depends on the creativity and open-mindedness of the participants to explore new areas and arrive at solutions that could not possibly result from individuals working alone. The true benefit of cooperative activity is thus creative thinking. A conflict between cluster members presents a definite challenge to the cluster to come up with a solution that every member will support. There can be no losers in such a process—only winners.

The ability of a cluster to resolve successfully internal conflicts between cluster members can be greatly enhanced by establishing ground rules for dealing with conflict when it arises. A cluster can more effectively handle a conflict if the members have agreed in advance on a set of guidelines for their actions when conflicts occur. Although there is no one correct set of ground rules, the following is an example of the types of guidelines a cluster might develop.

GROUND RULES FOR MANAGING CONFLICT

As collaborative members of a positive and supportive cluster, we agree:

- To keep to the issues in any discussion and to avoid arguments that are personal.
- That the future is a more constructive basis for discussion than the past.
- To help each other see what is best for the cluster and to help each other look beyond self-interest.
- Not to judge, evaluate, or criticize before we understand.
- To stay open to new ways of thinking and new ways of doing things.
- To help clarify the key interests and needs of conflicting cluster members and to help identify alternatives that might assist in the conflict resolution.
- That when the cluster is locked in conflict, members will stop and brainstorm creative options.
- To paraphrase what has finally been agreed upon to make sure that true agreement has been reached and that the cluster has elicited the commitment and support necessary to carry out the solution.
- That the other side of the conflict always has a point of view that is just as legitimate and reasonable to him or her as mine is to me.

Obviously, these ground rules do more than just help the cluster members deal with conflict. They are a recipe for success in all aspects of the cluster's activities. They reflect the state of mind required for effective and successful cluster activity: "You are just as important as I am."

Conflict is a vital aspect of the collaborative process. It is inevitable. Moreover, it is the key to growth and creativity in the Self-Directed School. If people who work together do not have conflicts, then something is wrong. Either people are not voicing their opinions or they are acting in ways that do not accurately reflect their true thoughts, ideas, or opinions.

Since conflict is natural, inevitable, and desirable, Stakeholders must learn how to deal with it. By creating a positive atmosphere for resolving conflict, working together to clarify perceptions, and establishing ground rules for managing conflict, the Stakeholders can turn conflict into an exciting opportunity for creativity and constructive development.

Conclusion

Success in the Self-Directed School is based on the three C's: communication, coordination, and conflict resolution. Effective Stakeholders can communicate and exchange information, plan and coordinate effective and productive meetings, and work together to resolve conflict when it arises. Armed with these skills, the Stakeholders will be able to work together as a team to handle any problems that occur in the course of the development of the Self-Directed School.

Appendix 5–1 Sample Inservice Meeting
October 2, 1992
Primary Facilitators: Chicken Tribe

AGENDA

Clock Time	Meeting Time	Topic	Objective
• 8:00–8:45	45 min.	Mathematics curriculum articulation	Staff will review curriculum developed this summer by math cluster
• 8:45–9:00	15 min.	Effective group meetings (Dr. Mac)	Review characteristics of effective meetings
• 9:00–9:30	30 min.	Review and discuss meeting evaluation form (Tribes)	Reach consensus on evaluation form
• 9:30–9:45		BREAK	
• 9:45–9:55	10 min.	**I.O. test**	Determine who goes to lunch first & who receives $5 certificates
• 9:55–10:15	20 min.	Using "HOTS" concept in regular classroom (Aixa & Louri)	Understand philosophy of "HOTS" & uses for regular classroom
• 10:15–10:45	30 min.	Tribe preparation time (each tribe will work on its project)	
		Lambs—discipline plan	Formulate evaluation of discipline plan
		Lions—student attendance plan	Prepare presentation
		Owls—morning problem	Prepare for discussion of problem
		Ducks—Fabulous Friday	Finish details for implementing FF
		Chickens—inservice	Brainstorm future inservice programs
• 10:45–11:10	25 min.	Campus Improvement Plan for Attendance (Lions)	Get consensus on attendance plan & how money will be spent

AGENDA

Clock Time	Meeting Time	Topic	Objective
• 11:10–12:00	50 min.	Higher-level thinking (Janice)	Present new ideas on higher-level thinking
• 12:00–1:00		LUNCH & DISCUSSION GROUPS	
• 1:00–1:15	15 min.	ENERGIZER (Chickens)	
• 1:15–1:35	20 min.	Ducks—Fabulous Friday	Communicate final details for Fabulous Friday
• 1:35–1:55	20 min.	Lambs—discipline plan	Communicate changes to discipline plan
• 1:55–2:15	20 min.	New Jersey Writing Project (Pixie)	Introduce New Jersey Writing
• 2:15–2:30		BREAK	
• 2:30–3:00	30 min.	Needs assessment—what at McQueeney needs to be changed or refined	Brainstorm list of needs
• 3:00–3:30	30 min.	Core funds	Brainstorm how we should use core funds, PTA funds, & Lions Club funds
• 3:30–4:00	30 min.	New techniques in cooperative learning	Learn three new techniques for cooperative learning

Appendix 5–2   Sample Meeting Evaluation Guide

1. The meeting started on time and ended on time.

   10   9   8   7   6   5   4   3   2   1
   right on time   very late—10 minutes or more

2. During our meetings, people arrive late, ask to be excused early, are frequently called out to answer the telephone, etc.

   10   9   8   7   6   5   4   3   2   1
   meeting not disrupted   many disruptions

3. If the objective of the meeting was not reached by the time limit, we scheduled a follow-up meeting rather than extend the discussion and run overtime.

   10   9   8   7   6   5   4   3   2   1
   always   run overtime or do not reschedule

4. Discussions do not begin until it is clear that everyone understands the issue to be decided or the objective to be reached.

   10   9   8   7   6   5   4   3   2   1
   everyone understands   much confusion

5. Our decisions are always reached by consensus, with everyone agreeing that they are the best we can make under the circumstances.

   10   9   8   7   6   5   4   3   2   1
   consensus   do not reach agreement

6. The facilitator established and maintained a supportive atmosphere throughout the group and encouraged every member to participate.

   10   9   8   7   6   5   4   3   2   1
   supportive & good participation   not supportive & little participation

7. One or two members dominate or talk excessively during the meeting.

   10   9   8   7   6   5   4   3   2   1
   seldom or never   sometimes   often

8. After the meeting, it is clear what was decided and who is responsible for the implementation.

   10   9   8   7   6   5   4   3   2   1
   always   sometimes   not clear

6

Making Decisions and Reaching Agreement in Clusters

It has been well observed, that the tongue discovers the state of the mind no less than that of the body; but in either case, before the philosopher or the physician can judge, the patient must open his mouth.

Caleb C. Colton
English clergyman (1780–1832)

Collaborative Decision Making: The Basis of the Self-Directed School

In traditional, hierarchical organizational structures, the highest-ranking "leaders" make all the important decisions. Using the accepted methods of gathering information in which they have been trained (which typically are limited to scientific studies, statistical spreadsheets, and other "official" compilations of data), these individuals obtain whatever information they deem to be relevant and make executive decisions which they then impose on other members of the organization. Executives in traditional organizational structures have been well taught that effective leadership is based on the ability to make and implement decisions quickly.

In the Self-Directed School, most decisions are not made by administrators. Instead, they are made by the Stakeholders. We believe that the participation of the Stakeholders in the decision-making process is not only logical and desirable, it is fundamental—since the Stakeholders are the individuals most closely involved in, and affected by, the teaching process and the educational environment.

Obviously, many school administrators may feel threatened by the Self-Directed School concept. In a collaborative environment such as that of the Self-Directed School, administrators are no longer prized for their executive abilities; that is, their abilities to make and carry out decisions. Therefore, at first blush it might appear that in a Self-Directed School there is nothing for a principal or superintendent to do. As we shall see in Chapters 8 and 9, however, Self-Directed Schools create new and highly diverse roles for administrators. New demands are placed on both the principal and the superintendent, and in many ways administrators of Self-Directed Schools are much busier and much more challenged than their counterparts in traditionally organized school systems.

The implementation of the collaborative process in a Self-Directed School is likely to evoke a number of reactions from the individuals who are affected by such an action. Many superintendents, school board members, and district office administrators may feel nervous and uncertain about the ability of the school's Stakeholders to make the kinds of policy, curriculum, and other decisions that have traditionally been made at the district office level. Principals may feel threatened and ill at ease because of the demands placed on them to become listeners, facilitators, and information providers rather than decision makers and doers. Even parents, teachers, community members, and business leaders, who for the first time are offered a chance to become involved in a meaningful way in the educational process, may experience uneasiness as they face the challenges of such an opportunity.

The shift to a Self-Directed School is not easy. It cannot be accomplished with a simple snap of the fingers or a wiggle of the nose. As we have seen, the successful implementation of the Self-Directed School requires a commitment to training. *Everyone* involved in a

Self-Directed School needs to learn the types of skills required in a collaborative management environment. We have already discussed the group interaction skills of communication, coordination, and conflict resolution. These skills form the basis of group activity and allow the clusters in the Self-Directed School to establish the safety and security necessary to support the decision-making process. This chapter examines the decision-making process itself and explores some of the ways in which clusters can become more effective decision makers.

Reaching Agreement: Coming to a Consensus

> *And so we've agreed together that we can't never agree.*
> William McKendree Carleton
> "Betsey and I Are Out," stanza 3

Defining Consensus

Webster's Ninth New Collegiate Dictionary defines "consensus" as "the judgment arrived at by most of those concerned." It also defines it as "a general agreement."

Collaboration depends upon the ability of the individuals who are working together in groups to reach a consensus. Although consensus can be a rather slippery concept, we believe that *Webster's Dictionary* provides a fairly accurate definition when it states that consensus represents "a general agreement." In this sense, consensus requires unity but not unanimity. A consensus is reached when all of the members of a group support a particular decision. This does not necessarily mean that all of the group members agree with the decision. Rather, it means that all of the group members either agree with the decision or do not so strongly disagree that they will work to undermine the decision.

Consensus is far more complex than the simple concept of majority vote. In a pure majority vote, there are winners and losers. In a collaborative environment, there can be no winners and losers because losers will not support the decision made by the group. In some cases, losers become so disenchanted that they actually seek to undermine the group's decision. Obviously, such divisive activity makes it virtually impossible that the group will be able to implement its decision successfully. More important, however, the existence of "losers" jeopardizes the group's ability to function effectively over the long term. Once an individual has experienced the feeling of being a "loser" in the group process, it is extremely difficult for that person to reestablish feelings of being a part of the group. The net result is that the individual will have a tendency to remain an outsider—the death knell of collaborative activity.

The solution, then, is to arrive at a consensus in the first place. In that way, a group can avoid the destructive effect of creating outsiders. Majority vote may in some cases play a role in a group's efforts to reach an agreement, but it is rarely if ever relied upon as the primary method of arriving at a consensus.

In this chapter we examine some of the strategies groups can use to reach consensus in a collaborative environment. Before doing so, however, let us address some of the myths that seem to surround collaborative decision-making activity.

Myths About Decision Making and Collaboration

In any kind of human activity, the existence of one or more myths can be exceedingly detrimental. Although most myths incorporate some grain of truth, more often than not myths are more fiction than fact. As such, they can be misleading to anyone attempting to understand and succeed in the activity to which the myths relate.

In the case of collaborative decision-making activity, three myths have proved to be particularly "popular" among those involved in the discourse concerning the feasibility of Self-Directed Schools. While the three myths vary greatly in terms of their implied positions either for or against collaborative decision making, they are equally misleading and can cause serious problems for those interested in implementing the Self-Directed School. Therefore, each of these myths needs to be addressed, understood, and explained.

Myth 1: Unanimous consent is the only way to make decisions in the Self-Directed School.

Many people who argue against moving toward a Self-Directed School focus on the issue of consensus. They argue that collaborative decision making will not work because consensus requires unanimity, and unanimity is an unrealistic concept in our diverse society. We agree—at least with the part of the argument which states that unanimity is unrealistic. We wholeheartedly reject, however, the part of the argument that relies on the belief that consensus requires unanimous agreement.

As we have already discussed, consensus and unanimity are *not* synonymous. In some cases, consensus is achieved through unanimous agreement, but consensus does not necessarily require unanimity.

Consensus reflects a willingness on the part of all members of a group to support actively the decision of the group. It does not necessarily mean that all members of the group agree with the group's decision. What it does mean is that to the extent that any group member disagrees with the decision, such disagreement is not so deep as to cause the group member to attempt to undermine the group's decision.

In most cases, consensus occurs naturally in clusters that maintain safe and supportive environments and that practice and develop effective communication skills. In other words, consensus is frequently the by-product of the types of skills we discussed in Chapter 5. The reason for this is that in most cases what people really want is the opportunity to have their opinion heard and considered. In clusters that successfully establish and maintain supportive environments, cluster members know that they can state their opinions honestly and without fear of rejection or personal attack. Members of these clusters also know that their opinions will be listened to and discussed in a serious manner. In many cases, all that the cluster members want is the opportunity to express their views. In effective clusters, members have that opportunity. Having had the chance to express their views and to try to convince others to adopt their views, dissenting members are frequently willing to embrace the decision of the group—even if the decision contradicts their own opinions and beliefs.

In some instances, however, the opinions of a cluster member are so strong and so deeply rooted that he or she cannot support the position taken by the cluster. In those cases, cluster members will need to work together to fashion a new position that all members are willing to support. The cluster may be able to employ one or more of the techniques described later in this chapter for achieving consensus. Alternatively, after exploring and exhausting all known options—which could include having another cluster attempt to develop a solution—the cluster members may be able to agree that in this particular case the best way to achieve a consensus is to rely on a majority vote. Notwithstanding his or her objections to the proposed course of action, the disagreeing member may, after seeing that all known alternatives have been explored, be willing to accept the decision reached by the majority.

We believe that as clusters develop effective communication, coordination, and conflict-resolution skills, the instances of strong dissent leading to extensive negotiations and ultimately to reliance on majority vote will be rare. Effective clusters, which foster safe and secure environments for exchanging ideas, offer members the opportunity to engage in give and take in an open and honest manner. This kind of respect for individuals and their ideas will lead to an amicable and effective resolution of most issues brought before the cluster.

If the Stakeholders of a Self-Directed School accept the myth that consensus requires unanimous consent, then in all likelihood the school will fail. Unanimous consent is simply not a workable concept. In most cases, Stakeholders will have varying opinions about a particular matter. This divergence of thought constitutes the strength of the Self-Directed School. If unanimity is required on every issue, then one of two things will happen: The school will develop a lot of uncreative, unproductive, and nonparticipating Stakeholders as Stakeholders simply rubberstamp the decisions made by others without thinking through the ramifications of those decisions. Or absolutely nothing will get done as Stakeholders wait for agreement by the entire group before taking any action. Obviously, neither scenario is productive.

Rather than relying on unanimity, Stakeholders should accept the fact that consensus can in most cases be achieved relatively easily once the Stakeholders have developed communication, coordination, and conflict-resolution skills. In rare cases, where individual opinions are extremely divergent and very strongly held, arriving at consensus can be a difficult and painful process. Still, because the process encourages involvement and participation, it creates a sense of commitment and teamwork among the participants. Arriving at a consensus in a collaborative environment is a far more effective way of making decisions than through the type of decision-making process that exists in traditional, hierarchical organizational systems.

Myth 2: Clusters always make good decisions.

Many people who extol the virtues of collaborative decision making point to the value of having many people involved in the process. These advocates of collaborative decision making emphasize the quality and creativeness of group decisions. We agree with this argument.

The problem, however, is that in their zeal to push for collaboration, many advocates of group involvement assume that collaborative groups will never make mistakes or bad decisions. This is not true. History is replete with examples in which individuals working together in groups have made bad decisions.

One factor that can cause groups to make bad decisions is "groupthink." According to Irving Janis,[1] who originally developed the concept, groupthink occurs when individuals in groups allow their desire to reach agreement to override their ability to appraise realistically alternative and, in some cases, better courses of action.

Janis developed his theories on the group decision-making process when he began looking at what he considered the classic decision-making fiascos of modern history—Pearl Harbor, the Bay of Pigs invasion, President Harry Truman's crossing of the 38th parallel (leading to the start of the Korean War), and the decision to launch the ill-fated "Challenger" spacecraft (despite serious design flaws and poor weather conditions). All of these "disasters" were the result of group decisions. Janis undertook his study in an attempt to identify a common thread, some unifying element, that could lead reasonable, even accomplished, group decision makers to embark upon what turned out to be disastrous courses of action.

What struck Janis most was the inability of the decision makers in question to see beyond their own narrow focus, to consider alternatives, and to foresee how their own interests and agendas could seriously threaten the groups' goals and objectives. Also striking to Janis was the extreme desire among group members to "please one another," to be perceived as team players and to retain their sense of membership in the group.

In his study, Janis was able to identify eight symptoms that serve as indicators of the existence of "groupthink." The presence of

---

[1]Irving L. Janis, *Crucial Decisions: Leadership in Policy Making* (New York: Free Press, 1989).

these symptoms can give clusters an early warning sign that group-think may be occurring. The more of these symptoms that are present in any decision-making group, the higher the probability that the group's decisions will be unsuccessful.

1. Illusion of Invulnerability. A feeling of power and authority is important to any decision-making group. If cluster members do not believe that they have the power and authority to make a decision, they will have no incentive to invest their time, energies, and talents to arrive at a reasoned and well-articulated decision. It can be devastating, however, if cluster members believe they have more power than they actually have. If cluster members come to believe that *any* decision they reach will be successful—because of their omniscience as a group or otherwise—then they will have fallen prey to an illusion of invulnerability. Groups which believe that their judgments are invulnerable can become careless and lazy in exercising the type of analytical skills that must exist for group decision making to be effective.

2. Belief in the Inherent Morality of the Cluster. All of us, whether we take part in decision-making clusters or not, have a need to believe in the rightness of our actions. In the extreme, this need to be morally "right" has led people to justify what appears to be questionable activity with the exhortation that "God is on our side." (As this book was being written, the city of Waco, Texas, witnessed a perfect example of this moral rightness issue in the religious compound headed by David Koresh.) What happens in those cases is that the individuals involved adopt the view that their opinions and actions are morally right, regardless of any argument to the contrary. People who believe strongly in group decision making sometimes have a tendency to believe that collaborative activity is the panacea for all problems and that group decision making is "pure" and above reproach. To the extent that group members adopt this belief, they may, during times of stress, have a tendency to abandon rational procedures and pursue courses of action that have not been fully explored.

3. Rationalization. In finalizing any decision, it is normal and natural for individuals to downplay the drawbacks of the chosen course of action. All of us want to emphasize the positive aspects of our decisions and minimize or ignore the negative ones. As a result, we tend to rationalize our decisions by explaining them in terms of the anticipated benefits or advantages and downplaying any perceived disadvantages. The problem in group decision making arises when the drive to make a decision becomes so strong that the need to rationalize the decision overshadows any legitimate objections to the decision. In some cases, the group simply ignores any objections that are voiced regarding the direction the group is taking. In other cases, group members who disagree with the decision of the group choose to remain silent on the issue being considered for fear that the other group members may, in their eagerness to arrive at a decision, ostracize them for speaking out.

4. Rejection of Out Groups. Sometimes individuals who are directly involved in an activity—whether the endeavor involves education, space exploration, the manufacture of goods, or anything else— begin to believe that they are the only ones who know anything about the matter before them. As a result, they reject any input that is offered by anyone "outside" the activity in question. In his video "The Business of Paradigms," Joel Barker[2] explores this concept. As Barker explains, the greatest hindrance to creativity and progress is often the tendency of the individuals who are involved in an activity to assume that their paradigm (that is, their set of rules for looking at their activity) is the only one that exists. As a result, these individuals ignore suggestions or ideas offered by people outside the activity. Among the examples Barker cites is the case of the Swiss watch manufacturers, who at one time enjoyed world-wide market dominance. In the late 1960s, the Swiss watch manufacturers ignored the development of quartz technology, preferring to continue manufacturing watches as they always had. As we all know, this turned out to be a mistake of gargantuan proportions. Sales of Swiss watches plummeted as Seiko and other manufacturers inundated the market with attractive and highly reliable quartz watches. When a cluster adopts the position that its way is the only way, it falls prey to "us against them" thinking. The result is that the cluster becomes less receptive to ideas, suggestions, and constructive criticism from outside sources—even when these suggestions are valid.

---

[2]Joel Barker, *The Business of Paradigms* (Minneapolis, MN: Chart House International Learning Corp., 1990).

5. *Self-Censorship.* Almost all of us reject attempts by others to censor what we think, feel, or believe. What many of us fail to realize, however, is that the most powerful, and frequently the most all-encompassing, form of censorship is that which we impose upon ourselves. In order to fulfill our need to be accepted and to feel like a member of the team, we sometimes suppress our doubts about or our disagreements with the position being taken by the group rather than appear as disagreeable "malcontents." We want the group's decision to be right—and we want to be a part of the group. As a result, we choose not to voice our concerns, to the detriment of the group, which no longer is afforded the benefit of our ideas.

6. *Peer Pressure.* This is the corollary to symptom 5. Because of our need as humans to feel like a part of the group, we succumb to peer pressure. Peer pressure in the group decision-making process can take a number of forms, ranging from direct pressure (as in a specific instruction from a "superior" to remain silent on an issue) to far more insidious, and more common, forms of indirect pressure (which can range from derogatory and negative gossiping about individuals to informal ostracism and nonacceptance of those who speak their minds and disagree with the group). The net effect of peer pressure, regardless of its form, is that cluster members are conditioned to keep dissenting views to themselves. The result, again, is that the cluster is deprived of valuable information that could spell the difference between success and disaster.

7. *Mindguards.* A bodyguard is someone charged with the responsibility of protecting another person's physical being. In groupthink what sometimes becomes evident is something that can be described as the mental equivalent of a bodyguard—a mindguard. The term "mindguard" refers to the phenomenon by which individuals choose to "protect" other members of the group from disturbing or bothersome ideas. In other words, an individual may possess important information not known to others in the group and may choose not to share that information. Generally, a mindguard decision is based on what may seem to the group member possessing the information to be rational reasons—for example, the group is subject to time limitations that prohibit discussion; the information is not directly pertinent; or the group has already made up its mind. Once again,

though, the net result is the failure of the group to consider all relevant information before making a decision.

8. Illusion of Unanimity. When a group engages in discussion, particularly a heated or emotionally charged discussion relating to a critical concept or idea, it is sometimes possible for the group to reach what appears to be a position of unanimity when, in fact, there really is no consensus. Sometimes this illusion of unanimity is simply the result of confusion or the failure of the group to restate adequately and accurately what has been discussed and agreed upon. In other cases, the illusion of unanimity is created by exhaustion— the group members express "agreement" and accept the decision simply because they are fatigued by the struggle and are looking for relief.

Notwithstanding the potential existence of groupthink, the fact remains that the group decision-making process is better than the individual-based decision-making process. In general, decisions made by groups in which individual members are involved in meaningful ways are more creative, more informed, and more effective than decisions made by individuals "in charge" who dictate decisions and impose those decisions on others.

Fortunately, there are a number of positive strategies and techniques that can be employed by clusters to reduce the chances of lapsing into groupthink. These strategies and techniques can help ensure a rational, well-balanced study of all available alternatives. These strategies and techniques were discussed earlier in this book in connection with the training and development of clusters. They include:

- *Maintain an open climate.* As we have stressed throughout this book, the maintenance of an open and supportive environment in which to discuss and solve problems is crucial to the success of the Self-Directed School. Toward this end, clusters should work to develop and maintain safe environments in which members feel free to share their true thoughts and opinions. In order to encourage high involvement and promote open discussions, each cluster member needs to focus on learning how to be nonjudgmental and accepting of divergent styles and ways of thinking. The skills discussed in Chapters 3 and 5 of this book must serve as the building blocks for a cluster environment that permits free and open sharing of information and ideas.

- *Avoid the isolation of clusters.* Stakeholders must be on guard not to develop the attitude that they know everything there is to know about the issues and problems facing the public education system. Too often when highly involved and committed individuals such as Stakeholders work together to try to solve a problem they fail to consider what individuals outside the organization might think about the problem. This kind of thinking is petty, short-sighted, and in some cases disastrous. As Joel Barker has pointed out, it is often the people "on the inside" who create problems in an organization. By blocking out new and innovative ways of looking at things and instead continuing to rely on traditional paradigms, individuals on the inside sometimes perpetuate problems rather than solve them. To avoid this trap, clusters should constantly emphasize the need to obtain information and points of view from individuals outside the mainstream of education. Sometimes this means consulting an expert in a particular field, as a cluster developing a science curriculum might do when it asks for help from a local scientist. In other cases, it might mean searching for an individual who has had experience dealing with a particular issue in an area outside of education. For instance, a cluster that is responsible for assisting the school district to locate a new principal might consult with human resource directors of local companies who have had experience in identifying and locating qualified candidates for challenging positions. While clusters should not rely blindly on the advice or opinions of outside consultants (after all, thinking that experts have all the answers is just as dangerous as members themselves thinking they have all the answers), it is important that clusters be willing to consider the input of individuals outside the cluster. Such input can shed light on what otherwise might seem to be an unsolvable problem, thereby allowing the cluster to explore avenues of thought that had not previously been considered. The cluster may then be able to snatch success from the jaws of failure.
- *Maintain cluster balance or assign a cluster member to play the role of critical evaluator.* The concept of cluster balance is

discussed in Chapter 3. As noted there, it is important that clusters be composed of individuals with a variety of personal styles. If all of the members of a cluster have the same personal style, they may find it very easy to get along and therefore may experience a great deal of success in arriving at a consensus. The problem, however, is that in a cluster of like-minded people, it is frequently too easy to come up with a solution. Because the group members think in similar ways, they do not challenge each other to explore new or different approaches to an issue. As a result, the cluster is not forced to consider all possible alternatives. Granted, a cluster made up of individuals with similar personal styles may sometimes succeed. In the long run, however, a cluster that is so limited will be less creative and less innovative than a cluster that can successfully blend diverse personal styles.

In cases where cluster members do not represent diverse personal styles, it is sometimes possible to create such a situation by having cluster members play the roles of any personal styles that are not represented. While this solution may not be as effective as actually having varying personal styles represented in the cluster, it can, if the members playing the roles of other personal styles are convincing, serve as a mechanism for creating the kind of positive conflict that leads the cluster to consider new ways of looking at the issue at hand.

- *Don't let the principal use his or her power as a leader.* Perhaps the single most important step that principals in Self-Directed Schools can take is to remove themselves from leadership roles. As we discuss in Chapter 8, a principal in a Self-Directed School is a facilitator, not a leader. As such, the principal has responsibilities that in many cases are far more challenging and demanding than the responsibilities facing the principal in a traditional school.

With respect to collaborative decision making, the role of the principal is not to dictate decisions or ways of thinking. If the Stakeholders of a Self-Directed School sense that the principal is acting as a leader as opposed to an equal participant, they will be less willing to share what they really think about an issue. As we have stressed throughout this book, if the Stakeholders begin to feel that someone is "in charge" of them or is superior in rank to them, then the success of the overall process is seriously threatened. Rank and position are fundamentally inconsistent with the notion of collaborative management and decision making. Individuals working in groups must feel like equal and valued participants. If they feel inferior in rank, they will be less likely to share their inner thoughts. Fearing repercussion from the "higher ups," they will frequently choose to remain silent—thereby depriving the group of their input. The principal of a Self-Directed School must strive to be a facilitator and not a dictator. This is particularly true during the initial phases of the Self-Directed School when Stakeholders are just beginning to experiment with the concept of collaborative management and are likely to be very wary of the principal's reassertion of his or her traditional power as an administrator.

Myth 3: Clusters make all decisions concerning the Self-Directed School.

Proponents of collaborative management emphasize, quite correctly we believe, the importance of involvement and participation in the decision-making process by all of the individuals affected by a particular decision or course of action. In fact, collaboration as a philosophy demands that the Stakeholders participate actively and enthusiastically in the decision-making process. It is essential, however, that the nature of the Stakeholders' participation be clearly specified and understood. Collaboration in the Self-Directed School does not mean that all school decisions will be made by, or subject to the review or approval of, the Stakeholders.

Some educators who oppose collaborative management and the other concepts underlying the Self-Directed School do so on the grounds that the Stakeholders cannot be trusted to make decisions because they do not have sufficient knowledge of federal and state laws and regulations affecting public education. Consequently, the argument goes, Stakeholders cannot be expected to make informed decisions. More strongly stated, these educators who oppose collaborative management argue that Stakeholders who lack complete knowledge of governing laws and regulations can be expected from time to time to make decisions that directly conflict with those laws and regulations. In order to avoid the potential problems created by "uninformed" Stakeholders, the critics say, it is better not to have them involved in the first place.

We believe that this kind of thinking is both short-sighted and close-minded. Collaboration by the Stakeholders does not mean that every decision affecting the educational process is entrusted to the Stakeholders. Nor does it mean that principals, superintendents, and other administrators are relieved of their responsibilities for ensuring that decisions made within the school or school district comply with applicable laws and regulations. The continuing roles of the principal and central office administrators in a Self-Directed School are discussed in more detail in Chapters 8 and 9, respectively.

It is a fact of life that our system of public education is subject to an intricate web of laws and rules. Some decisions affecting an individual school are dictated by these laws, and those decisions cannot be changed by the Stakeholders. Other decisions involve matters that affect all of the schools in a district. Those decisions are best handled at the district level where the various interests of the individual schools can be coordinated and considered in a single forum. Payroll issues and coordination of busing routes come to mind as issues that are most appropriately handled at the district level.

Notwithstanding the issues that are controlled by federal or state laws and regulations and those that rightly fall within the purview of the district office, there is an enormous number of issues affecting the educational process that can be addressed on an individual school basis. These are the kinds of issues that should be considered by the Stakeholders of an individual school. Chapter 7 explores the process of determining which decisions are to be made by which parties.

A Format for Solving Problems, Making Decisions, and Arriving at a Consensus

Stakeholders in a Self-Directed School need to develop skills in problem solving, decision making, and arriving at a consensus. Although the skills can be listed separately, in practice they constitute part of an integrated process of considering and acting upon issues in a collaborative environment. Since the purpose of this book is to provide a practical guide for implementing a Self-Directed School, we discuss the skills of problem solving, decision making, and arriving at a con-

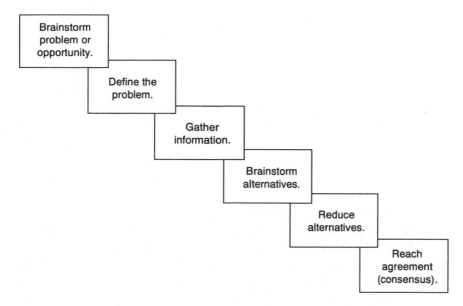

Figure 6–1. An Integrated Model for Problem Solving, Decision Making, and Arriving at a Consensus.

sensus as they are used in practice—as integrated and interdependent skills.

Figure 6–1 depicts a relatively simple and straightforward model for working through the problem-solving and decision-making process to arrive at a consensus. The figure represents a conglomeration of a number of good decision-making and problem-solving models discussed in the literature relating to collaborative management. We have modified the models for use in the setting of the Self-Directed School.

Step 1: Brainstorm the Problem or Opportunity

The first step in the decision-making process is to brainstorm the problem or opportunity to be considered. This might seem to be an unusual place to start—after all, most of us are used to functioning in a system in which the problems are obvious. In such an environment, there does not appear to be any reason to waste time "guessing" what the problems are. Rather than spending valuable time brainstorming about the problem, our inclination is to move directly toward attempting to solve the problem.

The problem with the foregoing scenario is that it is *reactive* in nature. Once a problem arises, the individuals involved react and deal with it—often too late to prevent significant damage. By contrast, the goal of a Self-Directed School is to be *proactive*. Rather than waiting for problems to arise, the Stakeholders should be continually working to improve the educational environment. The Stakeholders must adopt the attitude that "whatever we are doing is not good enough." Obviously, that is true in our schools and school systems today, since over half of our students are failing.[3] There is a great deal that can and must be done to improve our system of public education.

We are not suggesting that obvious or pressing problems which are threatening to undermine the educational environment of a school be ignored in favor of identifying new problems to be solved. Rather, we are stressing that the focus of a Self-Directed School should be to work proactively to *prevent* problems from occurring. Where a pressing problem exists, the Stakeholders should skip step 1 and proceed to step 2.

Whenever possible, however, we believe that it is helpful for the Stakeholders of a Self-Directed School to brainstorm about the problem or opportunity to be considered. Brainstorming, of course, is a critical ingredient of the collaborative decision-making process. It is a given that during a brainstorming period *all* ideas, comments, thoughts, and suggestions are welcomed. There should be no attempt to evaluate the pros or cons of any idea, and no filtering of comments should occur. Instead, the group should simply list all thoughts, comments, and suggestions that are offered.

The purpose of brainstorming is to open up the discussion. Creative, even off-beat, ideas should be encouraged. There will be plenty of time later to examine the content of individual ideas for their validity or applicability. During brainstorming, the focus should be on new ways of looking at things.

Brainstorming the Problem—An Example

One of the best ways for the Stakeholders to start thinking about the kinds of things that can be done to improve the educational and

---

[3]David T. Kearns and Dennis P. Doyle, *Winning the Brain Race* (San Francisco: Institute for Contemporary Studies, 1989).

operational environment of the school is for them to compile a list of all of the things that need to be changed about the school. At the same time they should also list all of the things that do not need to be changed. Without simultaneously looking at the good things about the school, the Stakeholders may become overly negative and discouraged about the conditions that prevail at the school, thereby dampening the enthusiasm to support needed changes and reforms. We suggest that these lists be generated by Stakeholders working individually or in established clusters as opposed to one large group, in order to make the brainstorming environment as nonthreatening and nonjudgmental as possible.

Once the individual or cluster lists have been submitted, they can be combined into a single list and presented to the Stakeholders for further consideration. Having been presented with an exhaustive list of "needs," the Stakeholders are then in a position to narrow their focus and address only the needs they designate as the most important.

Figure 6–2 (p. 176) illustrates the way in which Stakeholders at McQueeney Elementary School in McQueeney, Texas, identified the problems that needed the most attention at their school. First, the Stakeholders worked in clusters and listed the things that needed to be changed. The lists were combined into a single list and resubmitted to the Stakeholders. The Stakeholders were then asked to rate each issue on a scale of 0 to 4 to reflect the importance of immediately addressing the issue, with a 4 indicating that the issue needed the most immediate attention. In order to prevent Stakeholders from saying that every problem needed immediate attention, the Stakeholders were allowed to rate only seven items with a 4.

The results of the brainstorming process showed that the Stakeholders at McQueeney judged discipline to be their biggest problem. The issue of discipline was then given to one of the cluster groups in the school to evaluate. As we shall see shortly, that cluster engaged in each step of the decision-making process as it sought a creative solution to McQueeney's discipline problem.

Step 2: Define the Problem

After engaging in brainstorming sessions to identify problems to be addressed, the next step for Stakeholders is to define the nature of the problems to be addressed. As we shall see, the proper definition

Needs Assessment

Several weeks ago, we asked all teachers to work in groups and develop a list of things that need to be changed, added, or refined at the McQueeney School. The following list is a summary or combination of all lists developed. This list is to be completed by you. Please circle 4 if a statement is something that must be changed, circle 3 if it is something that should be changed, circle a 2 if it is a maybe, circle a 1 if it should not be changed, and circle a 0 if you don't know or don't care. There are 30 statements. You may circle only 7 number 4's and 9 number 3's. The results of how all teachers answered will be given back to you. The results will be used to help develop our school's new school improvement plan.

1.	Need more consistency in math program across age levels.	4	3	2	1	0
2.	Need to clarify and publish the rules for the "good behavior button."	4	3	2	1	0
3.	Bus traffic problem in A.M.	4	3	2	1	0
4.	Need a back-up supply of laminating film.	4	3	2	1	0
5.	Return to previous computer, music, PE schedule.	4	3	2	1	0
6.	Approval of increased disciplinary actions.	4	3	2	1	0
7.	Advance notice on assemblies.	4	3	2	1	0
8.	Fix air conditioning/heating problem.	4	3	2	1	0
9.	Sometimes we do not get our phone messages.	4	3	2	1	0
10.	More 3rd grade material to 4th grade.	4	3	2	1	0
11.	More communication between grade levels, including 3rd and 7th grades.	4	3	2	1	0
12.	Full-time counselor.	4	3	2	1	0
13.	Problems at lunch/recess time.	4	3	2	1	0
14.	In-service and help on how Anglo teachers relate to the Hispanic population.	4	3	2	1	0
15.	Lack of self-esteem among students.	4	3	2	1	0
16.	Getting students to turn in assignments.	4	3	2	1	0
17.	More communication (events, activities).	4	3	2	1	0
18.	Need more teacher manuals.	4	3	2	1	0

19. Need more teacher supplies.	4	3	2	1	0
20. No consistency in writing program across grades.	4	3	2	1	0
21. Discipline is inconsistent.	4	3	2	1	0
22. Discipline should be teacher initiated.	4	3	2	1	0
23. Need a school-wide discipline plan— teacher designed and implemented.	4	3	2	1	0
24. Allow good students to go outside in mornings.	4	3	2	1	0
25. Lack of faculty softball games.	4	3	2	1	0
26. Need "school spirit-building" activities and assemblies.	4	3	2	1	0
27. Air-condition gym.	4	3	2	1	0
28. Earlier starting time next August.	4	3	2	1	0
29. Rainy day lunch/recess is chaotic.	4	3	2	1	0

Figure 6–2. Things That Need to Be Changed at McQueeney.

of a problem is one of the keys to the success of collaborative decision making.

To encourage creative and effective solutions by the Stakeholders, it is very important that the problem be defined as broadly as possible. An action-oriented question must be framed that permits the cluster to get to the root of the problem. In other words, the cluster has to address the *cause* of the problem as opposed to treating and dealing with the *symptoms*.

To better illustrate the importance of defining the nature of the problem to be solved, let's return to the example of the needs assessment at McQueeney Elementary. Based on the results of the needs assessment, it was apparent that discipline problems were of major concern to the McQueeney Stakeholders. If the Stakeholders are meeting with frustration in dealing with the issue of discipline and the students are wearing them down, they might ask, "What are we going to do with the students who cause discipline problems?" If they were to define the problem in this way, however, the McQueeney Stakeholders would be limiting the scope of their evaluation and the possible alternatives for resolving the problem. If, on the other hand, the McQueeney Stakeholders ask, "What is causing the discipline problems?" they open up a much broader type of inquiry, one that will, in turn, allow them to explore a much greater variety of options for resolving the problem and for preventing it from occurring in the first place.

If the Stakeholders at McQueeney limited themselves to the first question—"What are we going to do with the students who cause discipline problems?"—they would in all likelihood study only ways to punish the students who are problems. Consequently, the "solution" to the problem would probably be limited to deprivation of privileges (such as field trips), after-school detention, in-school suspension, and so on. These kinds of punitive solutions deal only with the symptoms of the discipline problem, of course; they do not address the actual causes. By asking the second and broader question, "What is causing the discipline problems?" the Stakeholders of McQueeney would be forced to look at a number of different kinds of issues: Are the rules and the consequences for violating the rules clear to all students and staff members? Do students have acceptable outlets for their feelings? Are the curriculum and instruction boring? Are the faculty members using good conflict-resolution techniques when problems first develop?

A cluster that can successfully define a problem in broad terms allows its members to delve into the causes of the problem and not be limited to a discussion of how best to deal with the symptoms. The proper definition of a problem requires more work on the part of the cluster members as they are forced to gather information and consider alternatives. The net result of such a process, however, is a better reasoned, better constructed, and more effective solution.

Step 3: Gather Information

The cluster responsible for developing a solution to a problem or determining how best to take advantage of an opportunity should make no assumptions about the problem or where the opportunity lies. One of the biggest mistakes an individual can make is to assume that he or she has all of the necessary facts at hand to arrive at a well-reasoned and logical conclusion. This can especially be a problem for an experienced administrator or decision maker. These individuals tend to think that they have seen it all before and that the answer is obvious. The weakness in this thinking is that such persons only know what they know—and the answer may lie in what they don't know. In education, at least, we *know* that the answer must lie in what we don't know—otherwise we would not be in the terrible position that we are in.

No decision should be made until the individuals responsible for making the decision possess all of the relevant information that can reasonably be acquired—taking into account time limitations and cost factors—pertaining to the decision to be made. In the case of the Self-Directed School, this means that once a problem or opportunity has been defined, the cluster responsible for developing a plan to solve the problem or take advantage of the opportunity should engage in a comprehensive information-gathering effort. The three major areas to be considered when gathering information are asking the right questions, consulting with "experts," and evaluating outside influences.

Asking the Right Questions

The first step in gathering information is to start asking questions. Again, it is important for the questions to be framed properly. The most effective questions are open-ended ones that lead to divergent kinds of thinking. Posing open-ended questions allows cluster members to collect a variety of data, which can then be used to formulate new and innovative alternatives for dealing with the problem or opportunity at hand.

The following are sample questions that a cluster might use when digging for facts and information:

> *What is the true scope of the problem or opportunity? Is the problem bigger, or is it less important, than it originally appeared to be? Are deeper issues involved?*

In the case of the discipline problems at McQueeney Elementary, the cluster given the responsibility for tackling the problem asked questions such as: What are the current discipline procedures in the school? Are the discipline procedures clear to all of the students and staff members? Are staff members sure about what their responsibilities are concerning discipline? What specific complaints about the discipline procedures do the staff members have? Do the staff members have the training to be able to mainstream special education students? What effect have the changes in the school day had on the discipline problems? (At McQueeney, the school day had recently been extended by approximately forty minutes, with the start of the school day having been moved back by about twenty-five minutes. The result was a lot of wasted time in the morning since students continued to arrive by bus at approximately the same time as before the changes in the school day were implemented.)

Who is affected by the problem or new opportunity? Is everyone affected or only one group of people? Is everyone affected in the same manner?

Sometimes school discipline problems can be traced to a relatively limited number of students. In other cases, it may be that only certain teachers are having severe discipline problems. In still other cases, the discipline problems that exist at a particular school may reflect a deep and underlying problem in the relationship between the students and the teachers; or they may be symptomatic of a curriculum that is not meeting the needs and satisfying the interests of the students. In each of these cases, the solution to the problem will be entirely different. Therefore, before it is possible to construct a solution, information must be obtained regarding the specific type and pervasiveness of the problem being encountered.

At McQueeney, the school discipline cluster asked questions such as: Can the discipline problems be isolated to a few students? Are the discipline problems limited only to certain teachers, or are all of the teachers having problems? Are there some teachers that seem to have more discipline problems than others year after year? What subjects are being studied in the school? Are students involved in the creation of their own learning? What steps have the teachers taken to create a curriculum that is challenging, useful, and relevant to the students?

Some of the questions that a collaborative cluster will ask may cause discomfort and may require a fairly painful analysis of the existing situation. However, without this kind of probing and honest evaluation of the facts, no true progress can be achieved.

Have other schools or school systems (or other organizations) encountered our problem or addressed our opportunity? How do their situations compare with ours? What have they done to handle the problem or address the opportunity?

In the case of schools like McQueeney, which are trying to deal with discipline problems, this phase of the information-gathering process could involve studying and reading about other schools that have successfully overcome discipline problems and become quality schools. A number of studies have been done and books written about successful discipline programs.[4] In their search for information, the Stakeholders should be asking questions such as: How have other schools gone about developing discipline programs? Who was involved? How long did it take? Are the theories underlying the successful programs compatible with ours? Are the educational environments similar enough that comparable results can be expected at our school?

The process of gathering data need not be limited to schools or other educational institutions. Frequently the problems encountered in an educational environment are really quite similar to those encountered in a business environment. If businesses have been able successfully to overcome or handle issues that seem to be creating bothersome roadblocks for a school, the Stakeholders would be well advised to find out what those businesses have done to solve the problem or take advantage of the opportunity in question.

For example, a Self-Directed School that is in the process of hiring a new principal can learn a lot from corporate America. Many corporations have experienced tremendous success in revamping their organizational structures to implement greater employee participation. In these companies, the roles of middle managers—the positions most similar to that of the principal in the "industry" of education—have changed dramatically. Instead of being leaders and dictators, middle managers have had to become facilitators and helpers. To succeed in these new roles, individuals have had to develop new skills, new attitudes, and new approaches. At the same time, the corporate personnel responsible for hiring middle managers have had to develop new techniques for identifying the types of people who will be successful middle managers. The Stakeholders seeking a new principal could be asking questions such as: What are the characteristics of a successful middle manager in a collaborative environment? What strategies have been used to identify quality candidates? What makes a search for a candidate successful?

---

[4]See, for example, William Glasser, M.D., *The Quality School: Managing Students without Coercion* (New York: Harper Perennial, 1990).

It should be noted that schools looking to restructure their leadership positions can now also find a growing data base of experience from other schools and school systems. A number of schools across the country are in the process of reevaluating the role of the principal—so much so that some school systems are currently considering having schools *without* principals (a concept that just a few years ago would have been greeted with derision).

The issue of restructuring the leadership role in schools is starting to be discussed. Stakeholders should not close their eyes to the experiences of other schools. There is no need to be constantly reinventing the wheel.

Consulting with "Experts"

Once the right questions have been posed, it is time to start obtaining information. Toward this end, the Stakeholders will need to consult "experts." As we are using the term, "expert" refers to *any* source of data or information. So defined, the term "expert" can include a variety of sources.

One way to obtain information—in fact, the most traditional way—is to read books, articles, and studies on the subject being considered. Books and other printed material, then, constitute one form of an expert source.

As we proceed in the technological age, a rapidly growing portion of the "hard data" that has traditionally been published only in printed form is becoming available as computer software or on videotapes, laser disks, or other forms of electronic media. Stakeholders who do not take advantage of the huge amounts of data available in electronic form will be doing a disservice to their schools.

People represent perhaps the greatest source of information for Stakeholders searching for data. Acknowledged and respected experts exist in virtually every area of human knowledge and are usually no more than a phone call away. These experts are individuals who have devoted a tremendous amount of time and effort to developing their knowledge in a particular area. It would be foolish *not* to take advantage of their efforts.

In talking about the process of consulting with experts, we do not mean that the Stakeholders should be limited to consulting with renowned academic or intellectual experts. To the contrary, some of the most valuable information sources are other Stakeholders.

In Self-Directed Schools, the Stakeholders soon discover a wealth of information that has not been tapped or used in any way. Given their diverse backgrounds and experiences, the Stakeholders of a particular school possess a broad range of information. Some may have ideas about how to handle a particular situation based on their experiences in other schools or in other communities. Others may have accumulated knowledge or practical experience in a particular area that interests them. Moreover, as the Stakeholder base changes, as happens continually, new sources of information become available.

Consultation with other Stakeholders should not be limited to a single school. Sometimes Stakeholders' own ethnocentric views prevent them from talking to Stakeholders of other schools in their district. If Stakeholders begin to feel that their own school is superior to other schools, then it will be extremely difficult for them to develop the kind of unfettered access to information that is crucial to becoming effective and efficient problem solvers.

As a word of caution, Stakeholders need to remember that in consulting with experts, as in every aspect of the decision-making process, there are no absolutes or guarantees. Information, no matter how detailed or persuasive, doesn't guarantee success. Moreover, information changes rapidly and constantly. For example, remember all those schools that took out walls to create open classrooms in the 1960s and 1970s only to spend hundreds of thousands of dollars putting the walls back after both teachers and parents concluded that the experiment did not work?

Evaluating Outside Influences

When gathering information, there are often external factors such as legal, social, ethical, and political issues that may be relevant to the Stakeholders' decision and that should be considered.

Suppose that some Stakeholders are urging the use of paddling as part of the discipline plan for their school. Although paddling was once used in almost every school in America, some states have passed laws prohibiting the use of the paddle. In addition, many parents and teachers oppose paddling for psychological or emotional reasons. Lastly, many boards of education have strong policies concerning the practice. Obviously, the Stakeholders should take all of those factors into account in considering the possibility of using the paddle in their school.

As another example, let's return to the no principal concept. For any school system thinking about implementing schools without principals there are many important outside factors to be considered. For instance, some states have strong administrator certification laws and regulations that require schools to have principals. In addition, parents may have strong opinions about having a principal at their children's school. They will want to know who they can talk to if their children are having problems in school. The district superintendent and board members are also likely to have strong opinions about the issue of principals in schools. They will want to know who will be accountable for the performance of the school if there is no principal.

A myriad of outside influences surround virtually every decision made by the Stakeholders of a Self-Directed School. In fact, it is these outside influences that typically cause most of the concern when making decisions. All of the influences must be considered, and reasonable forums must be provided for the Stakeholders and other interested parties to express their views before a sensitive and reasoned decision can be made.

As a final comment about step 3 of the decision-making process, we would note that the quest for knowledge, understanding, and information can be an endless project. All issues considered by the Stakeholders of a Self-Directed School will involve time constraints and deadlines. Accordingly, the Stakeholders will have to set limits on their efforts to obtain information. They should attempt to obtain all of the information that they can in the time period allotted and then move on to step 4.

Step 4: Brainstorm Alternatives

Once all of the relevant information that can reasonably be obtained in the time available has been gathered, the cluster responsible for the issue in question should engage in a brainstorming session as a means of identifying possible alternatives for solving the problem. As we discussed earlier, the focus of brainstorming is creativity. Innovative, even off-beat, suggestions should be welcomed. All criticisms and judgments regarding the merits or practicalities of particular suggestions should be withheld until a later time.

As the brainstorming process continues, the Stakeholders may be able to see combinations of ideas that had not previously been envisioned, or they may be able to see new ways to improve existing ideas.

The brainstorming process may be limited to the Stakeholders of the cluster responsible for the issue at hand. Alternatively, that cluster may decide to open the brainstorming session to all Stakeholders of the school. The decision as to who will be included will depend on a number of factors, such as the amount of time available, the scope and complexity of the problem, and whether the issue is of a confidential or sensitive nature. The ultimate goal of the brainstorming process, however, is to solicit a long list of suggestions regarding potential alternatives for handling the problem or opportunity. Accordingly, it is advisable to include as many Stakeholders as possible in the brainstorming session.

As we have stressed throughout this book, the real advantage of Stakeholder involvement in the operation of a school is the commitment, enthusiasm, experience, and creativity the Stakeholders bring to the school. The brainstorming process gives the Stakeholders the opportunity to use their originality, experiences, and unique perspectives in a focused but limitless way—all to the advantage of the school.

Step 5: Reduce Alternatives

After completing the brainstorming process, the cluster responsible for handling the issue in question should have in hand a relatively long list of alternatives. The goal at this point is to pare down the list to a workable number of alternatives so that a final decision can be made. In narrowing the list of possible alternatives, the cluster may benefit from considering the following:

- *Clarify options.* After making a written list of the alternatives or options, the cluster should review each alternative to make sure it is clearly stated and understood by each member. Any ambiguity or confusion should be addressed and rectified.
- *Check the goal or objective.* Cluster members should take a moment to revisit the specific goals of their activity. Given the problem or opportunity being considered, what exactly does the cluster wish to accomplish? Was the problem or

opportunity clearly defined? Does it need to be restated? By asking these types of questions, cluster members can ensure that they are all "on the same page." If the alternatives are going to be evaluated on their merits, then it is critical that each cluster member understand the objectives that are being sought. Only then can the substance of each alternative be fairly evaluated.

- *Eliminate or combine options.* Each alternative should be examined to determine whether it fits the objectives of the cluster. If it does not, the alternative should be eliminated. Some alternatives can be eliminated even if they meet the objectives of the cluster because of outside factors—time limitations, cost, limitations of physical facilities, and so on—that make them impractical. Other alternatives may be eliminated because of a lack of support among the cluster members or other Stakeholders. Duplicate or repetitive alternatives can be combined and restated as a single, comprehensive alternative.

- *Restate and renumber options.* To ensure that every cluster member understands the remaining alternatives, the options should be written down and restated. The cluster will then know exactly which alternatives are to be considered in making the final decision.

If after completing the foregoing steps the cluster has pared down the list of possible alternatives to a relatively small number, for example, two or three, the cluster can proceed to the last step of the decision-making process (step 6: reaching agreement). If the list of remaining alternatives is still relatively long, however, the cluster may need to use one of the following techniques for identifying the "best" or most supported alternatives:

- *Forced ranking.* The process of forced ranking involves having the Stakeholders rank each alternative in terms of its anticipated effectiveness or applicability. This is the process the Stakeholders at McQueeney Elementary used to identify the most important problems at their school. In this forced ranking, the list of alternatives is presented to the cluster, and each member is asked to evaluate the anticipated effectiveness of each alternative on a scale of, say, 1 to 10 (with 1 being the least effective and 10 the most effective). In order to force cluster members to be critically evaluative, only a certain number of alternatives may be ranked as being most effective. For example, if there are fifteen alternatives, the cluster may decide that cluster members can give a 10 ranking to only five alternatives. Once the members have completed their individual rankings, the rankings can be tabulated and a single list compiled. The small number of alternatives deemed to be most effective, that is, those with the highest scores, can then be evaluated in terms of making a final decision.

- *Voting with "dots."* Rather than using a forced ranking system, the cluster may prefer to utilize a simpler form of voting. This technique begins with making a written list of alternatives that is posted for everyone in the cluster to see. Each cluster member is then given two or three adhesive, colored dots to place on the list. In voting with the dots, each member places his or her dots next to the alternatives he or she believes are the best. If a cluster member feels that only one alternative should be considered, the person is free to put all of his or her dots on that alternative. Once every cluster member has voted, the most popular alternatives should be fairly easy to see. These alternatives can then be evaluated for a final decision.

Step 6: Reaching Agreement (Consensus)

Once the cluster has prepared a relative short list of alternatives that are both practical and meet the objectives of the cluster, it is time to carefully evaluate each alternative with a view toward making a final decision. Although there may be cases in which there is no need to settle on the one best solution or alternative, most of the time the implementation of a solution will require the cluster to agree on a single approach. It is during the process of making a final decision that cluster members will be most challenged to use their newly acquired communication and conflict-resolution skills. Mutual respect and the supportive atmosphere engendered by the feeling of being a member of a unified team are critical to the Stakeholders' ability to arrive at a consensus.

In discussing each proposed alternative, it is best if the cluster can establish in advance certain criteria for judging the relative merits of each alternative. The following is a short list of factors that cluster members might consider:

- Which alternatives give the greatest results with the least effort?
- Which alternatives will solve the problem or exploit the opportunity with the least disruption?
- How much change does each alternative require? Does an alternative require significant change immediately, or does it require gradual change over time?
- What are the potential risks of each alternative?
- Which alternative takes the best advantage of the school's resources, both its personnel resources and its physical resources?
- How will the Stakeholders be affected by each alternative?

The first three questions relate to the concept of change. Change is difficult in any organization because it requires individuals to abandon the way they have always done things and adopt new and possibly uncomfortable attitudes and behaviors. Therefore, it is always best if the amount of required change can be minimized. A solution that requires only a small amount of change on the part of organization members is far more likely to be successful than a solution that requires the members to make sweeping changes in their accepted ways of doing things.

What we have just said about change, however, should not be interpreted as a recommendation to avoid change at all costs. Sometimes change is necessary, even vital, to the success of a proposed solution and should be undertaken. All we are saying is that if two proposed solutions can be anticipated to yield the same results, it is probably better to adopt the solution that requires the fewer number of changes—since that solution is far more likely to be successful than the one that calls for the greater number of changes.

In engaging in the final analysis of alternatives, the cluster should be especially careful not to accept blindly the popular front runner among the alternatives. Each alternative should be examined in detail—even the alternative that appears to have unanimous support. If the front-running alternative is adopted too quickly, the cluster members may fail to see some inherent weaknesses in the alternative that could ultimately create more problems than are solved by that alternative.

Reaching agreement and gaining consensus is the ultimate goal of the decision-making process. We believe that in a mature cluster—

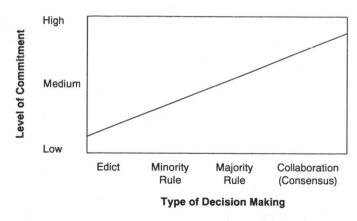

Figure 6–3. Commitment and Decision-Making Styles.

one in which the cluster members have developed feelings of inclusion and have established acceptable norms for group communication and behavior—arriving at a consensus is the natural conclusion of the decision-making process. Since each cluster member has been involved in each step of the process, and since each member has had ample opportunity to share and contribute ideas in a safe and supportive environment, then each member will be highly motivated to arrive at a decision that all cluster members support.

As we have already discussed, consensus requires unity but not unanimity. A consensus is reached when all members of the cluster can say that they either agree with the decision or that they have had their day in court and can accept the decision that is being made. In the final analysis, consensus means that everyone in the group agrees to support the outcome.

Consensus also means that each group member will feel committed to the final decision because each member has had a chance to influence it. Consensus spurs commitment. Figure 6–3 illustrates how the commitment of participants in the collaborative decision-making process increases as they are given a greater opportunity to take part in the decision-making process.

Conclusion

Clusters engaged in the collaborative decision-making process must allow enough time to make good decisions, and they must have the patience to work through as many options and alternatives as can be generated by cluster members or other Stakeholders. During the decision-making process all members of the cluster must have an opportunity to have their say and to share their thoughts, ideas, and suggestions. It is imperative that a cluster maintain an atmosphere of mutual respect and support, so that each member feels safe in voicing even the slightest concern or reservation.

With effective communication skills and a clear respect within the cluster for everyone's contributions, the areas of agreement will widen. Eventually the cluster will come to a point where conflicts and disagreements will melt away. Group members will begin to realize that they are approaching a decision that is acceptable to all. Consensus may then emerge quite suddenly.

The belief in collaborative decision making is based on the assumption that a cluster of individuals working as a team can produce a more effective, more creative, and more supported decision than can one or more individuals working separately. Taking the necessary time to get to consensus is critical to the successful implementation of the final decision.

Part III

From Hierarchy to Stakeholder Empowerment

7

Deciding Who Decides: Determining Which Decisions Are Made at Which Levels

I keep six honest serving men
(They taught me all I knew);
Their names are What and Why and When
And How and Where and Who.

Rudyard Kipling, *The Just-So Stories,*
"The Elephant's Child," 1902

Despite our obvious bias in favor of moving responsibility for making decisions that affect the nature, quality, and content of the educational process to the individuals who are the closest to the schools and the students—the Stakeholders of individual schools—we acknowledge that there is and always will be an organizational hierarchy in the field of public education. As we see it, this hierarchy is divided into three basic levels: the federal and state administrative agency level, the school district level, and the individual school level. Strange as it may seem given our repeated arguments for the removal of the rigid, bureaucratic top-down management form, we believe that *some* amount of *limited* hierarchy is essential to the efficient operation of the public education system. We do not advocate the complete usurpation of authority and control by individual schools. Such a system would, we believe, result in chaos and anarchy. What we do advocate is an organizational structure in which federal and state educational agencies, district offices, and individual schools work together to operate an educational system that is creative, challenging, exciting, and responsive to the ever-changing needs and interests of our society and our students. The key in such a system is for participants to understand their roles. Each participant must know *who* is responsible for making which decisions. That is what this chapter is about.

Allocating Decision-Making Authority: Some Introductory Examples

At first glance, it may seem relatively easy to allocate decision-making authority among the participants in the educational process. The following examples, however, demonstrate how complex and confusing the allocation of authority can actually be:

Case 1: A superintendent of a medium-sized school district declares that in the coming year the school district will emphasize site-based decision making. He then announces that the primary goal of the district will be to improve student achievement, as measured by the students' scores on nationally normed tests. To help raise the mathematics scores in each school, he asks a well-known consultant to work with the central office staff to develop inservice training for all mathematics teachers in the district.

Case 2: A superintendent convinces her board of education of the merits of site-based decision making and announces that the ultimate power to change the public schools is in the hands of the classroom teachers. She states, "Decisions must be made where the action is, and the important action is in the classroom." The superintendent's new plan calls for the school district to divide all revenue on a per student basis and to hand it over to school site councils, which are then responsible for determining how the resources are to be used. The site council are to consist of parents, community members, the principal, and classroom teachers. Each school site council is to make all decisions affecting the operation of its school and is to enter into whatever contracts or agreements are necessary to conduct school business—including insurance contracts, utility agreements, employment contracts, and payroll service contracts. The superintendent believes that bypassing the district office allows for a more effective allocation of resources to meet the needs of students in the district.

These two short case studies illustrate how educators who want to give schools and their staffs more freedom can, instead of solving problems, create a panoply of new problems that can eliminate any chance of achieving success. In the first case, the superintendent announced his intention to give new power to the schools, but then turned around and started to make important curriculum decisions by himself. He "talked the talk but didn't walk the walk." It is doubtful that school staffs would buy into and accept his form of site-based decision making.

In the second case, the superintendent and the board renounced responsibility, ceding all authority to the individual schools without considering the need for training Stakeholders in the skills necessary to make the kinds of decisions created by such a system of site-based decision making. Even if training had been provided, however, it is unlikely that a system of site-based decision making that places complete authority in the hands of individual schools would work. There are simply too many details involved in the day-to-day operation of a school for such details to be handled efficiently at the individual school level. Any school that attempts to assume responsibility for day-to-day operational decisions will probably find itself too bogged down by daily operations to be very effective in fashioning a creative, exciting, and challenging curriculum and educational environment. Schools should be in the business of educating—not entering into food service contracts and paying utility bills.

What is apparent in the two cases is that there is a great deal of confusion regarding who has the responsibility for making decisions in a site-based–managed school. Traditionally, school districts and central offices have willingly assumed the authority to make most decisions relating to both the operation of schools and the development of curriculum and educational strategies. The result has been an educational system that is woefully inadequate to meet the needs of its students. Reform is obviously necessary; however, simply recognizing the need for reform does not solve problems. As the foregoing examples demonstrate, the movement toward instilling more control at the individual school level generates many views of how this new-found authority is to be exercised. We believe that the differences in interpretations stem from a fundamental lack of understanding of the issues involved in school decision making.

A Framework for Deciding Who Decides

Step 1: Determining the Level at Which a Decision Is to Be Made

In discussing decision making, it is possible to isolate two distinct issues:

1. Who should be responsible for making a particular decision?
2. Once the decision maker has been identified, how is the decision to be made? (This is often referred to as the decision-making process.)

Chapter 6 discussed the decision-making process in detail. Here we present a framework for determining who should be responsible for making which decisions in our educational system.

For the past three decades educators have debated whether decisions should be made at the central office level or at the school level. This debate has crystallized as a battle between centralized decision making and decentralized decision making, with proponents of both sides claiming superiority in efficiency and effectiveness.

The terms "centralized decision making" and "decentralized decision making" are value-laden. Supporters of decentralization equate decentralization with autonomy, self-determination, and self-actualization, whereas they view centralization as a system steeped in bureaucracy, rigidity, and authoritarianism. Proponents of centralization argue that centralization provides uniformity, control, and informed leadership, whereas they see decentralization as resulting in anarchy, chaos, and aimlessness.

Based on the literature published in the last thirty years, it appears that the majority of educators and other individuals interested in the field of education believe that decentralization of our public education system would yield enormous benefits. Despite this strong support for decentralization, very few schools and school systems in the United States have attempted to shift a significant amount of decision-making authority to the individual school level. In essence, decentralization has been a nonevent during the past three decades.

The problem with the decentralization movement to date, we believe, is that no one has been able to define clearly what decentralization means in terms of responsibility for making decisions. In any system, whether it is education, politics, or business, there must be an accepted framework for determining who is responsible for making which decisions.

Proponents of decentralization have tended to focus their arguments on the need for allowing teachers, parents, community leaders, and business representatives to have more discretion and authority in shaping the educational environment of individual schools. Their arguments are based on the assumption that the Stakeholders of a school are the individuals who are in the best position to make decisions about the scope and content of the curriculum. But does decentralization mean that Stakeholders will make *all* of the decisions? *most* of the decisions? *some* of the decisions? To date, these questions remain unanswered.

What is needed, we believe, is a framework for allocating responsibility for making decisions. Such a structure must define clearly and succinctly the responsibilities of each participant in the decision-making process. Once these responsibilities are clearly identified, all participants will understand their roles and the extent to which they should be involved in a particular decision.

The first step in creating an understandable framework for allocating decision-making authority is to identify broad areas of responsibility and to rank order these areas—in other words, to determine which areas will control or supersede decisions made by other areas. We have seen that there are three distinct areas or levels of responsibility for making decisions: federal and state administrative agencies, school district offices, and individual schools. Moreover, there is a definite ranking to the decision-making authority of each level: Decisions made by federal and state administrative agencies control decisions made at the school district level, which, in turn, control decisions made at the individual school level. In a centralized model of school management, most decisions are made either by federal and

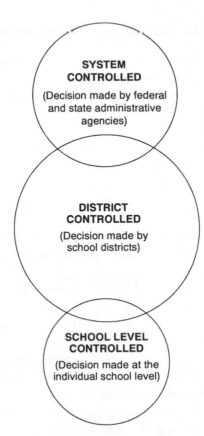

Figure 7-1. Allocation of Decision-Making Authority in a Centralized Model of School Management.

state administrative agencies or by school district offices. Hence, the allocation of decision-making authority in a centralized model of school management may be depicted as in Figure 7-1.

The figure represents the prevailing structure of decision-making authority in most public education systems in the United States today. It is a structure with which most professional administrators are comfortable. After all, it entrusts most of the important decisions affecting the educational process to professional administrators. Unfortunately, it is a structure that does not work—one that has proved to be too rigid, too static, and too unresponsive to meet the needs of America's youth.

For a Self-Directed School to succeed, there must be a reallocation of decision-making authority. This does not mean that *all* authority is transferred to the Stakeholders. It does mean that responsibility for making the majority of decisions affecting the curriculum and the educational environment of an individual school is transferred to the Stakeholders of that school. Of course, all of the decisions made by the Stakeholders will still be subject to overriding federal, state, and district interests. It's just that in a Self-Directed School system, those federal, state, and district interests are clearly defined and specifically limited to interests that are truly outside the control or interest of the individual school. In short, the allocation of decision-making authority in a Self-Directed School system may be depicted as in Figure 7–2.

System Controlled Decisions

Some decisions are beyond the authority of the school district or the individual school to make (see Fig. 7–2). The U.S. Constitution, U.S. Supreme Court decisions, and numerous federal laws, rules, and regulations establish and define the civil and other rights of every U.S. citizen. These federal rights override any action by a school district or individual school that is inconsistent with these rights.

Examples of decisions that are set and determined by federal laws, rules, and regulations include:

- Prohibition of prayer in school.
- Prohibition of school segregation.
- Prohibition of employment discrimination.
- Due process for students.
- Requirement of "reasonable grounds" for searches and seizures.[1]
- Requirements governing the rights of students with special needs.
- Chapter 1 guidelines requiring schools to enter into a formal improvement process if their Chapter 1 students do not meet minimum achievement standards.

In addition to federal laws and regulations, a number of issues affecting education are governed by state laws and regulations. Any

---

[1]*New Jersey v. T.L.Q.*, 469 U.S. 325 (1985): Search and seizure are acceptable if the methods adopted are "reasonably related to the objectives of the search and are not excessively intrusive in light of the age and sex of the student and the nature of the infraction."

decision made by a school district or individual school must also be consistent with these state laws and regulations. One of the most prominent areas in which state laws and regulations affect educa-

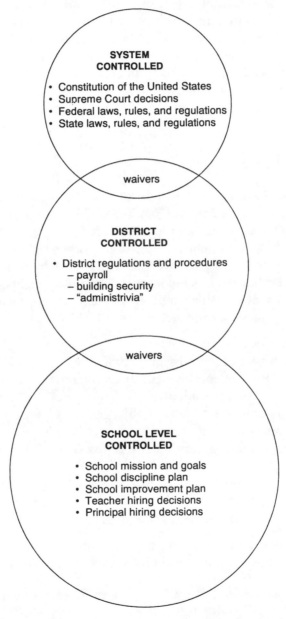

Figure 7–2. Allocation of Decision-Making Authority in a Self-Directed School System.

tional decisions is the issue of school funding. In the past twenty years, the highest courts of ten states have found the system of school funding established by the state legislature to be unconstitutional. As a result, the legislatures in those states have been forced to redefine their methods of financing public education. Other examples of state-determined educational decisions include regulations regarding the number of students who can be placed in each classroom and requirements dictating the subjects to be taught in schools (as well as the amount of time to be spent on each subject).

The issues governed and controlled by federal and state laws and regulations are beyond the authority of school districts and individual schools. Reform of the organizational structure of our public education system will not change the fact that certain decisions will still be dictated by these laws and regulations. Occasionally waivers from these federal and state requirements can be obtained, but in most cases the rights and interests protected by federal and state laws are paramount and supersede any attempt by a school district or individual school to change or undermine them.

Federal and state laws determine decisions made throughout the public education system. That is why we have referred to the decisions governed by federal and state laws, rules, and regulations as *system controlled decisions*.

District Controlled Decisions

After taking into account the decisions that are going to be controlled by federal and state laws and regulations, the next level of decision-making responsibility is the local school district (see Fig. 7–2). Regardless of the size of the district, a number of issues, for reasons of efficiency and administrative convenience, are most appropriately handled at the school district level. Areas of concern that are best addressed at the school district level include:

- Management of payroll.
- Purchase of materials (cumulating the needs of the schools in the district to take advantage of economies of scale).
- Transportation of students.
- Provision of food service.
- Facility maintenance and repair.
- Establishment of district-wide goals and objectives.

In a decentralized model of school organization, such as a Self-Directed School system, the focus of the district office changes from one of leadership, control, and direction of educational policy to one of facilitation and management of day-to-day operations. This shift in focus, in turn, creates the opportunity and freedom necessary for individual schools to develop their own educational programs and procedures to best take advantage of the needs, interests, and talents of the students. This transformation of the role and scope of the district office is a key to the success of the Self-Directed School. The ability of the central office to function effectively in the area of *district controlled decisions* will determine to a great extent the ultimate success or failure of the Self-Directed School.

School Level Controlled Decisions

Notwithstanding the breadth of the areas covered by system controlled decisions and district controlled decisions, an enormous number of decisions can be made at the individual school level—*school level controlled decisions* (see Fig. 7–2). Traditionally, these are the decisions that have been made at the district level by "trained" professionals. They include:

- Hiring principals and teachers.
- Developing and implementing educational programs and curricula.
- Creating and developing school improvement plans and educational missions and objectives.
- Establishing school budgets and plans.
- Establishing school missions.

The experience of business and industry has demonstrated that success, enthusiasm, commitment, and creativity can be achieved by transferring responsibility for as many decisions as possible to the individuals who are most directly involved in and affected by the decisions. Through participatory management and self-directed teams, many U.S. companies have been able to take advantage of the incredible creativity and productivity of employees to remain competitive in an increasingly challenging global economy.

By increasing the involvement and decision-making responsibility of the Stakeholders, Self-Directed Schools can expect to achieve the same kind of success experienced by businesses that have emphasized employee involvement.

Distinguishing between District Controlled Decisions and School Level Controlled Decision

To help differentiate between district controlled decisions and school level controlled decisions, Table 7–1 presents a simple typology for school system decisions.

Category I decisions are decisions that relate primarily to the day-to-day management of the school district and the individual schools within the district. By taking care of the intricate details involved in running the schools within the district, a district office in a Self-Directed School system can greatly assist its schools in developing and maintaining the type of world-class schools that can be achieved through high Stakeholder involvement. Chapter 9 examines

Table 7–1 A Typology of School System Decisions

CATEGORY I DISTRICT CONTROLLED DECISIONS	CATEGORY II SCHOOL LEVEL CONTROLLED DECISIONS
Characteristics	*Characteristics*
Decisions that are routine, recurring, and certain; they are procedural, predictable, andwell defined and have definite decision criteria; there is a need to rely upon uniform processing and accepted methods for handling.	Decisions that are unique, creative, innovative, or inspirational in nature; the desired solution may be novel and complex; there may be incomplete information, and the decision criteria may be uncertain; there is a need to rely on judgment, intuition, and creativity.
Examples	*Examples*
• Procedures for the purchase of supplies and materials.	• Finding approaches for raising test scores.
• Standard accounting procedures for handling school funds.	• Recommending a teacher for the science department.
• Procedures for accounting for staff absences.	• Developing the school improvement plan.

the role of the district office in implementing and supporting Self-Directed Schools.

Category II decisions are decisions that relate primarily to the development and implementation of educational and other programs designed to accomplish the objectives of the school district and of the individual schools. Category II decisions revolve around the question: How can we as Stakeholders best achieve the educational goals that have been established for our school by the school district and by ourselves as Stakeholders? As the individuals most directly involved in the lives of the students, the Stakeholders are in the best position to know how most effectively to translate high-minded objectives into concrete educational programs that can prepare the students for the challenges of the twenty-first century. Category II decisions demand creativity, commitment, and a willingness and ability to consider and conceptualize new and innovative ways of thinking and doing things. By developing their communication skills and abilities to work together in clusters, Stakeholders of Self-Directed Schools can position themselves to be effective decision makers with respect to category II decisions.

Recognizing Decision-Making Responsibility

As we stated earlier, all participants in a Self-Directed School system must be aware of and must accept the allocation of decision-making authority as just outlined. Although it may take time, participants in a Self-Directed School system should, with practice, become fairly adept at identifying which decisions are to be made at which levels of the overall educational structure. Although there may be some overlap of decision-making responsibility on some issues, we believe that most decisions fit distinctly into one area of responsibility.

Recognizing and accepting the area of responsibility into which a decision falls is critical to the success of the Self-Directed School. For example, Stakeholders who work diligently to fashion a creative solution to a problem that is controlled by federal or state law will be wasting their time and energy (unless a waiver has been obtained—a subject we will address in a moment). Similarly, a district office that attempts to usurp authority for making a decision which is clearly within the realm of the Stakeholders as a school level controlled decision will engender confusion and mistrust among the Stakeholders and district office personnel, thereby seriously impairing the Self-Directed School's chances for success.

As we shall see in Chapter 8, the principal plays an important role as an adviser to the Stakeholders regarding the decision-making process. Since the Stakeholders will not have been professionally trained in understanding federal and state law or in knowing all of the intricacies of district policies and procedures, it is the principal who will serve as their primary source of information regarding "external" matters affecting the education of the students. The principal must be well versed in all federal and state laws, rules, and regulations relating to the educational system as well as in all district policies and procedures governing the operation of the schools in the district. In addition, the principal must be knowledgeable in preparing and submitting requests for waivers, whenever such waivers are possible, from federal, state, or district controlled issues or policies.

Requests for Waivers

Most issues, we believe, can be identified as system controlled, district controlled, or school level controlled decisions. Moreover, in most cases, we believe that in order to foster efficiency and clarity, it is in the best interests of the participants in the educational process, including the Stakeholders, to accept the decision-making authority of another level in the system whenever responsibility for making that decision falls within the realm of the other level. In some cases, however, the issues that fall within the realm of another level may be such a critical aspect of the Stakeholders' effective implementation of a successful educational program that the Stakeholders may want to try to assume responsibility for that issue at the school level. In those cases, it may be possible to obtain a waiver from the federal, state, or district policy that otherwise would prohibit the Stakeholders from exercising control over that issue.

Waivers are not always available. Some issues are considered so important and so fundamental that they cannot be changed or modified. Constitutionally mandated equality of educational opportunity is one example of a policy for which no waiver can be obtained. There are other cases, however, in which federal, state, or district rules and/or regulations do not address fundamental rights but instead exist primarily for purposes of convenience of administration or record keeping. In these cases, it is often possible to obtain waivers. As an example, take the state-mandated laws requiring teachers and students to attend school a specified number of days each year. These laws have traditionally been interpreted (or are specifically written) to require that each school day be a "full" school day (unless otherwise approved by the state). Stakeholders in some states, recognizing the importance of dedicating time to working together in teams, have petitioned and successfully received waivers from the state law allowing them to close school early up to one day a week to create the time necessary to meet in clusters.

Again, one of the primary responsibilities of the principal of a Self-Directed School is to be knowledgeable in all aspects of the waiver process. The principal must know how to prepare and submit requests for waivers and must know which issues are subject to waivers and which are not. Given the demands that are going to be placed upon the Stakeholders and the severe time constraints within which they will have to work, every effort must be made to focus Stakeholders' energies on issues over which they have control. Investment of time and energy in preparing a request for a waiver when there is ultimately little chance of obtaining a waiver on a particular issue will only serve to undermine the Stakeholders' enthusiasm and commitment to the process.

Collaboration of District Office and Individual Schools

As we have stated, we believe that the majority of decisions affecting the operation of public schools can be identified as either system controlled, district controlled, or school level controlled decisions. This does not mean, however, that the assignment of a decision to a particular level will always be easy or that the individuals involved will always agree on the appropriate level at which a particular decision is to be made. Disagreement is especially likely to occur at the beginning of the process of implementing a Self-Directed School. Administrators and other district office personnel, who have been accustomed to assuming responsibility for making decisions which in a Self-Directed School system should be made by the Stakeholders, may have a difficult time letting go of the authority necessary to make the decision. Similarly, the new Stakeholders, in their quest to be meaningful contributors to the educational process, may have a tendency to overestimate the nature and extent of their authority.

Over time, as the respective roles of district office personnel and individual school Stakeholders become clearer, fewer disagreements should occur.

Some school systems that have commenced the process of implementing Self-Directed Schools have answered the question, "What are the decisions that individual schools can make?" by having the district administrators list the decisions they would be willing to allow schools to make. We believe that this district-directed process of deciding who decides what issues is fundamentally inconsistent with the principles underlying Stakeholder participation and the Self-Directed School.

A better way to allocate responsibility, we believe, especially at the beginning, is for district office personnel and individual school Stakeholders to discuss which issues will be handled by the district office and which will be handled by the Stakeholders at the school level. The focus should be on transferring as much authority as possible to the Stakeholders. However, the Stakeholders at some schools may not be as prepared to assume responsibility, in terms of their stages of development as team members, as those at other schools. That is why the allocation of responsibility between district office personnel and school Stakeholders must be made on a school-by-school basis.

In these meetings between district office personnel and school Stakeholders, the district office personnel are no longer the givers of directions, but instead are the providers of support and needed services. The primary role of the district office in a Self-Directed School system is to facilitate the decisions made by the Stakeholders. This is a far cry from the dictatorial posture assumed by most district offices today.

Once the district office personnel and school Stakeholders have identified an issue as being within the responsibility of the Stakeholders, they should discuss in detail how the district office can best facilitate the decision-making process and assist the Stakeholders in accomplishing their objectives. We suggest that the Stakeholders and district office personnel follow the steps outlined in Figure 7–3:

1. Develop a concept or objective statement for the issue.
2. Develop elaboration statements that address the specific ways in which the concept or objective statements will be achieved.

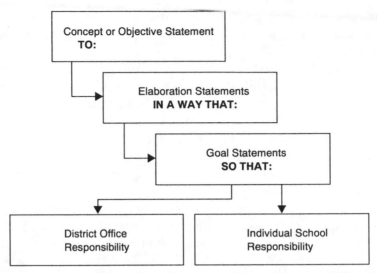

Figure 7–3. Joint Allocation of Responsibility (District Office Personnel and School Stakeholders).

3. Develop specific goals.
4. Allocate responsibility for action between the district office and the individual school.

The following is an example of how the district office personnel and school Stakeholders might jointly decide how to handle the issue of creating a challenging curriculum for the students in a Self-Directed School:

CONCEPT STATEMENT FOR CURRICULUM

TO: Develop a visionary curriculum that will assist our students to meet the needs of the twenty-first century.

ELABORATION STATEMENTS

IN A WAY THAT:

• Shifts the curriculum, instructional techniques, and assessment practices of our school to reflect the needs and skills necessary for the real world in the twenty-first century.
• Emphasizes an approach that consciously applies knowledge and methodology from more than one subject or discipline

to examine a central theme, issue, topic, or experience (that is, interdisciplinary studies).
- Allows a child's placement to be changed at any time it is determined to be in the best interests of the child's development considering his or her physical, intellectual, emotional, and social characteristics.

GOAL STATEMENTS

SO THAT: Students will be employable in a globally competitive marketplace—which results in an improvement in the quality of life for everyone.

ALLOCATION OF RESPONSIBILITY TO DISTRICT OFFICE

District office personnel will be responsible for:

- Facilitating the gathering and dissemination of research information.
- Allocating the time and money necessary to provide training and staff development.
- Coordinating the process of integrating the curriculum.
- Coordinating the resources for staff and Stakeholder development.
- Developing waivers for issues that may be in conflict with board policies or state regulations.

ALLOCATION OF RESPONSIBILITY TO SCHOOL STAKEHOLDERS

School Stakeholders will be responsible for:

- Evaluating the current curriculum in light of student and societal needs and what is known about future changes or developments in society or particular curricular areas.
- Conducting an assessment of the new skills needed by staff members and Stakeholders.
- Identifying new means of assessing student achievement.
- Determining how best to deliver the curriculum.
- Planning and implementing campus training activities (with the support of district office personnel).

The foregoing provides just a rough illustration of how district office personnel and school Stakeholders might allocate responsibility for a particular issue. It is not intended to serve as a comprehensive model or guide for responding to the needs of any particular district or school. Obviously, the ultimate plan agreed upon by district personnel and school Stakeholders will vary substantially from district to district and from school to school.

Step 2: Determining Which Stakeholders Participate in School Level Controlled Decisions

Once a decision has been identified as being a school level controlled decision, the next issue is to determine how the Stakeholders will work together to make the decision. This is a more complex issue than it might appear to be at first glance because not every Stakeholder will participate in the same capacity in every decision that is brought before the Stakeholders as a school level controlled decision.

There are many ways in which a Stakeholder—or any other person—can participate in the decision-making process. A Stakeholder may be an active decision maker with the power to cast a "vote," or he or she may just be serving in an advisory capacity, with the responsibility to provide information or make recommendations. In other cases, a Stakeholder may only need to be informed about a decision but play no active role in the making of the decision. The various roles that can be assumed by Stakeholders in the decision-making process are summarized in Figure 7–4. The letter abbrevia-

---

D   *Decision Maker.* Stakeholder is a member of the group that makes the decision.

S   *Suggestion Maker.* Stakeholder may suggest or recommend alternatives. In a healthy organization, any person should be encouraged to make suggestions and recommendations.

I   *Information Provider.* Stakeholder's role is to provide data or information.

Z   *Authorizer/Implementer.* Stakeholder is primarily responsible for making sure that decisions are initiated and implemented.

C   *Interested Participant.* Stakeholder must be informed of the results of the decision-making process in order to be able to take appropriate coordination action.

Figure 7–4.   Roles Played by Stakeholders in the Decision-Making Process.

tions in the figure will make more sense when considered in light of Figure 7–5, which we will discuss shortly.

In reviewing Figure 7–4, note that Stakeholders are not limited to a single role in the making of a particular decision. In fact, it is quite common for Stakeholders to assume more than one role at a time. This is especially true with respect to the role of suggestion maker, which is a role played by most Stakeholders most of the time—regardless of any other roles they assume. What is important is not that Stakeholders be limited to a single role. What matters is that all of the Stakeholders who are members of the decision-making body understand the roles they are assuming *before* the group starts to deliberate the issue at hand. Knowing the roles of each Stakeholder before discussions begin helps to clarify what is expected of each Stakeholder and to minimize the confusion and frustration that can result from a debate in which the participants are unsure about the nature and scope of their roles.

Recognizing the various roles that Stakeholders can assume is only the first step in understanding the logistics of the decision-making process at the Self-Directed School. The next step is to agree upon the roles each category of Stakeholders will assume on each particular issue presented for a decision. In some cases, all of the Stakeholders will be acting as decision makers. In other cases, some may be decision makers, some may be suggestion makers, and some may be information providers. The role assumed by each category of Stakeholders will depend on the nature of the issue being considered.

As with virtually every aspect of the Self-Directed School, there is no one right way to assign or agree upon the roles to be played by the Stakeholders in the decision-making process. We believe, however, that the development of a decision-making structure chart can help to simplify the process of assigning roles and to minimize any confusion concerning which Stakeholders are playing which roles on which decisions.

The decision-making structure chart (Fig. 7–5) constitutes a simple graphic representation of how the site council of a Self-Directed School might begin to assign to the Stakeholders who are members of the site council the roles to be assumed by those Stakeholders in the deliberations on various issues to be brought before the council. The left-hand column of the chart lists the issues that are to be considered by the site council for decision. Across the top of

ISSUE OR QUESTION TO BE CONSIDERED	CATEGORY OF STAKEHOLDER					
	TEACHERS	PARENTS	BUSINESS LEADERS	COMM. REPS.	DIST. OFFICE	PRINCIPAL
Selecting new teachers	D, S, I	S, I	S, I	S, I	C, Z	D, S, I
Developing school budget						
Discipline plan						
Homework policy						
Grading policy						
Student grouping						
Teacher training program						
Site council training program						

Figure 7–5. Decision-Making Structure Chart.

the chart is listed each category of Stakeholders serving on the site council. For each issue to be considered by the site council, a letter of the alphabet (taken from Fig. 7–4) appears below each category of Stakeholders to indicate the role of that category of Stakeholders in deliberating on that particular issue.

The chart in Figure 7–5 reflects that the site council of this school has decided that with respect to the hiring of new teachers the primary decision makers will be the principal and the teachers who are site council members. Other Stakeholders on the site council (parents, business leaders, and community representatives) are to serve as suggestion makers—with responsibility for providing input and making recommendations but with no final decision-making authority. The district office representative on the site council must be informed of any hiring decision and is responsible for taking the actions necessary to implement that decision (for example, ensuring that the necessary paperwork is completed).

Figure 7–5 is obviously incomplete. As the site council matures and begins to tackle the other issues listed, it will be very important for the site council to assign specific roles to each of its members for each issue the council is to consider.

A decision-making structure chart cannot be imposed on a school by command. Instead, it needs to be developed by the Stakeholders working together in clusters. A separate decision-making structure chart should be prepared by each cluster since each cluster will vary in its Stakeholder membership and in the issues it considers.

The primary advantage of a decision-making structure chart is that it clarifies in advance the roles to be played by each cluster member on each issue brought before the cluster for a decision. As a result, the members do not have to make guesses about what the nature of their participation should be or about what is expected of them during the course of deliberations. This, in turn, helps to ensure an orderly discussion that enables the group to deal thoroughly and effectively with the issue being considered.

Conclusion

In a Self-Directed School system, significant decision-making authority is transferred to the Stakeholders of the individual schools. Stakeholders are not, however, empowered to make all decisions affecting the operation of the school or its educational environment. Even in a decentralized model of public education, three basic levels of hierarchical structure will continue to exist: the federal and state level, the school district level, and the individual school level. What is unique about a Self-Directed School is that the vast majority of decisions affecting the educational environment of a school are made at the individual school level (as opposed to the school district level, as is presently the case in traditionally organized school districts).

The allocation of decision-making authority is one of the keys to success in a Self-Directed School. Each Stakeholder must understand who is to be responsible for making which decisions. For the Stakeholders of a school to spend time wrestling with developing solutions to problems that are ultimately governed by state or federal law or by school district policy will not only waste the Stakeholders' time and resources, it will also undermine the Stakeholders' enthusiasm for and commitment to the collaborative decision-making process.

We believe that the models presented in the chapter for identifying the levels of decision-making authority and for identifying the various roles that can be assumed by Stakeholders involved in the decision-making process will help clarify the roles played by each participant in the Self-Directed School and help maximize efficiency and effectiveness.

8

What's Left for the Principal to Do?

> *As for the best leaders, the people do not notice their existence. The next best, people honor and praise. The next, the people fear; and the next, the people hate. When the best leader's work is done, the people say, "We did it ourselves."*
>
> Chinese philosopher Lao-Tzu

Throughout this book we have emphasized the importance of the roles played by Stakeholders in Self-Directed Schools. In a successful Self-Directed School, the Stakeholders formulate strategies, identify objectives, establish policies, and implement plans and programs—all with a view toward serving the school's mission, which itself is a reflection of the Stakeholders' vision for the school.

In fact, Stakeholders are so vital to the viability of a Self-Directed School that one might conclude that the principal is no more than a symbolic figurehead—an unnecessary appendage that may be severed from the school without having any significant impact on the operation or performance of the school. But the contrary is true. The principal of a Self-Directed School remains a critical determinant of the success or failure of the school, albeit in a far different role than that played by the principal of a traditional school. The challenge confronting principals of Self-Directed Schools is that their responsibilities are more diverse and less obvious than the responsibilities of principals of traditional schools. The principal of a Self-Directed School must therefore be more sensitive, more aware, more flexible, more informed, and, in the end, more qualified and capable than his or her counterpart at a traditional school.

The role of the principal in a traditional school is pretty well defined. The principal in such a system is, first and foremost, an enforcer of rules. In this capacity, the principal's primary responsibility is to control behavior and to dictate to the staff the methods and procedures for accomplishing the stated objectives of the school. The district office supports the principal's efforts through numerous policies, practices, and procedures that define acceptable and unacceptable conduct within the school. The district also provides a generous supply of district administrators who work in conjunction with the principal to maintain close supervision of the operation of the school. A strict chain of command exists, with the principal clearly in charge of, and responsible for, the operation and performance of the school.

The principal of a Self-Directed School does not function within the same sort of guidelines that apply in traditional school settings. "Control," "rules," and "chain of command" are out. "Facilitation," "teamwork," and "shared responsibility" are in. Principals of Self-Directed Schools must be able to play a number of roles. Moreover, they must be able to recognize in an instant the role required of them in each particular situation. This chapter examines the various roles played by principals of Self-Directed Schools. We shall see that a Self-Directed School puts *greater* demands on a principal than a traditional school. These demands, while challenging, are certainly not impossible to meet. The Self-Directed School principal will, however, have to learn new behaviors and assume new leadership styles. The old methods of administration simply will not work.

The Changing Role of the Principal: The Evolution of Principal Leadership

While so far we have referred to only two types of principals—those of traditional schools and those of Self-Directed Schools—it should be noted that there are at least three distinct schools of thought about school management and the appropriate role of the principal as the administrative head of an educational institution. The first school of thought about principal leadership centers on traditional, hierarchical management. In this type of system, the principal's role is, as we have just stated, clearly defined and a part of a highly detailed and rigidly maintained chain of command.

The second view of principal leadership arises from the numerous studies conducted in recent years attempting to identify the key components of effective schools. Many of these studies have concluded that the single most important factor in the success or failure of a school is the performance of the school's principal. On the basis of these studies, many proponents of school reform have argued for the decentralization of school management and the granting of additional power and authority to individual principals. Under the principal empowered model, the principal of a school assumes much of the decision-making power and authority formerly reserved to the superintendent and/or the school board. This new-found power granted to the principal obviously broadens the principal's role in the overall performance of the school. Principals are free to impose their own ideas and to contribute their own creativity in ways precluded under the traditional system of school management. Schools functioning under a principal empowered model tend to be more individualistic and less structured than those in traditional systems. Still, the principal in a principal empowered model remains the authoritative head of the school and, as such, imposes the same sort of hierarchical structure that is present in traditional school systems.

The third school of thought about principal leadership is the Self-Directed School concept. Self-Directed Schools require a new vision of principal leadership—a complete rethinking of the role of the principal as the leader of a group of actively participating Stakeholders. The principal in a Self-Directed School does not give orders or attempt to control behavior or dictate policy. Instead, the principal shares his or her responsibilities with the Stakeholders.

Figure 8–1 summarizes the respective roles of the principal under each of the school management theories we have just discussed.

We have briefly reviewed the various schools of thought about school management and the corresponding roles of the principal under each model. The purpose of such discussion has been to highlight the confusion that arises in education circles concerning the

Traditional Management	Principal Empowered Model	Self-Directed School
Direct people	Consult people	Build trust and inspire teamwork
Make decisions	Get input for decisions	Facilitate and support cluster decisions
Contain conflict	Resolve conflict	Assist clusters to resolve conflict
Train individuals	Develop individual performance	Expand cluster capabilities
Superintendent has the power	Principal has the power	Stakeholders have the power
Superintendent determines principal evaluation	Superintendent and staff determine principal evaluation	Superintendent and site council determine principal evaluation

Figure 8–1. The Three Views of Principal Leadership.

role of the principal under a collaborative, or a Self-Directed School, model. One of the issues that has attracted the most attention and engendered the most debate is whether shared decision-making authority means that clusters are to function as advisers to the principal or as equal decision makers. In attempting to resolve this issue, some groups (most notably and most predictably, state principals' associations) have concluded that shared decision-making authority requires that ultimate authority reside with the principal and that school site councils and other clusters serve only as advisers to the principal. In some states, both the elementary and the secondary school principals' associations have questioned the legality of schools' site-based decision-making plans on the grounds that such plans place the principal in a political environment that, in some cases, makes it impossible for the principal to exercise independent judgment and maintain authority.

This type of thinking is both short-sighted and destructive. The true impediment to excellence in schools is excess structural and hierarchical control. Empowering principals does result in incrementally better schools than are possible under traditional theories of school management because layers of unproductive bureaucracy are eliminated. The principal empowered model will not, however, result in the type of innovative and creative schools that are necessary in order to produce students capable of functioning in the competitive global environment of the twenty-first century. Principal empowered models simply transfer power from one hierarchical level to another. Stakeholders are still stifled. The enormous pool of talent and energy offered by Stakeholders is still not tapped.

Those who argue for what is essentially a principal empowered model (that is, site-based management with school clusters limited to serving as advisers) are prisoners of the past. They are bound by their training and experience to outdated methods of hierarchical management. Site-based decision making, as it exists in Self-Directed Schools, does *not* mean concentration of power in the hands of the principal. It also does not result in the erosion of the principal's authority, as state principals' associations argue. Effective principals of Self-Directed Schools are individuals who are able to learn new ways of leading, new ways of interacting, and new ways of behaving. The resulting system will be one of truly *shared* decision-making authority and responsibility.

Moving to Self-Directedness: How Fast Can It Be Done?

Moving a school from a traditional management style to a self-directed, collaborative institution will require training, as we discussed in Chapter 4, and, perhaps most importantly, *time*. Simply abandoning all traditional, hierarchical methods and implementing new, collaborative styles will not work. The principal must give up control and decision-making authority only when and to the extent that the Stakeholders are ready to assume and exercise such control and authority. Indeed, the most difficult task for the principal to accomplish will be to strike the right balance, at any particular time, between exercising power and relinquishing control.

The principal will need to know when to make tough decisions and when to allow Stakeholders to make those decisions; when to step in to accomplish a task and when to sit back and permit others to work out a solution. Given the techniques that are taught in most university administration programs and enforced in most school systems, there will be a tendency for principals to err on the side of exercising too much control and allowing too little room for cluster growth and development. While these sorts of judgment errors by principals may be excusable during the early stages of a Self-Directed School, principals must be ever vigilant of being tied to their past ways and must continually strive to be sensitive to the demands imposed by collaborative activity at a truly self-directed school.

Just as too much control will stifle the capability, initiative, and creativity of Stakeholders, so too will too little guidance, direction, and discipline if Stakeholders are unprepared to assume the responsibilities of self-governance. The transition to a Self-Directed School must be gradual, with the principal slowly relinquishing authority as the Stakeholders acquire the skills and knowledge necessary to function effectively in collaborative groups. In Chapter 2 we discussed the three stages of cluster development in the establishment of a Self-Directed School. These three stages correspond to distinct changes in the evolution of the leadership roles assumed by the principal as a school becomes self-directed. As the school evolves, so do the roles and responsibilities of the principal.

Stage 1: The Traditional Role of the Principal

During stage 1 of cluster development, the principal functions primarily in the familiar role of direction giver in a hierarchical management system. Because few, if any, of the Stakeholders will have had any experience working in collaborative, self-directed groups, there is likely to be a lot of confusion, uncertainty, and frustration— at the beginning. It will be up to the principal to keep the Stakeholders focused on the goal of becoming self-directed. The principal will need to use skills and energy to harness and direct the natural excitement that will be created by the prospect of change. As Stakeholder clusters grow in experience, the principal must learn to provide more information and relinquish more responsibility to the clusters.

The key word during stage 1 of cluster development is *training*. The greatest responsibility of stage 1 principals is to arrange for training for all of the Stakeholders, including themselves. It is essential that the principal and other Stakeholders receive training in all of the team skills required for effective collaborative activity, including problem solving, decision making, reaching a consensus, and team-building techniques. The principal needs to be trained in such skills as facilitating effective team meetings and managing and supporting change. Only by providing a basis for team activity can the principal ensure a transition to stage 2.

Stage 2: The Principal Empowered Role

During stage 2, cluster members become united and develop feelings of belonging (to each other) and independence (from the restrictions of traditional hierarchies). By this stage, the principal is functioning in the role contemplated by the principal empowered model of school management. Instead of unilaterally dictating plans or directing activity, the principal increasingly solicits input from Stakeholders before making decisions. With the opportunity to have a greater voice in the operation of the school, Stakeholder clusters begin to discover their potential and slowly begin to assert themselves and demand more responsibility. The principal must recognize this growth in confidence and must respond by pulling back from in-depth involvement in the clusters and allow the clusters to manage their own projects and programs. The principal can then concentrate on coordinating cluster activities and working with clusters on long-range planning.

The Stakeholders of a school that is in stage 2 may have a tendency to revert from time to time to old ways of doing things. This regression to dependence on the principal is natural, just as it is natural for children experiencing the tremendous changes of adolescence to occasionally revert to childlike dependence on their parents. Nevertheless, the principal must resist falling into the old ways, which would, in essence, "fulfill" the Stakeholders' dependence. Instead, the principal must give the cluster members the support and training necessary for them to overcome their dependence and assume an even greater level of leadership and responsibility.

Stage 3: Collaborative Leadership

The principal of a Self-Directed School that has achieved stage 3 uses collaborative leadership techniques and does very little directing of the activities of others. Instead, the principal's focus is on guiding and facilitating.

By stage 3, clusters are carrying out their own tasks, running their own programs, and developing new plans and strategies. Cluster members have developed the necessary trust, security, and confidence to be actively involved in every aspect of the operation of the school and to strive continually for improvement and excellence.

By being flexible, supportive, prepared, knowledgeable, and open minded, the principal can encourage and inspire the Stakeholders to develop the creative solutions and programs so necessary to achieving greatness in education. We now turn to a discussion of the skills needed by stage 3 principals.

Being Strong Enough to Be Weak: What Principals Do in Self-Directed Schools

Empowered clusters in Self-Directed Schools take on many of the responsibilities traditionally reserved for the principal in hierarchically managed schools. These tasks include hiring new staff members, setting goals and objectives, designing and implementing staff inservice programs, developing curriculum plans, and whatever other matters the Stakeholders may decide to become involved in. As clusters assume more responsibility for the operation of the school, the role of the principal changes radically. As one might imagine, such change may elicit fear and resistance. For many principals the transition is not easy.

The real weakness of traditional principals is that they fail to tap into the enormous wealth of talent offered to schools by Stakeholders. Most traditional principals operate under the quasi-military model of management, which emphasizes conformity and adherence to command rather than creativity, innovation, and productivity. Traditional principals are judged on their ability to run a tight ship and to maintain an efficient operation. By contrast, the strength of the new, collaborative principal is measured by the ability to take advantage of the full potential of the school's Stakeholders. A successful principal is a principal who can effectively facilitate the self-leadership of others.

Some people believe that a Self-Directed School will diminish the principal's ability to create a great school by eliminating the principal's power base. The fundamental flaw in this type of thinking is that without the meaningful involvement of truly empowered Stakeholders, there cannot be a "great" school. The demands placed on education by our rapidly changing world have made it impossible for one person to know it all and lead others to the desired goal.

Empowered Stakeholders, contributing their talents, skills, and insights, are the key to building successful schools. And the effectiveness of the principal is the single most important factor in developing empowered Stakeholders. During the early stages of cluster development, effective principals encourage self-direction to happen. During the later stages, they allow it to happen.

Principal leadership clearly does not mean the same thing in a Self-Directed School as it does in a traditional school. In Self-Directed Schools principals play roles that are quite different from those assumed by principals in traditional schools. The skills required of Self-Directed School principals are complex and not easy to master, particularly for individuals who have received all of their training and experience in traditional management systems. Many principals who make the transition from traditional management models to collaborative, site-based decision-making models may feel torn between attending to the needs, interests, and demands of their Stakeholders and responding to the priorities established by their superintendents and school boards. They may feel pulled in two directions at the same time, perhaps even developing feelings of incompetence and inferiority as they live out the old cliché about serving two masters and serving neither one well.

We believe that much of this apparent conflict results from confusion about the role of the Self-Directed School principal. Principals are accustomed to thinking of themselves as the most important figures in the operation and performance of their schools. By definition, the word "principal" refers to someone or something that is foremost in importance or the leading person or main participant. In such a role and in such a capacity, the principal is the person responsible for the actions taken and the programs instituted by the school. The traditional principal's master is the school superintendent and/or the school board.

The master of a Self-Directed School principal is, without question, the Stakeholders. Although the principal of a Self-Directed School retains ultimate accountability for the school's performance, responsibility for the operation of the school rests with the Stakeholders. Whereas the role of the traditional principal is to "manage" the Stakeholders, the role of the collaborative principal is to motivate, inspire, and support the Stakeholders.

We believe that it is a serious misnomer to talk about the "role" of a principal. In fact, all principals are required to serve in a number of roles. Even in a traditional management system, the principal is a manager, administrator, counselor, and so on. Some of these activities are performed by the new collaborative principal, but many new roles are added. One way to view the job of the collaborative principal is as an assortment of roles, not all of which are internally consistent and some of which may, in fact, compete with one another from time to time. This partially explains why it is necessary to use a medley of terms to describe the principal of a Self-Directed School: administrator, coach, facilitator, coordinator, instructional leader, and principal. The terms give us just a flavor of the sheer diversity of the roles that the Self-Directed School principal will be required to perform.

The Five Hats of the Self-Directed School Principal

The Self-Directed School principal will be required to wear at least five hats: attitude builder, facilitator, administrator, coach, and adviser (Fig. 8–2). As an attitude builder, the principal is required to model and implement the principles of collaboration and teamwork. As a facilitator, the principal must assist clusters in accomplishing their goals by providing support and guidance. As an administrator, the principal must handle the day-to-day details of operating the school and maintain a functional system for communicating information to Stakeholders. As a coach, the principal is required to serve as an inspirational leader and assist in the development and maturation of school clusters. As an adviser, the principal must provide the Stakeholders with information concerning applicable federal, state, and district laws, rules, regulations, and policies, as well as any additional information that might affect cluster operations or Stakeholder decisions. The challenge facing each principal will be not only to master each role but to recognize which role applies, or which roles apply, in each particular situation.

The Principal as an Attitude Builder

Traditionally, principals have been hired based on a set of specifications—good management skills, strong leadership abilities, and so on—that are largely inappropriate in the context of the Self-Directed School. Some principals who were hired according to these requirements will find it difficult to adapt their behaviors enough to achieve

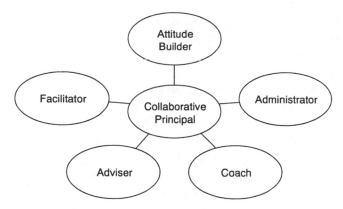

Figure 8–2. The Five Hats of the Self-Directed School Principal.

success in a collaborative environment. Other traditional principals will flourish in their new roles as facilitators and motivators, as opposed to direction givers and managers.

We believe that one of the most critical ingredients in determining a principal's ability to adapt to the collaborative world of the Self-Directed School is attitude. Successful principals in Self-Directed School environments possess the following characteristics:

- They do not believe that any one person has all the answers. Therefore, they do not insist on providing answers or dictating decisions, nor do they allow any one other person to do so.
- They believe that principals do not need to make all key decisions—so they don't.
- They believe that neither they nor the school can succeed without the combined contribution of *all* of the Stakeholders, and therefore they avoid action that might intimidate Stakeholders or constrain their input.

All of the foregoing characteristics are indicative of an open mind, a willingness to consider new ideas, and an honest respect for alternative points of view. These are all attributes of the type of attitude that must be present in all Stakeholders in order for a Self-Directed School to be successful. The role of principals is to create such an attitude through their actions and by means of Stakeholder training programs designed to develop self-esteem and mutual respect. The principal who is successful as an attitude builder creates a climate in which:

- Active participation and involvement by all Stakeholders is accepted and encouraged.
- Risks are viewed as valuable learning experiences and not as failures waiting to happen.
- Everyone feels a high degree of involvement in formulating tasks and experiences a concomitant commitment to accomplishing them.
- The Stakeholders are comfortable with each other and with their working environment and are willing to take risks.
- Communication is open and honest among Stakeholders so that people feel free to express their thoughts, feelings, and ideas.
- Conflict and disagreement are considered natural and are dealt with positively with an emphasis on resolution and not on personality quirks.
- Cluster members experience a sense of security and a strong sense of belonging to both their group and the school.
- Diversity of opinions and ideas is encouraged.
- Flexibility in thinking and sensitivity to others are practiced.
- Cluster members work together to arrive at high-quality consensus decisions and have the acceptance and support of the group members to carry them out effectively.

The Principal as a Facilitator

Facilitating a group means exactly what it appears to mean—doing the things that are necessary to make it easier for the group to accomplish its goals and perform its tasks. For the principal of a Self-Directed School, facilitation of cluster activity takes two distinct forms: guidance in group interactions and assistance in carrying out group decisions. Since providing assistance in implementing group decisions is by far the easier role to perform, we will discuss it first.

To a certain extent, a Self-Directed School principal is a hired gun. Once a cluster has made a decision on a matter that has been delegated to it for action, it is the principal's responsibility to carry out that decision. Accordingly, the principal will need to provide whatever materials, equipment, communications, or other forms of support may be necessary to implement the cluster's decision.

Facilitation of cluster activity *prior* to the reaching of a final decision is a much more complex concept for a principal to master. In this sense, facilitation means providing guidance to clusters in resolving conflicts or formulating ideas without unduly influencing the cluster with the principal's personal biases or opinions. Frequently clusters may call the principal into cluster meetings in order to obtain assistance in the resolution of personal conflicts or to answer questions about laws, regulations, or other matters. In their role as facilitators, principals must confine their participation in discussions *solely* to matters on which they have been consulted. The principal who becomes embroiled in the relative merits of the discussion risks upsetting the delicate balance of trust and respect established by the cluster members. The result may be the substitution of the principal's judgment for that of the cluster—with the ultimate cost being the destruction, or severe disruption, of the cluster's confidence and independence.

Subordinating personal ideas and opinions to the responsibility of acting as a facilitator may be difficult for some principals. After all, most principals have been trained to be efficient administrators—they have learned to identify the problem, make a decision, and implement it. When acting as facilitators, principals may become privy to discussions of issues on which they have strong personal opinions as administrators. Principals must remember that they are present as facilitators and not as cluster members and must be careful not to exercise their positions as principals to influence or control the decision of the group.

Some people have argued against Self-Directed Schools on the grounds that acting as a facilitator requires a principal to surrender administrative control—to the detriment of the school. At first blush it might appear that this is true. After all, a principal who becomes aware of a cluster issue by virtue of his or her involvement as a facilitator may, because of background, training, or experience as an administrator, have definite ideas about what the ultimate resolution of an issue should be. That principal will certainly be tempted to substitute his or her judgment for that of the cluster, either to ensure efficiency (that is, avoid a long drawn-out discussion) or prevent a mistake. But the principal who imposes his or her judgment will really end up causing long-term *inefficiency* by undermining Stakeholder confidence and development. With respect to the temptation to avoid mistakes, we make two observations:

- Mistakes are often valuable learning experiences, and making a mistake can often be more beneficial in the long run than not making one.
- What may appear to the principal to be a mistake might, in fact, constitute a creative and effective solution to the problem being discussed.

Principals who can remain faithful to their roles as facilitators will be rewarded with seasoned, competent, reliable, and creative Stakeholders who will take initiative and assume responsibility.

Principals are effective facilitators of collaborative activity among cluster members if they can do the following:

- Accept the reality that the principal's primary responsibility is to help the cluster members achieve their objectives rather than to lead or control the cluster in its decision making.
- Accept that the cluster members may achieve their objectives in ways and with methods that are different from those the principal might choose.
- Accept that the group interaction in which cluster members engage is a far more valuable learning process for the cluster members than listening to what the principal might say about the process.

The Principal as an Administrator

The principal's role as an administrator goes hand in hand with the role of facilitator. As a facilitator, the principal's primary function is to provide support to the clusters. As an administrator, the principal's primary responsibility is to provide the one resource that is a prerequisite to effective cluster management: *information*. Information is power, and power leads to control.

In traditional management systems, information is jealously guarded by the elite individuals fortunate enough to be in positions of power. These "leaders" rightly understand that if they were to share their information with the "masses," their authority, that is, their ability to control the behavior of others, would be undermined. That is why most school districts and school administrators treat budgetary, personnel, and certain other "sensitive" issues as *top secret*. It's as if the revelation of such information to teachers or other Stakeholders would threaten national security. As a result, teachers and other Stakeholders are in most school systems forced to work in the dark. They are asked to do their best for the school but are not given access to the type of information (for example, budget allocations, educational programs, and physical facility planning) that would allow them to develop truly effective curricula.

It's easy to see, then, that the role of administrator in a Self-Directed School is perhaps the principal's most important role. It is up to the principal to maintain an efficient system for communicating information. As the visible figurehead of the school, the principal remains the primary liaison between the school and the district office. All district policies, rules, and goals, as well as any other matters communicated by district personnel to the principal, need to be disseminated to the Stakeholders.

In addition to serving as a conduit for the communication of district matters, the principal is responsible for maintaining open lines of communication between and among Stakeholders. Thus, it is up to the principal to assist and administer the communication of information between clusters. Each cluster must be fully cognizant of, or at least be able to easily obtain complete information about, the workings of every other cluster. Without a strong and effective system of sharing information, a school attempting to implement cluster management will quickly disintegrate and implode on itself in a chaotic state of *non*management. The left hand must know what the right hand is doing—and it is up to the principal to see that it happens.

In carrying out the responsibilities of an administrator, the principal of a Self-Directed School will have to perform the following tasks:

- *Manage relationships with people outside the school.* As we mentioned above, the principal of a Self-Directed School remains the figurative leader of the school. As such, the principal is expected, especially by people outside the school (the superintendent, district administrators, board members, and so on), to manage the school's contacts and relationships with the school system and with the community. This does not mean that the principal will be the only one who makes such contacts. As the clusters mature and develop, cluster members will become increasingly more visible as school leaders and will gradually play more important roles in interacting with individuals outside the school. The principal will remain, however, the person most responsible for coordinating and facilitating relationships outside the school.

- *Coordinate the state and district planning process with the Self-Directed School.* While Self-Directed Schools are highly autonomous—and we advocate as much independence and autonomy from the district office as possible—it is a fact of life that no school can be completely autonomous. All schools, no matter what their degree of self-governance, remain subject to certain rules, regulations, and policies established by district offices. One of the areas in which the district's policies will continue to apply is the area of goals and strategic plans. The state may also establish plans or goals. The principal needs to make sure that these state and district policies are taken into account in any school planning process.
- *Coordinate the school's planning process.* In addition to communicating information about state and district policies (to ensure that strategic plans established by the school are complementary to state and district policies), it is the responsibility of the principal to coordinate the school planning process itself. It is not the principal's responsibility to develop the plan, but it is his or her responsibility to coordinate the planning process with all of the Stakeholders.
- *Manage "administrivia."* We have coined the term "administrivia" to refer to all of the small and highly detailed matters arising in the administration of any organization or entity. If such details are not handled, the result will be the gradual suffocation of the organization or entity in its own paperwork or red tape. In a school, administrivia includes record keeping (attendance, lunch program, enrollment, and so on), conference planning (parents and students), correspondence, and, in the case of a Self-Directed School, communication of information. The principal needs to ensure that all administrivia is managed properly.
- *Terminate employees.* As a coach, the principal works with teachers to improve and support their teaching methods and abilities. As an administrator, however, it remains the principal's responsibility to terminate any staff member deemed, after training, feedback, and other support, by the employee-evaluation cluster to be ineffective. Termination and nonre-

newal of a contract is highly regulated and subject to administrative details, particularly in union states. It is up to the principal, in carrying out this distasteful but often necessary task, to see that all i's are dotted and t's are crossed in the termination process.

* *Manage tasks and responsibilities not yet delegated to the clusters.* It will take several years for the clusters to assume responsibility in most of the areas that are appropriate for collaboration. Until the clusters have accepted this responsibility, the principal needs to continue to manage these areas.

The Principal as a Coach

The coaching role of the principal focuses primarily on developing team players and instilling a sense of teamwork. Just as a sports coach must work to mold a unified team from a collection of diverse individuals, so, too, must a principal work to bring together diverse Stakeholders to function as an effective, collective unit. In reality, professional sports coaches have an advantage: Their team members possess the specific athletic skills and talents necessary to make contributions. The coach's primary responsibility is simply to instill the athletes with a sense of team play, whereby they can then contribute their skills to the collective good of the team.

The principal of a Self-Directed School, by contrast, is frequently put in the position of working with Stakeholders who do not have the skills necessary to make contributions. Most Stakeholders—in fact, most people in the United States—have no training or experience in working in groups. Our society has emphasized individual accomplishments over group activities. As a coach, then, the Self-Directed School principal must not only develop a team but must also arrange for training of the Stakeholders to provide them with the skills necessary to be effective team players. (The concept of training for the Self-Directed School is discussed in detail in Chapter 4.)

Of course, the principal must also receive training to become an effective team player. As the principal develops in this area, his or her behavior can serve as a valuable model for other Stakeholders.

A crucial element of the principal's role as coach is to sense the level of maturity of a particular cluster and to strive continually to extend this maturity by delegating more and more responsibility to the cluster. Eventually, the principal will withdraw completely from active participation in all but a few selected clusters in which he or she serves as a regular, equal member.

As a coach, the principal engages in the following tasks:

- *Allows and assists clusters to develop their own goals.* In order to be effective, a cluster must shape its own goals and performance standards. As a coach, the principal's role is to assist in the development of independent clusters. At the outset, the principal is deeply involved in virtually all of the clusters. As part of this involvement, the principal models effective team player behavior and provides guidance regarding group problem-solving strategies and methods for building consensus. As the clusters mature, the principal assumes less of a role until he or she is involved as an active participant in only a limited number of clusters. Even in those clusters, the principal needs to remember that he or she is only a member of the cluster and not the leader or dictator. The principal may provide suggestions and input, but he or she should be careful not to have his or her comments interpreted as mandates. This is especially important in contexts in which Stakeholders are accustomed to hearing "orders" from the principal. Principals must let clusters struggle with the issues of developing goals, performance standards, and plans. Principals must demonstrate patience and keep their silence when clusters discuss the specifics of their plans.

- *Builds commitment and confidence.* As an integral part of developing the independence and confidence of clusters, Self-Directed School principals must work to build the commitment and confidence of individual Stakeholders. This is done through training activities, effective modeling techniques, and positive reinforcement of individual Stakeholders. As Stakeholders learn the skills and attitudes necessary to be effective team players, their level of involvement and participation in cluster activities will increase. With increased participation will come a deepening of Stakeholder commitment. Confident and committed Stakeholders will accept both individual and group accountability for cluster decisions—the ultimate sign of mature cluster interaction and management.

- *Empowers others.* An effective Self-Directed School principal nurtures the power of others. If Stakeholders are to become involved, they must believe their participation is more than a token display of magnanimity on the part of the principal. They must believe that their input will be taken seriously and that their efforts will result in changes. In short, they must feel a true sharing of power. Empowering others allows the principal to take full advantage of all of the skills and talents offered by the Stakeholders. Stakeholders may be suspicious, especially at the outset, of a principal's attempts to share power. The principal must convince the Stakeholders that the sharing of power is legitimate and lasting. The "empowering" principal will be more of a colleague than a boss, working side by side with Stakeholders to resolve problems and develop plans.

- *Develops Stakeholders.* In developing effective Stakeholders, the Self-Directed School principal needs to monitor the level of sophistication achieved by individual Stakeholders. In any given situation, some Stakeholders may need individualized training, some may need informal coaching, some may require only positive reinforcement or role modeling, and some may be ready for the delegation of additional responsibility. The principal's challenge is to recognize the type of support required by each Stakeholder and respond in kind. Thus, the principal may serve as a coach by discussing teaching strategies with a classroom teacher or by working with a parent who is a chairperson of a cluster to develop techniques for running effective meetings. By encouraging representatives from the community to become involved in school projects and later asking them to be responsible for the coordination of such projects, the principal can, through training, coaching, and delegation, provide an opportunity for the school to benefit from the expertise of all Stakeholders.

The Principal as an Adviser

The principal acts in an advisory role on such issues as laws, rules, regulations, court decisions, and policies. In addition, as we have discussed, the principal has the initial responsibility for the appropriate training of individual Stakeholders and clusters. Thus, as an adviser, the principal is involved in the following tasks:

- *Strengthens the level of cluster skills.* The principal's role in training consists of analyzing and determining each Stakeholder's ability for working in a collaborative environment. Since most Stakeholders will have had no significant training or experience in group interactive activities before becoming involved in a Self-Directed School, the principal needs to either provide training programs for Stakeholders or make arrangements for them to attend workshops. The specific kinds of skills Stakeholders need and the types of training activities advisable are discussed in Chapters 5 and 4, respectively. In addition to arranging for formal training activities, however, the principal can, through effective role modeling, provide valuable informal training. Principals who are effective role models behave the way they would like Stakeholders to behave. For example, to encourage others to arrive on time for meetings, the principal should consistently be on time. Similarly, if principals want others to listen carefully to what they say, then they too should be careful listeners. Modeling is probably the most powerful teaching technique available to the principal.

- *Keeps clusters informed about laws, regulations, and policies.* This is a *critical* responsibility of the Self-Directed School principal. Empowered Stakeholders bring enthusiasm, commitment, and creativity to a school. They do not, however, bring with them any significant knowledge of federal, state, or local laws or regulations governing the administration of public education. It is up to the principal, then, to educate the Stakeholders about all laws, regulations, and policies that may be applicable to the management of the school. This will require the principal to conduct at least a minimal amount of formal training regarding the legal aspects of school administration. More importantly, the principal must constantly be aware of the issues that school clusters are dealing with so he or she can step in to provide guidance concerning applicable laws and regulations whenever necessary.

- *Assists the site council in making waiver requests.* As we have seen, in some school districts and in some states, a school may apply for a waiver of a law or policy. As an adviser, the principal needs to keep clusters informed of the exitence of and possibilities offered by such waivers. The principal may also be required to prepare applications for obtaining waivers.

A Day in the Life of a Self-Directed School Principal

We have briefly reviewed the various roles that the principal of a Self-Directed School must play in order to be successful. During the course of each day, the principal will, in all likelihood, have to assume all five roles. For purposes of illustration, we have outlined below a "typical" schedule for a Self-Directed School principal. Obviously, a one-day example cannot give a complete picture of the challenges faced by a Self-Directed School principal. Still, a one-day schedule can help to identify the differences between the traditional principal's roles and the roles of a Self-Directed School principal.

TYPICAL SCHEDULE FOR A SELF-DIRECTED SCHOOL PRINCIPAL

7:15 A.M.   Arrive at school and check electronic mail for messages from teachers, other principals, or the district office. Review schedule for the day, noting list of things to be accomplished that day and the rest of the week.

7:30 A.M.   Take walk around campus to see that all duty personnel are in place.

7:45 A.M.   Join technology cluster meeting. The cluster is attempting to build a technology budget for the next school year. The budget will be presented first to the total faculty for consensus and then to the site council for approval. The technology cluster has already developed a technology improvement plan, which has been approved by the faculty and the site council. The cluster is now struggling with

	budget issues. Leave the meeting to join another cluster meeting.
7:55 A.M.	At cluster's request, join inservice cluster meeting already in progress. Cluster members are designing an inservice program to be presented to the faculty the following month. The cluster submitted an initial plan to the faculty two weeks ago, and the faculty suggested several revisions. Make a short presentation on ways to get to consensus on a matter when there is disagreement. Cluster works to finalize new inservice plan to be presented to the faculty that afternoon for approval.
8:05 A.M.	Bell rings to start school. Take a quick walk through the school to see if there are any problems with substitutes or other personnel. Sometimes a teacher may just want to tell the principal something very quickly before school starts. Being available to students, teachers, the school secretary, and parents is an effective way to obtain information that may help the principal anticipate where problems will occur during the day.
8:15 A.M.	Do a teacher evaluation. The faculty has developed a new teacher evaluation program for teachers on the highest level of the state's teacher classification system. The faculty had been upset with what they consider to be the demeaning nature of the state-mandated appraisal procedure. After developing an alternative evaluation system, the faculty had applied for, and received, a waiver from the district and the state. The principal's evaluation is only one aspect of the overall appraisal.
9:15 A.M.	Two students arrive at the office as a consequence of fighting in the bathroom. Under the teacher-and-student–designed discipline plan, teachers have the authority to assign lunch detention, after-school detention, and other forms of discipline. In cases where students will be placed in in-school suspension, the principal is required to listen to the students' stories and conduct an investigation prior to the suspension.

9:45 A.M.   Begin preparing weekly faculty bulletin. The bulletin lists meetings for the week and other information that needs to be communicated to staff members (for example, status of cluster meetings, agenda for faculty meeting, and applicable developments in education). The bulletin is prepared on computer and sent by electronic mail to each teacher. A paper copy of the bulletin, when finalized, will be placed on the staff bulletin board.

9:47 A.M.   Receive telephone call from parent asking why her child received a C in Science rather than her usual A. Suggest that the child's teacher call the parent after school. Parent indicates that she would like to know before noon. Inform parent that teacher will call before noon and parent is happy. At a Self-Directed School students and parents are priorities.

10:00 A.M.   The teacher responsible for assisting the principal with the faculty meeting agenda walks into the principal's office and requests assistance in finalizing the agenda for the afternoon faculty meeting. The agenda is finalized.

10:15 A.M.   Meet with the teacher who gave the student a C to ask him to call the parent. Provide the teacher with details of the phone conversation with the parent.

10:20 A.M.   Teach class while the teacher calls the parent.

10:40 A.M.   Return to office to resume work on faculty bulletin.

10:47 A.M.   Representative from the local bank drops in to talk about a problem he is having in working with the "Shrimps Are Us Corporation." The "Shrimps Are Us Corporation" is a cluster of students, teachers, and business leaders working together to establish a small business as part of a curriculum emphasizing economics and social skills. (The bank representative is a member of the cluster.) The corporation intends to travel to the coast to purchase shrimp for resale to residents of the community. The corporation needs $2,000 from the bank to purchase the shrimp. The students have pre-sold $1,500 worth of shrimp. The bank representative

	notes that the principal's old pickup is paid off and suggests that the principal use it as collateral on the loan. As a team member, the principal agrees to the request (but is thankful that his wife's name is not on the title).
11:15 A.M.	The first student group arrives in the cafeteria for lunch. Walk to cafeteria and talk to students. Take a quick walk around the school. Visibility and availability are keys to achieving success.
11:35 A.M.	Resume work on faculty bulletin. Finish typing bulletin on the computer and send via electronic mail to each staff member. Place one hard copy on the staff bulletin board.
11:50 A.M.	A teacher drops in to discuss the status of the school garden cluster's work and request the principal's attendance at a meeting. The cluster apparently has an issue on which it cannot reach consensus and wants the principal to be the facilitator at this one meeting in an effort to reach an agreement.
12:05 P.M.	Go to cafeteria to observe and talk to students. Walk to outside areas where students are enjoying recess. Observe and talk to students.
12:20 P.M.	Return a call to another principal to discuss a student who has moved to her school. The conversation also focuses on a recent article in the local newspaper regarding a school board member who had stated a preference for using homogeneous groups in district schools. Note that this school's site council has already taken the position that grouping is a teacher decision. Prepare a letter to the superintendent informing him of the school's position on this issue. Remind the superintendent that the board has agreed the matter is for individual schools to decide.
12:35 P.M.	Eat lunch with students.
12:50 P.M.	Work with the school secretary to review the details of amounts spent by each cluster and send the report to clusters by electronic mail. Bemoan the fact that the computerized district budget is not yet available to teachers.

1:00 P.M.	Make a short visit to all classrooms.
1:30 P.M.	Meet with mathematics department head to develop a waiver that would allow the school to use a math book that is not on the state adopted list.
1:55 P.M.	Return telephone call to a secretary in the district office confirming receipt of a message from the superintendent about a scheduled meeting next week. Note that district personnel still do not trust electronic mail or fax machines.
2:00 P.M.	Return call to parent wanting to know the school's policy on whether her children can take a week's vacation to go on a family trip.
2:10 P.M.	Return call to a vendor requesting permission to substitute an item on a school order.
2:15 P.M.	Two students arrive in the office to work with the principal in learning how to use a new interactive computer program on navigation.
3:00 P.M.	Visit a classroom in which teacher had requested a principal visit to review the discipline plan with her students. The teacher had been having problems with the class and wanted to make sure that her students understood what would happen if inappropriate behavior continued.
3:30 P.M.	Bell rings for end of school day. Observe loading of buses and departure of students.
3:35 P.M.	Attend faculty meeting. One cluster has the responsibility to conduct an energizer (a quick three- to five-minute activity to revitalize the faculty, who typically have a low level of energy by 3:35 P.M.). Three clusters report to the total faculty on projects and plans they have been working on. The inservice cluster gets faculty approval for the next month's program and activities.
4:05 P.M.	At conclusion of faculty meeting, meet with the attendance cluster at its request to discuss the writing of strong letters to parents of some students who have been arriving at school late on a regular basis.
4:15 P.M.	Leave school for home, taking the day's mail and three telephone calls to return to parents.

In the course of a workday, an effective Self-Directed School principal navigates many roles, changing roles as circumstances evolve. The principal relies on one set of behaviors when working with a parent who has a concern about a teacher, another set when working with a cluster to design a new discipline plan, and still another set when ensuring that the lunch schedule fits the needs of the staff members and students. Depending on the situation, then, the principal serves one or more of the following functions: attitude builder, facilitator, administrator, coach, and adviser.

Who's Accountable?

In the Self-Directed School, the principal is presented with what may appear to be a dilemma: "If I successfully empower my Stakeholders and pass authority and responsibility on to them, will I be held accountable for the successes and failures of the school, or will the Stakeholders—the real decision makers—be held responsible?" Although it may seem anti-intuitive at first, it soon will be very clear to the superintendent, the board, and the principal that the principal remains accountable.

In a collaborative, high-involvement environment such as a Self-Directed School, the principal is not prized for the ability to keep the lid on or to run a tight ship. Instead, the principal is judged on the basis of his or her ability to listen effectively, use conflict resolution, build consensus, build teams, facilitate Stakeholder problem solving, and delegate and hold individuals and clusters responsible for their performances.

If a Self-Directed School is successful, it is because the principal facilitates and empowers the Stakeholders to make decisions. If a Self-Directed School fails, it is because the principal exercises too much power over the Stakeholders or otherwise fails to empower the Stakeholders to become decision makers. In what appears to be a contradiction, a Self-Directed School principal must be strong enough to be weak. The principal must be strong enough as an attitude builder, facilitator, administrator, coach, and adviser to release the power and authority that has traditionally been reserved for the position of principal. Through modeling, coaching, advising, and providing training, the principal must allow a new leadership to emerge—the collective leadership of the Stakeholders working together in teams. The principal is then held accountable for the performance of the Stakeholders. Principals of Self-Directed Schools are subject to the same types of pressures (and will ultimately be prized for the same types of abilities) as are coaches of professional athletic teams. These involve the ability to motivate, guide, and facilitate success through the delegation of responsibility to those who are closest to the performance being sought. Some principals will survive and flourish in this new collaborative style, whereas others will not.

Evaluating the Principal

The principal of a Self-Directed School does not perform the same type of job that the principal of a traditional school performs. A traditional school principal is, basically, a manager who is responsible for making and implementing the decisions that shape the school's curriculum and work environment. The principal of a Self-Directed School is neither a manager in the traditional sense of the word nor a decision maker. Instead, a Self-Directed School principal is an attitude builder, facilitator, administrator, coach, and adviser, working with Stakeholders to make and implement decisions.

Given the dramatic differences between the job of a traditional principal and that of a Self-Directed School principal, it is apparent that the established techniques for evaluating the effectiveness of a principal are woefully inadequate for assessing the effectiveness of a Self-Directed School principal. In most cases today, principals are evaluated—usually by their "superiors" (the superintendent)—based on their ability to efficiently manage the school environment. "Successful" principals, under this kind of evaluation system, are principals who can effectively control the behavior of the faculty and other staff members, either through motivation or intimidation, or some combination of the two.

The Self-Directed School requires a new kind of evaluation system. Principals are not judged on their management, or control, skills but on their ability to work with others. This means that the people with whom the principal works—the Stakeholders—should play a major role in the evaluation of the principal. The superintendent may still have a say in assessing a principal's performance, but it is the Stakeholders who know the most about the principal's true skills and abilities. Accordingly, their evaluation should be given significant weight.

As we have stressed throughout this book, there is no one correct model for a Self-Directed School. As such, there is no one correct form for assessing the principal's performance. Appraisal techniques and methods vary from school to school based on the input and judgment of the Stakeholders. As a starting point, however, we have included in Appendix 8–1 the principal evaluation form drafted by the Stakeholders of McQueeney Elementary School. We believe it is illustrative of the kinds of things upon which an evaluation of a Self-Directed School principal should be based.

Conclusion

We began this chapter with the question, "In a Self-Directed School, what's left for the principal to do?" The supposition of many educators, particularly principals, is that self-directedness, or the sharing of power with Stakeholders, so undermines the authority of the principal that there is nothing left for the principal to do. Thus, the principal becomes a figurehead, a mere scapegoat for any problems that arise. We believe that this position is ludicrous. In fact, the demands placed upon a Self-Directed School principal are so great and so diverse that the issue is not whether there is anything left for the principal to do. Instead, the question that should be asked is, "How can we find individuals with the skills, talents, and abilities necessary to be successful principals of Self-Directed Schools?"

Traditionally, principals have possessed the authority to command the school and make all of the "tough" decisions. This power is so ingrained in our thinking about education that it has sometimes been referred to as the "divine right of principals." Well, as Bob Dylan might say, "the times, they are a-changin'." We can no longer afford to have our educational curriculum and environment controlled by one individual. Society today is simply too complex, too diverse, and too rapidly changing to be understood by any one individual. The role of the principal must be redefined. The divine right must be delegated and shared with others—with Stakeholders who are actively and enthusiastically involved in shaping the educational environment of our youth.

As we move to Self-Directed Schools, the challenge is to successfully reshape the role of the principal. The principal is so central to the traditional authoritarian system of school governance that the first question to be asked of any plan to modify a school's management system is, "What does it do to the role of the principal?" Any plan that leaves the principal's traditional role intact is fraudulent and will ultimately fail. Fundamental change is required. Business as usual is not acceptable. It is the dawning of a new day. What is needed is principals who are strong enough to be weak—principals who can build attitudes, facilitate, administer, coach, and advise. The challenge facing schools, indeed facing all of us, is to locate and develop individuals with vision, commitment, and ability who can succeed in the new world of the Self-Directed School.

Appendix 8–1 Evaluating the Collaborative Principal

The Principal as an Attitude Builder

1. Our principal encourages participation by everyone.

   10   9   8   7   6   5   4   3   2   1
   encourages   encourages   not at all
   everyone   some groups

2. Our principal believes that each Stakeholder is a resource and can make a significant contribution to the school.

   10   9   8   7   6   5   4   3   2   1
   strongly   believes that   believes that
   believes   some can   a few can

3. Our principal establishes an environment in which everyone feels a high degree of involvement in formulating tasks and has a commitment to accomplishing these tasks.

   10   9   8   7   6   5   4   3   2   1
   everyone   some feel degree   no one
                          of involvement

4. Our principal creates a climate where diversity of opinions and ideas is encouraged.

   10   9   8   7   6   5   4   3   2   1
   almost always   some of the time   never

5. Our principal creates a climate in which communication is open and honest among Stakeholders and people feel free to express their thoughts, feelings, and ideas.

   10   9   8   7   6   5   4   3   2   1
   almost always   some of the time   never

6. Our principal is an effective listener and truly hears and evaluates what is said by Stakeholders.

   10   9   8   7   6   5   4   3   2   1
   effective   somewhat   ineffective
                          effective

The Principal as Facilitator

7. Our principal accepts the reality that his or her primary responsibility is to help clusters achieve their objectives rather than to *lead* the clusters.

   10   9   8   7   6   5   4   3   2   1
   facilitates clusters   takes leadership
   role for each cluster

8. Our principal makes it easier for the cluster to do its work by supporting the group interactive process. The principal provides guidance, when requested, in resolving disputes and reaching consensus.

   10   9   8   7   6   5   4   3   2   1
   helps each cluster   provides little
   assistance

9. Our principal effectively implements cluster decisions.

   10   9   8   7   6   5   4   3   2   1
   effective   somewhat   ineffective
   effective

10. In carrying out cluster decisions, our principal does not attempt to substitute his or her personal judgment for that of the cluster.

    10   9   8   7   6   5   4   3   2   1
    does not substitute   substitutes his or
    his or her judgment   her judgment

The Principal as Administrator

11. Our principal has a good working relationship with the rest of the school system and community.

    10   9   8   7   6   5   4   3   2   1
    excellent   fair   poor

12. Our principal keeps the school's Stakeholders informed about the district and state planning process.

    10   9   8   7   6   5   4   3   2   1
    Stakeholders   Stakeholders
    well informed   not informed

13. Our principal manages the day-to-day operation of the school—such as facilities maintenance, lunch program, and student attendance.

10	9	8	7	6	5	4	3	2	1
well managed								poorly managed	

14. Our principal is an effective communicator of information relevant to school matters.

10	9	8	7	6	5	4	3	2	1
effective				somewhat effective				ineffective	

15. Our principal maintains and manages a communication system whereby all Stakeholders, on a daily basis, are aware of, or can receive information about, the status of all cluster activity or other matters within the school.

10	9	8	7	6	5	4	3	2	1
excellent communication				fair communication				poor communication	

The Principal as Coach

16. Our principal delegates appropriate responsibilities to clusters.

10	9	8	7	6	5	4	3	2	1
appropriate delegation to clusters								little delegation to clusters	

17. Our principal allows clusters to develop their own goals and plans.

10	9	8	7	6	5	4	3	2	1
excellent				fair				poor	

18. Our principal inspires commitment and confidence by effectively empowering Stakeholders and trusting in their judgment.

10	9	8	7	6	5	4	3	2	1
excellent				fair				poor	

19. Our principal is a team player and effectively models the skills required to work with others.

10	9	8	7	6	5	4	3	2	1
effective				somewhat effective				ineffective	

The Principal as Adviser

20. Our principal keeps clusters informed about laws, rules, regulations, and policies relating to school decisions.

10	9	8	7	6	5	4	3	2	1
excellent				fair				poor	

21. Our principal has provided, or arranged for, training on a continual basis in group skills (how to work in groups, how to reach consensus, how to solve problems, and so on).

10	9	8	7	6	5	4	3	2	1
excellent training				fair training				poor training	

9

Facilitating the Self-Directed School

It is time for a new generation of leadership, to cope with new problems and new opportunities. For there is a new world to be won.

John Fitzgerald Kennedy
Television address, July 4, 1960

There are those who manage schools and there are those who teach students. You would think it would be a natural collaboration. Unfortunately, the relationship between the district office—the managers—and individual schools—the Stakeholders—often results in something akin to a private cold war. There has always been a joke told at schools about how the district office has all the money and the schools have all the kids. And, as Rudyard Kipling observed about the directions East and West in *The Ballad of East and West* ("Oh, East is East and West is West, and never the twain shall meet"), the money and the students seem to occupy hopelessly separate camps—with little or no chance of getting together. In addition, there is a feeling in many schools that district office personnel are out of touch with the reality of education. After all, how can they know what is best for the students when they have not been in the classroom in years?

248

These are old jokes, but no one is laughing anymore. Today there is a dire need for reform in our school systems. We cannot afford the confusion, waste, miscommunication, mismanagement, inefficiency, and low staff morale that are the products of the prevailing cold war between most district offices and their schools. If we do not do a better job of coordinating the management and teaching functions of our school systems, we will continue to operate an educational system in which 50 percent of the students fail. Will our customers, that is, students, parents, and business leaders, stand for this? We think not. They will look, and in some cases are already looking, for satisfying alternatives to the public school system.

The Traditional "Dysfunctional" District Office

The problem with our public education system lies in its organizational structure. Most school systems in the United States today are stratified into numerous levels or echelons. Consequently, teaching is performed at one level, school management at another, curriculum planning at another, staff development at another, budget decisions at another, and policy decisions at still another. Given the hierarchically stratified organizational structure of this kind of school system, it is almost impossible for these separate levels to interact or, more importantly, to understand one another. Only when these divergent groups are allowed to be equally involved in the design and process of educating our youth across organizational levels will we be able to maximize the power of our educational system.

The reason it is so hard for most school systems to deliver a quality educational program is that most systems are organized as hierarchies which resemble the military model. Under this kind of organizational structure, the superintendent is the general, supported by a cadre of deputy, associate, and assistant superintendents sprawled below him or her in pyramid fashion. Those working in this pyramid of power work at different levels with different perspectives. Formal communication in this context is primarily vertical, from boss to subordinate, and vice versa, with little or no emphasis on horizontal communication.

Fifty years ago, centralized, hierarchical district offices were effective for two reasons. First, the administrative bureaucracy was not as developed, not as complex, and not as enormous as it is today. Since fewer people were involved, there were fewer opportunities for miscommunication and inefficiency. In the past two decades, however, many district offices have increased the number of administrators by more than 200 percent. The result has been increased administrative red tape and inefficiency. The second, and more important, reason centralized district offices were effective fifty years ago is that society was much simpler then and the demands placed upon educators and the educational system were far less challenging than they are today.

Fifty years ago, information technologies were relatively primitive, and communication between locations was slow. Things happened at a slower pace and there was no need for school systems to respond quickly. Today, however, rapid advances in technology have created a world in which information is virtually limitless, and communication between remote locations is instantaneous. Changes occur with blinding speed—changes in our neighborhoods, in our states, in our country, and in the world. It is impossible to buy an accurate world map today. Names of countries change faster than mapmakers can print maps. The satellite-communicated newspaper *USA Today* has become one of our most accurate sources of information. When things change this fast, there is simply no time to wait for information to go up the chain of command and for decisions to come back down.

David Osborne and Ted Gaebler, in their book *Reinventing Government*,[1] give the following example of how technology has zoomed past the bureaucracy of the typical school district hierarchy:

> Consider the school principal who discovers students wearing beepers to stay in contact with their superiors in the drug trade. In a centralized system, the principal asks the school board to promulgate a regulation about beepers. By the time a decision comes down, six months later, the students are carrying mobile phones.

In today's complex, rapidly changing educational environment, the pressure for accelerated decision making by the district office is causing school boards and superintendents to rethink the way school systems are organized. Alvin Toffler,[2] in discussing alternative gov-

---

[1]David Osborne and Ted Gaebler, *Reinventing Government* (New York: Penguin Books, 1992).

[2]Alvin Toffler, "Introduction," in Clement Bezold, ed., *Anticipatory Democracy* (New York: Vintage Books, 1978).

ernment organizational structures, describes two possible responses to the need for an administrative structure that can respond quickly:

> One way is to attempt to further strengthen the center of government, adding more and yet more politicians, bureaucrats, experts, and computers in the desperate hope of out-running the acceleration of complexity; the other is to begin reducing the decision load by sharing it with more people, allowing more decisions to be made "down below" or at the "periphery" instead of concentrating them at the already stressed and malfunctioning center.

Traditional school boards and superintendents instinctively reach for Toffler's first alternative. When test scores drop or are not high enough to please the board, the board hires more central office administrators—that is, "experts"—to solve the problem. When one principal misuses a school's activity fund, the superintendent centralizes the accounting process for the activity fund accounts for all schools and hires two more accountants to manage the funds. Even school districts that seem to acknowledge the need for reform by "talking the talk" about implementing changes have a tendency to revert to Toffler's first alternative. This explains how some districts have talked about implementing site-based decision making and then turned around and hired a director of site-based decision making, which seems to us to be an oxymoron.

We believe that traditionally organized central offices are actually dysfunctional. Rather than supporting or creating an effective educational environment, they hinder the functions and purposes of the educational system.

School boards and superintendents who believe in the concept of the Self-Directed School accept Toffler's second alternative—the decentralized approach. They move responsibility for most decisions out of the central office to the periphery, into the hands of the Stakeholders at the individual school level. To transfer control to those who work down where the rubber meets the road, these superintendents need to develop a new and different approach to managing their school systems. They must find a way to utilize the strengths of both the traditional hierarchical model and the new nonhierarchical model.

The question addressed in this chapter is, "Can the Self-Directed School function in a school system that is operated in a bureaucratic, hierarchical manner?" Our conclusion, after working with and observing various types and kinds of leadership—or lack of appropriate leadership—at the district office level is that a Self-Directed School can only exist in a school system where collaboration, shared decision making, and respect for the concept and philosophy of the Self-Directed School exist. Most of the time this will mean working in a school system that is organized in a nonhierarchical manner.

Having just stressed the need for a nonhierarchical central office, we should point out that there are some responsibilities and activities managed at the district office that cannot be managed effectively in a completely decentralized organization. To attempt to manage the routine and structured functions of a business office (such as payroll or district budget) in a nonhierarchical way is not in the best interest of the Self-Directed School. *Complete* decentralization results in inefficiency and confusion that will negatively impact the operation of the Self-Directed School.

There are many areas in the operation and management of a school system in which there are routine and structured decisions and procedures. These are areas in which the problems have been encountered so often that the resolution and handling of the problems are routine. On the other hand, there are numerous other areas in which the problems are not simple or mundane. Instead, the problems are complex and challenging—requiring creativity and enthusiasm for their resolution. We believe that an effective central office is really a hybrid of hierarchical and nonhierarchical management. Routine or purely management problems are handled by the hierarchical side of the office. Unstructured situations, whose resolution calls for initiative and imagination, are entrusted to the nonhierarchical area of the district's organization. The remainder of this chapter explains how these two very different organizational structures can operate within the same school system at the same time.

The New Hybrid District Office

The new functional district office has both a hierarchical and a nonhierarchical organization (see Fig. 9–1). We believe that the district office must change from the purely bureaucratic, hierarchical model typically found in most school systems in the United States to include nonhierarchical strategies that use self-directed teams or clusters like the ones we have described in this book for the Self-Directed School. However, for the reasons discussed in Chapter 7, the district office must also keep some decision-making responsibilities and certainly must retain the management of such crucial functions as the purchasing of major equipment and the handling of payroll, food services, and transportation. Even though some of these functions, for example, food services and transportation, may be contracted out to private companies, the district office must still retain the responsibility for coordinating the activities to be performed by these private companies.

For several decades we have had good examples of highly decentralized school systems: Clark County, Nevada, in the 1960s; Cherry Creek, Colorado, in the 1970s; and Dade County, Florida, Salt Lake City, Utah, and Edmonton, Alberta, Canada, in the 1980s and early 1990s. None of these highly decentralized school systems can be classified as a totally nonhierarchical organization. Each system has implemented both a hierarchical, vertical network and a nonhierarchical, horizontal network. Since most of us have worked in hierarchical organizations in the past and, as a result, understand how they work, we will not elaborate on the hierarchical side of these district offices. However, since few, if any, of us have worked in a nonhierarchical organization, we will examine the nonhierarchical side of district office organization.

The Nonhierarchical Organization

A nonhierarchical district office organization can perhaps be best envisioned in schematic form through the use of concentric circles. The left side of Figure 9–1 is what we believe a nonhierarchical organization looks like. The diagram suggests that a nonhierarchical district office organization can be conceived as a group of concentric and interlocking circles. At the center of the organization is the superintendent, whose overall responsibility for the organization justifies a central and separate position. Surrounding the superintendent is a small management team that works with the superintendent in a focused manner. Orbiting the small management team is a series of clusters, represented by circles, that contain school district facilitators working in teams.

The interrelated circles indicate that, unlike in a conventional hierarchy, there are no vertical lines of reporting, supervision, or responsibility. People in the various circles interact with each other in clusters as necessary and appropriate, but without the degree of structure inherent in a hierarchy.

It should be noted that the concept of a small management team is not reserved for nonhierarchical organizations. Many school systems and other organizations with elaborately defined hierarchical management structures are, in fact, operated by top management teams.

What distinguishes nonhierarchical organizations from hierarchical organizations is the way the middle managers work. Instead of being concerned about making reports to higher ups or feeling a constant need to justify their actions to supervisors, as is the case in a hierarchy, middle managers in a nonhierarchical organization work on an equal footing with everyone else in the organization. In Figure 9–1, we have depicted this kind of group interaction as a series of circles surrounding the superintendent and core management team. Each circle, or working group, is led by a facilitator and is made up of those individuals who are in the best position to work on the particular problem at hand. Membership in the working groups is fluid, not static, as needs change and situations evolve.

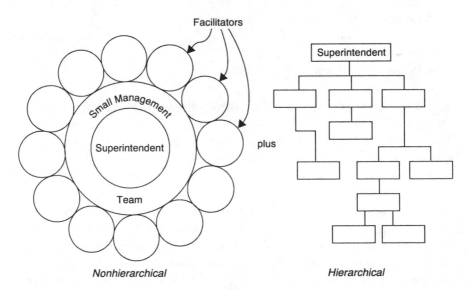

Figure 9–1. The Hybrid District Office.

To help understand how the nonhierarchical side of the hybrid district office works, we will discuss and describe the functions and roles of the superintendent, the small management team, and the facilitators.

The Superintendent

There are five leadership beliefs and skills that superintendents must understand and effectively utilize if they are to create and provide an environment that will support a collaborative or Self-Directed School system. First, superintendents must understand that their actions are critical to the development of Self-Directed Schools. Not only must the superintendent "talk the talk" of collaboration, but he or she must "walk the walk." The superintendent must adopt and implement the set of beliefs in collaborative activity that underlie every aspect of this book.

Second, the superintendent must understand that it is a particular kind of superintendent leadership that counts. It is not the charismatic, innovative high flyer that moves the whole collaborative school culture forward. Rather, it is a more subtle kind of leadership that makes collaboration meaningful to others. The superintendent's leadership style needs to take the form of facilitating the development of a collaborative school system by enabling and empowering the Stakeholders to identify and frame problems, to work collectively to understand and solve the problems, and to change the situations that resulted in the problems in the first place.

The third belief that an effective superintendent must have is that leadership should be shared with, and should come from, a variety of sources within the school system—that is, from individual schools and faculty members, community representatives, business leaders, and even students. In the fully functioning collaborative school system, many Stakeholders are leaders. As the culture of collaborative schools develops, leadership is shared almost equally by superintendents, district office administrators, principals, and Stakeholders.

The fourth, and possibly most difficult, task for the superintendent of a Self-Directed School system is to provide leadership in determining which issues and tasks will be handled by the nonhierarchical side of the organization and which are best assigned to the traditional hierarchy. The superintendent needs to work with the total school system, from the board of education to the staffs of the individual schools, to develop a system for identifying which issues are "pure" administrative management issues (and therefore best handled by a hierarchy) and which issues require the creativity and imagination of Stakeholder teams for effective resolution. The superintendent's ability to develop consensus support for this system of identifying issues will go a long way toward determining the overall success of the Self-Directed School system.

The fifth, and possibly the most important, challenge for the superintendent is developing an entrepreneurial environment in the district office. The superintendent should encourage the district office staff to develop new and innovative ways to assist schools. Communications should not be restricted by the boundaries of functions and levels within the district office. Everyone should be looking for ways to assist the schools within the district.

The Management Team

The nonhierarchical side of the hybrid district office rests responsibility in the hands of both individuals and teams. Although this seems to some superintendents and management team members to be a sure recipe for indecision, it is not. In fact, the sharing of power and responsibility among members of a small management team may be the easiest concept for a Self-Directed School system to implement. As we stated earlier, many hierarchical organizations in both business and education are operated by management teams. In these organizations, the members of the small management team work together as an effective group to manage the activities of the organization.

The key to the success of the central office management team is to avoid the elitism that is so easily acquired by management team members. If the team members view themselves as "managers" and as "mini-superintendents" with power over all others in the organization, then the Self-Directed School concept will fail. All that will happen is that another layer of hierarchy will have been created, and the school system will soon return to traditional ways of doing things.

Success, then, depends on the ability of management team members to become facilitators and supporters of the collaborative process. Each member of the team must receive training in and must adopt the same skills and beliefs identified here as crucial for the superintendent to have.

The District Facilitators

In the nonhierarchical district office, there are no subject area coordinators, no staff development coordinators, and no traditional middle-management administrators whose job it is to see that the schools in the district follow the district guidelines, philosophies, and beliefs. Instead, the district office is comprised of facilitators, some of whom are members of the management team, whose job it is to work with individual schools to identify school needs and to provide support to those schools.

We believe that much of the power that district offices have wielded in the past must be transferred to the individual schools. This transition of power cannot occur overnight, however. Instead, it must happen gradually and be accompanied by assistance and support. It is important to remember that many of the new responsibilities have never been assumed by the schools, and without support from the district office, the schools will surely fail.

The difference between the old way of doing things and the new way is that in the past the district administrators developed any new ideas and programs and then directed the schools to implement them. In a Self-Directed School system, the district facilitator works with the Stakeholders of the individual schools, as an adviser or facilitator, to help the Stakeholders develop and implement the programs they determine are the best for their schools. The district facilitator, working as a consultant to the Stakeholders, can usually provide valuable resources that would be difficult for a busy school staff to locate or even know about. Having worked with other schools in the district, the district facilitator will be able to share ideas about what other schools have tried and what has been successful.

Decentralization does not mean that each school must develop its own programs from the very beginning. It does mean that each school has the freedom to develop its own programs. This may mean that a school might select a program or idea from an array of programs that have already been developed. Alternatively, a school might modify or refine a program to fit its needs. Having a district office facilitator to assist in this process can save a lot of time.

To be able to assist schools that wish to become self-directed, the district office should have a limited number of facilitators whose job it is to work with individual schools to identify needs and to provide support. Each facilitator should be fully responsible to each school. The facilitators will serve as support for the schools desiring change.

Every school should have the right to communicate with and seek support from any facilitator. In many cases, several facilitators may join together to provide support to an individual school. By creating an entrepreneurial spirit among facilitators, the district office can create healthy competition. Facilitators who are effective and supportive will have many schools, or "clients," clamoring for their attention. Those who are not effective will not have clients and should therefore not continue to serve as facilitators.

Coordinating Hierarchical and Nonhierarchical Functions

The nonhierarchical side of the district office can be involved in both nonhierarchical functions, such as helping to develop new programs for individual schools, and hierarchical functions, such as developing new procedures to be followed district-wide. Figure 9–2 illustrates how this can happen. The left-hand side of Figure 9–2 depicts a cluster led by a district facilitator which is working to develop a new procedure for schools to use when accounting for student activity funds. This is clearly an issue where it is necessary for all schools in the district to follow the same procedures and guidelines (a hierarchical function). After the recommended procedure has been developed by the cluster, the procedure is given to the superintendent for comments or refinement. Once everyone has agreed on the procedure, the responsibility for auditing each school is given to the district internal auditor.

In addition to working on the development of new procedures for managing student activity funds, the district facilitators might also work with an individual school to help the Stakeholders develop a technology plan. (This kind of cluster is depicted on the right-hand side of Figure 9–2.) As part of his or her role as a consultant, the district facilitator might provide knowledge and experience in the development of computer programs. In addition, and perhaps more importantly, the district facilitator might assume responsibility for locating local business leaders or university professors who are experts

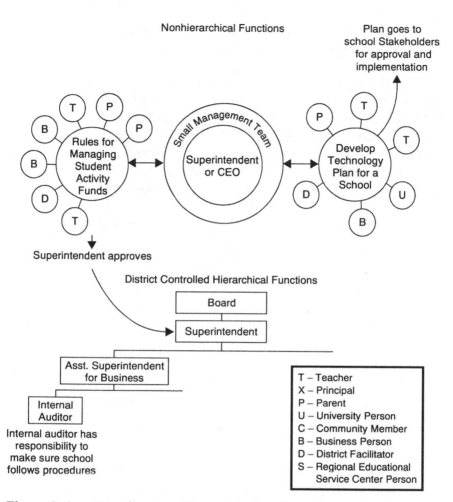

Figure 9–2. Coordinating Hierarchical and Nonhierarchical Functions.

in the field of technology to serve as cluster members. All of the parties then work together to develop an effective technology plan.

This random access characteristic of the district office cluster organization provides substantial strength. Because people are free to communicate without regard to hierarchical structure, full utilization of the district's communication network is permitted. The organization has dynamic fluidity and can continually create and extinguish elements without the complex issues of seniority, rank, and position that are raised in the reorganization of any hierarchy. In addition, the district office has low overhead because it has minimal administrative structure to support. There is high flexibility in using resources because each facilitator can easily assume different roles and assignments. The rigid, hierarchical organizational structure is absent. Meeting the needs of the schools is facilitated by the authority each facilitator has to initiate activities on a school's behalf and to involve other facilitators, teachers from other schools, university professors, and even corporate training specialists to implement the plans desired by each school. The facilitators work through informal networks and work groups that are defined by the needs of the school.

Epilogue

Moving Forward:
The Self-Directed Learner

I forget what I was taught. I only remember what I have learnt.

Patrick White

Tell me, and I'll forget. Show me, and I may not remember. Involve me, and I'll understand.

Native American saying

This book is about the need to reform the organizational structure of schools in the United States. Our current system of public education is failing at an alarming rate. Nearly 50 percent of our students either drop out of school before graduation or "successfully" complete their primary and secondary education with insufficient knowledge, abilities, and skills to function effectively in today's world. Something must be done. We can no longer blithely proceed with business as usual. If something is not done to reverse the snowballing trend of failure, we will soon find ourselves in the frightening position of being in the economic and competitive position of a Third World country.

We believe that our educational system can be successful only if there is a fundamental change in the way schools are managed and organized. The traditional, hierarchical organizational structure is inefficient, ineffective, outdated, and archaic, as this book has emphasized. It has simply outlived its usefulness. Whereas it might have been a satisfactory system of management fifty years ago when the global economy was dominated by the United States and there was virtually no competitive pressure for technological or informational advancement from any other country, it is woefully inadequate in today's highly competitive global economic environment. In the age in which we live, information is expanding and becoming available at an exponential rate. Computer technology, robotics, and advanced information-processing systems have revolutionized our society. The times, they are a-changin'—and our educational system must change just to keep up.

Minor tweaking of the educational system will not work. We have tried that before. New math, open classrooms, hooked on phonics, and whole language instruction are all examples of programs designed to increase student performance. Without commenting on the effectiveness of any of these (or other) programs to bring about incremental increases in test scores, grades, or other forms of assessment, we see that none of the innovations have gone far enough to bring about the kinds of fundamental changes that are necessary to achieve long-term success.

American businesses have learned painful lessons about maintaining the status quo or sticking to traditional ways of doing things. They have learned that the traditional ways no longer work. To compete with Japan, Germany, and other industrialized economies, U.S. businesses have had to restructure their organizations and rethink the way they do business. In many successful companies the hierarchical organization has been flattened, and much of the responsibility and authority for management and control of the company has been moved to the employees, who work on collaborative teams to develop strategies and solve problems.

The same kind of restructuring that has occurred in business needs to take place in education. For too long, decisions relating to education have been made by administrators and politicians—individuals far removed from the classroom and from any significant interaction with students. If we are ever going to achieve success, then we must transfer authority over the decision-making process to the individuals who are most closely involved in the actual process of education—the Stakeholders. By allowing the Stakeholders to become actively involved in the operation of our schools, we can take full advantage of the special skills and abilities offered by those individuals. In the end, the Stakeholders, working together in collaborative groups, can develop, design, and implement programs that are far more innovative, far more creative, and far more effective than those that could be achieved by a number of individuals working separately or independently.

The Self-Directed School will allow for the kind of creativity, involvement, participation, and Stakeholder enthusiasm that will be necessary to slay the dragon of educational failure. Stakeholders of the Self-Directed School will feel like members of a team. By being allowed to play a significant role in the operation of the school, they will develop feelings of ownership and will be more committed to the success of the school than Stakeholders of traditional schools.

But the Self-Directed School is not only about the adult Stakeholders who are involved in the educational process—the teachers, the parents, the principal, the community representatives, the business leaders, and the district office personnel. What the Self-Directed School is really about is the students. What we ultimately hope to create or imbue at the Self-Directed School is the self-directed learner.

We believe that the primary goal of our educational system is to create self-directed learners—students who are creative thinkers and problem solvers, students who are internally motivated to explore the universe of knowledge, and students who can successfully work with others in collaborative groups to develop and implement plans, programs, and strategies.

Self-directed learners are not passive recipients of information. Instead, they are actively involved in the exploration and search for information and understanding. The educational environment necessary to support the self-directed learner is depicted in Figure E–1. The self-directed learner guide presented in the figure is based on five postulates, which underlie the process of assisting students to become self-directed learners:

- *Most learning is not the result of direct instruction.* Instead, learning usually results from student participation in a meaningful setting that emphasizes real-world applications. In this kind of participatory environment, teachers are facilitators of learning rather than deliverers of information.

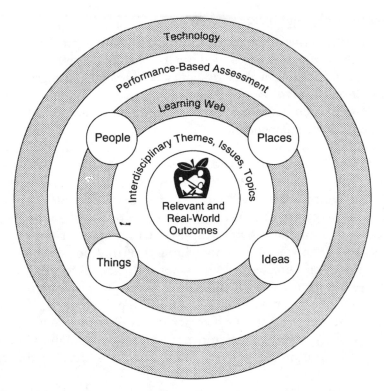

Figure E-1. The Self-Directed Learner Guide.

- *Students do not learn in neatly defined disciplines.* The human brain is not set up to receive math-only instruction from 8 A.M. to 9 A.M., reading from 9 A.M. to 10 A.M., and so on. Therefore, the artificial creation of "disciplines" can actually impede learning. Students should experience a range of interdisciplinary opportunities. Teachers and students should work together to create an educational environment that consciously applies a variety of disciplines, in a relevant manner, to examine a theme, issue, problem, or topic.
- *Learning is not confined to schools.* This point is almost so obvious that it may appear condescending to state it at all. However, all too often we ignore this statement of common sense and resort to efforts to confine our educational opportunities to the "school day." In a Self-Directed School, all Stakeholders work together all of the time to explore new

ways of thinking and new ways of learning. *Learning happens everywhere and all of the time.*

- *Student assessment is critical.* In a traditional school, the teacher assigns the work, the student does the work, and the teacher grades the work—"giving" the student the appropriate grade based on the quality of the work. This separation of doing the work and grading the work actually gets in the way of learning. Learning is most effective when the person who did the work, the student, is also involved in assessing the work. Self-directed learners work with their teachers and parents to develop a mechanism for assessing their work, and then participate with their teachers and parents in the actual evaluation of their work.

- *Technology is a tool for developing self-directed learners.* In our highly technological world it is naive and short-sighted to believe that students can learn the skills they will need in the "real" world without the implementation of technology in the educational environment. Technology in schools is not a luxury—it is a necessity. It provides new ways for students to manipulate and work with information. It also allows students to create real products that demonstrate their knowledge and understanding in a particular area. Technology allows students to apply their knowledge in relevant ways— thereby solidifying and extending their understanding.

The Self-Directed School is merely a means to an end. The goal is the Self-Directed learner. Before we can have students who are Self-Directed learners, we must first have teachers, parents, principals, community representatives, business leaders, and central office personnel who are themselves self-directed, who are themselves empowered, who are themselves collaborative thinkers and problem solvers, who are themselves Self-Directed learners.

Afterword

Learning to use collaboration and breaking out of the hierarchical mode of behavior in our schools and in our school systems is what this book is about. The very best learning environment for our children can occur only when the traditional hierarchical organization of our schools is changed dramatically and Stakeholders are empowered to become involved in an active and meaningful way in the operation and management of our schools. Only then will true commitment and enthusiasm occur. And only then will quality and excellence in our educational system be achieved.

Merely talking about the need for change will do nothing to solve the problem. We believe that the fundamental weakness in the current system of public education in the United States lies in the highly bureaucratic, overly rigid, and depressingly unresponsive hierarchical organizational structure in place in most school systems. What is needed is a revolutionary change in structure. We need to implement a system in which all of the individuals who have a stake in the education of our youth can become involved in an active way to create an effective and efficient educational environment. We need an organizational structure in which empowered Stakeholders work together in clusters to accomplish the missions and objectives of an effective educational curriculum and in which teams of Stakeholders have the opportunity to come up with solutions to the problems within our schools. It is through the solutions that the Stakeholders fashion—solutions that they believe in, are excited about, and are committed to—that real change will take place and excellence will be achieved. What we need in short, are Self-Directed Schools.

References

William J. Bailey, *School-Site Management Applied*. Lancaster, PA: Technomic, 1991.

Roland Barth, *Improving Schools from Within*. San Francisco: Jossey-Bass Publishers, 1990.

Warren Bennis, *Why Leaders Can't Lead*. San Francisco: Jossey-Bass Publishers, 1989.

Peter Block, *The Empowered Manager*. San Francisco: Jossey-Bass Publishers, 1987.

Joseph H. Boyett and Henry P. Conn, *Workplace 2000*. New York: Dutton Books, 1991.

Rexford G. Brown, *Schools of Thought*. San Francisco: Jossey-Bass Publishers, 1991.

William C. Byham, *Zapp*. New York: Harmony Books, 1988.

John E. Chubb and Terry M. Moe, *Politics, Markets and American Schools*. Washington, DC: The Brookings Institution, 1990.

D. Keith Denton, *Horizontal Management*. New York: Lexington Books, 1991.

Mark Van Doren, *Liberal Education*. New York: Henry Holt and Company, 1942.

Richard Elmore, *Restructuring Schools*. San Francisco: Jossey-Bass Publishers, 1990.

Michael Fullan and Suzanne Stiegelbauer, *The New Meaning of Educational Change*. New York: Teachers College Press, 1991.

Jeanne Gibbs, *Tribes*. Santa Rosa, CA: Center Source Publications.

William Glasser, *The Quality School*. New York: Harper Perennial, 1990.

Carl D. Glickman, *Renewing America's Schools*. San Francisco: Jossey-Bass, 1993.

John I. Goodlad, *A Place Called School*. New York: McGraw-Hill Company, 1984.

Jane Hannaway and Martin Carnoy (eds.), *Decentralization and School Improvement*. San Francisco: Jossey-Bass Publishers, 1993.

Wendy S. Hopfenberg and Henry M. Levin, *The Accelerated Schools Resource Guide*. San Francisco: Jossey-Bass Publishers, 1993.

Irving L. Janis, *Crucial Decisions: Leadership in Policy Making*. New York: Free Press, 1989.

Jon R. Katzenbach and Douglas K. Smith, *The Wisdom of Teams*. Boston: Harvard Business School Press, 1993.

David T. Kearns and Dennis P. Doyle, *Winning the Brain Race*. San Francisco: Institute for Contemporary Studies, 1989.

Edward E. Lawler, *The Ultimate Advantage*. San Francisco: Jossey-Bass Publishers, 1992.

Ann Lieberman, *Building a Professional Culture in Schools*. New York: Teachers College Press, 1988.

Gene I. Maeroff, *The Empowerment of Teachers*. New York: Teachers College Press, 1988.

D. Quinn Mills, *Rebirth of the Corporation*. New York: John Wiley & Sons, Inc., 1991.

National Commission on Excellence in Education, *A Nation at Risk: The Imperative for Educational Reform*. Washington, DC: Government Printing Office, 1983.

Jeanne Oakes and Martin Lipton, *Making the Best of Schools*. New Haven, CT: Yale University Press, 1990.

David Osborne and Ted Gaebler, *Reinventing Government*. New York: Penguin Books, 1993.

Thomas J. Peters and Robert H. Waterman, *In Search of Excellence*. New York: Warner Books, 1982.

Lorne C. Plunkett and Robert Fournier, *Participative Management: Implementing Empowerment*. New York: John Wiley & Sons, Inc., 1991.

Seymour Sarason, *The Predictable Failure of Educational Reform*. San Francisco: Jossey-Bass Publishers, 1990.

Phillip Schlechty, *Schools for the 21st Century*. San Francisco: Jossey-Bass Publishers, 1990.

Thomas J. Sergiovanni, *Building Community in Schools*. San Francisco: Jossey-Bass Publishers, 1993.

Joseph B. Shedd and Samuel B. Bacharach, *Tangled Hierarchies*. San Francisco: Jossey-Bass, 1991.

Mary Walton, *Deming Management at Work*. New York: Perigee-Putnam, 1991.

Richard S. Wellins, William C. Byham, and Jeanne M. Wilson, *Empowered Teams*. San Francisco: Jossey-Bass Publishers, 1991.

Index